JOHN H. HOWE, ARCHITECT

JOHN H. HOWE, ARCHITECT

FROM TALIESIN APPRENTICE TO MASTER OF ORGANIC DESIGN

JANE KING HESSION AND TIM QUIGLEY   FOREWORD BY BRUCE BROOKS PFEIFFER

UNIVERSITY OF MINNESOTA PRESS   MINNEAPOLIS · LONDON

Frontispiece (page ii): John Howe at the drafting table with Frank Lloyd Wright, circa 1950s. Photograph by Pedro Guerrero. Copyright 2015 Pedro E. Guerrero Archives.

Page vi: Stained glass detail at Sankaku. Photograph by William Byrne Olexy. Courtesy of of Modern House Productions.

Page 198: Howe's "House for Phoebe Point," Wyoming Valley, Wisconsin, circa 1945. Courtesy of the John H. Howe Papers (N14), Northwest Architectural Archives, University of Minnesota Libraries, Minneapolis.

The University of Minnesota Press gratefully acknowledges financial assistance provided for this book's publication by Mrs. Lu Sparks Howe.

In accordance with our specific areas of expertise, chapters 2, 4, and 6 were written by Jane King Hession, and chapters 1, 3, and 5 were written by Tim Quigley.

Published by the University of Minnesota Press
111 Third Avenue South, Suite 290
Minneapolis, MN 55401–2520
http://www.upress.umn.edu

Library of Congress Cataloging-in-Publication Data

Hession, Jane King, author.
John H. Howe, architect: from Taliesin apprentice to master of organic design / Jane King Hession and Tim Quigley; foreword by Bruce Brooks Pfeiffer.
ISBN 978-0-8166-8301-7 (hc)
1. Howe, John H., 1913–1997. 2. Wright, Frank Lloyd, 1867–1959—Friends and associates. 3. Architects—United States—Biography. 4. Howe, John H., 1913–1997—Criticism and interpretation.
I. Quigley, Tim, author. II. Title.
NA737.H67H47 2015
720.92—dc23   2015006582

Printed in Canada on acid-free paper

The University of Minnesota is an equal-opportunity educator and employer.

21 20 19 18 17 16 15

10 9 8 7 6 5 4 3 2 1

IN MEMORY OF LU SPARKS HOWE

THE LAND IS THE BEGINNING OF ARCHITECTURE. I DON'T HAVE A PRECONCEPTION FOR A HOUSE OR BUILDING. . . . I RELY ON TOPOGRAPHICAL MAPS, THE LOCATION OF TREES AND OTHER NATURAL FEATURES, THE VIEWS, AND THE POINTS OF THE COMPASS. THAT'S WHERE I START.
—JOHN H. HOWE

CONTENTS

FOREWORD

BRUCE BROOKS PFEIFFER

Among the thirty-two apprentices who arrived at Taliesin on October 20, 1932, was nineteen-year-old John H. Howe from Evanston, Illinois. From the age of nine, Jack, as he was called, was intensely interested in architecture. He regularly rode his bicycle to those places where he could see the architecture of Frank Lloyd Wright and Walter Burley Griffin. Later, when he heard about the Taliesin Fellowship, Jack was determined to be part of Wright's new school. A week after his high school graduation, he applied for membership and was accepted.

An eager student with youthful enthusiasm, Jack brought to Taliesin a love of architecture and an eagerness to learn from Wright. He also brought a pronounced gift for drawing. In the evening after the day's work was done, Jack would visit the storage cabinets in the drafting room, select a few of Wright's perspectives and plans, and sit down at his drawing board to carefully trace them—a process that further developed his own natural skill. Soon Wright noticed Jack's aptitude for drawing was accompanied by speed as his pencil would glide effortlessly across the paper almost as if it had a mind of its own.

Just as Wright had risen to become chief of design under Louis Sullivan, Jack became Wright's chief draftsman. Wright had Jack stand by his side while he drew—a ritual continued for as long as he worked in the drafting room. Jack was always there, listening to Wright as he explained the drawing he was making. Then it was up to Jack to develop the conceptual drawings, plans, sections, elevations, and—eventually—the perspectives that were presented to clients. After Jack completed a perspective, he showed it to Wright for approval. Often Wright would add some details, such as foliage or other landscape features, before initialing and dating the drawing in the red square provided for him on the sheet. For the most part, however, Jack's renderings proved sufficient to Wright, and he added nothing to the drawing but his signature.

Wright placed Jack in charge of the drafting room. As projects came in, and once Wright had developed the design to a certain degree, Jack assigned the rest of the work, or the process of preparing the working drawings and specifications, to other apprentices. He was always kind and patient (never expressing any air of superiority) and would tirelessly explain tasks to the newer apprentices.

In 1951 Jack married Lu Sparks. Trained as an English teacher, Lu was an invaluable asset at Taliesin. She was tasked with typing specifications for all design projects as well as Wright's manuscripts. She also assisted Wright's secretary, Gene Masselink, with the architect's voluminous correspondence. Lu was as essential to administrative work at Taliesin as Jack was in the drafting room.

Wright's buildings are architectural masterpieces, but the renderings of those buildings are masterworks as well. Without his cadre of skilled draftsmen, the great work of Frank Lloyd Wright from 1932 to 1959 would never have been accomplished. Although Jack was one of several apprentices of marked talent who worked at Taliesin over the years, undeniably he was the person most responsible for producing the avalanche of drawings for Wright's architectural designs during that twenty-seven-year period.

Bruce Brooks Pfeiffer
Scottsdale, Arizona

INTRODUCTION
THE LAND IS
THE BEGINNING

RHODODENDRON CHAPEL FOR MR E J KAUFMANN
FRANK LLOYD WRIGHT , ARCHITECT

Wright's design for the Rhododendron Chapel at Fallingwater, in Mill Run, Pennsylvania (1953), was not built, but
Howe captured the essence of the small building in this
perspective sketch.

John Henry Howe (1913–1997) claimed to have had "two lifetimes" in architecture.
The first life began in 1932, when, at age nineteen, he became a charter member of architect
Frank Lloyd Wright's Taliesin Fellowship in Spring Green, Wisconsin. Over the next
twenty-seven years, Howe would rise to become chief draftsman and eventually head of
the Taliesin studio. As such, he was the interpreter of Wright's concepts and supervisor
of the work flow in the studio. Howe was responsible for assigning tasks to fellows who
would move Wright's initial sketches forward through presentation sets to completed
working drawings. As "the pencil in Wright's hand," he produced hundreds of drawings of
the architect's designs. Many of them are among the finest—and most renowned—to have
emanated from the studio. Within the Taliesin community, Howe was respected for his
leadership skills and his ability to rapidly produce drawings of extraordinary beauty. Outside
that world, however, his talents were little known. Howe's name did not appear on a single
one of the drawings he produced during all the years he worked with Wright, nor did it
appear in any of the early published compendiums of Wright's work.[1]

Following Wright's death in 1959, Howe became a lead architect for Taliesin Associated
Architects (TAA), Wright's successor firm. After he left Taliesin in 1964 and worked
for three years for Aaron Green Associates in San Francisco, Howe's second lifetime in
architecture began in 1967. At the age of fifty-four, he established John H. Howe, Architect,
a one-man firm in Minneapolis, Minnesota. His wife, Lu Sparks Howe, managed the business
side of the office. During twenty-five years in practice, he designed more than two hundred
projects, and more than 120 of these were built. The majority of Howe's work was residential.
He was an expert at designing houses that appeared to grow out of the earth, as much a
part of the site as landforms and flora.

Although Howe distinguished between the two eras of his life, he also recognized they were inextricably linked by the common thread of organic architecture. Its principles, which guided Howe throughout his independent career, were firmly rooted in the lessons he learned from Wright during their long and close professional relationship. Arguably, no one understood Wright's architecture better than Howe. Of his own later work, Howe expressed "hope" that it constituted "a kind of continuity" with Wright's legacy.[2]

Simply stated, organic architecture promotes the idea of working with, rather than against, nature. Wright believed a building should take inspiration from and be in harmony with the land on which it stands. Although he did not invent the concept of organic architecture—the built works of many indigenous cultures and ancient civilizations were respectful of nature—Wright did make its precepts central to his architectural philosophies. He strove to emulate nature by creating an architecture of unity and integrity, in which all aspects of a building (including site, purpose, materials, and construction method) were as honestly and fully integrated as were the leaves, branches, and roots of a tree: each and every part related to the whole. Howe took the lessons to heart and would later state, "The philosophy of an organic architecture, perhaps more than the remarkable fruits of this philosophy, constitutes Mr. Wright's greatest contribution to the world."[3]

All of Howe's designs were shaped by his belief that "the land is the beginning of architecture," a phrase he learned from Wright. In fact, Howe often said that if a book were to be written about him it should be called *The Land Is the Beginning*.[4] The words were an apt description of Howe's design process. He said he had "no preconceptions about a building . . . until I have seen the site or gotten familiar with the site."[5] The contours and character of the land, climate, and the needs of his clients inspired the architecture he designed.

When it came to putting pencil to paper Howe was, by all accounts, an efficient designer. "I work carefully and I follow a direct path," a technique he adopted from Wright.[6] "He never switched horses in the middle of the stream, so to speak," Howe said of his mentor. Howe started every design with a topographical map of the prospective site, which he used as an underlay for his drawings. After orienting "the house to the compass points, to the view, and to preserve nice trees or rocks or natural features on the site," he decided on the geometric module—usually a triangle, square, or rectangle—that would generate the plan best suited to the conditions of the site. This was a critically important step in the design process, because "Mr. Howe believed if the plan isn't beautiful, the house can't be," recalled his apprentice Geoffrey Childs.[7] Once the plan was completed, Howe drew the sections and elevations. "It's very simple," he reasoned. Observers noted Howe's designs would spring rapidly and fully formed from his mind and be quickly transcribed to paper— an exemplar established by Wright. Of Howe's rendering skills, Japanese architect and former Taliesin fellow Raku Endo poetically said, "His drafting was always so beautiful and yet so promptly done."[8]

Howe employed Wright's process for creating presentation perspectives for clients. He began by making a pencil-and-ink drawing on vellum that conveyed the qualities of the site and showed the structure's fit into the surrounding landscape. A stippling technique of small dots was used to detail trees, plantings, shadows, and reflections. Once the drawing was finished, two "blue line" reproductions of it were made. Howe then hand-colored each copy with hundreds of densely packed parallel lines, which he believed was "the best

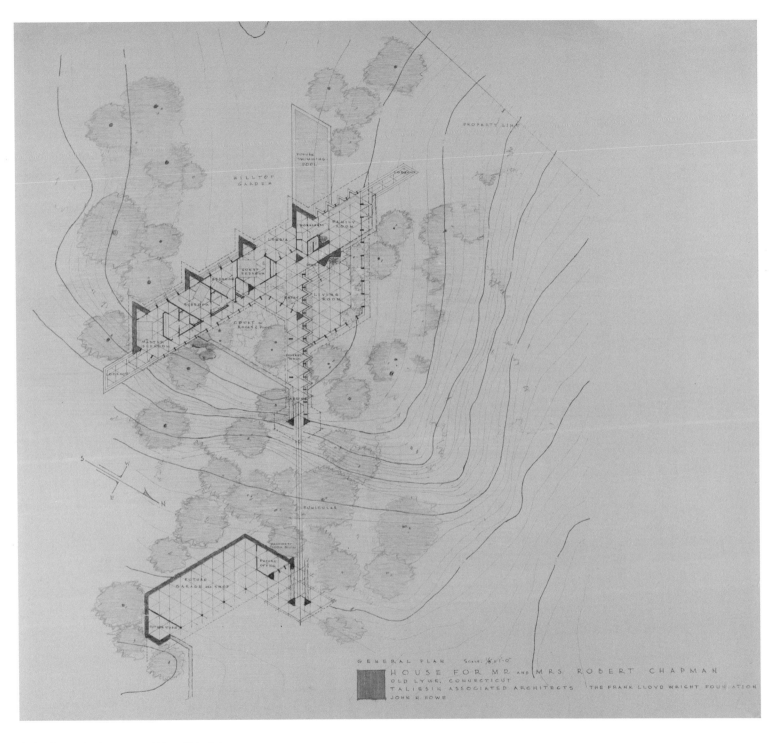

As this drawing for the unexecuted Mr. and Mrs. Robert
Chapman House, Old Lyme, Connecticut (1962), reveals,
Howe drew inspiration from the land when developing a
plan. Here he used a triangular module to create the plan
best suited to the site.

SANKAKU
HOME OF MR. AND MRS. John H. Howe

Howe used pencil and ink to render this perspective view of Sankaku, his residence in Burnsville, Minnesota, which was built in 1972. This was the first step in his process for creating a presentation drawing.

way to get an even covering of color."[9] Using this process he created, in effect, two unique drawings: one for the client and one for the architect. Howe understood that "the best powers of persuasion are beautiful drawings."[10]

A superb draftsman and a master of perspective, Howe used certain techniques to draw the eye into a rendering. After setting up a perspective, he framed two corners of the drawing with a continuous line, one end of which was linked to a foreground element and

HOUSE FOR MR. AND MRS. JOHN H. HOWE
WOODHOME, BURNSVILLE, MINNESOTA
JOHN H. HOWE, ARCHITECT

To create the final presentation drawing of Sankaku, a reproduction of the original pencil-and-ink perspective was hand-colored with hundreds of densely packed parallel lines.

the other end to a background element. This trick of the eye emphasized the perspective and allowed Howe to enhance the illusion of three-dimensionality on a two-dimensional surface. The framing also kept the eye from wandering off the paper and maintained focus on the rendered design. Howe claimed to have learned the technique by studying the drawings of Marion Mahony, a talented architect, draftswoman, and artist who worked in Wright's Oak Park studio in the late nineteenth and early twentieth centuries.[11]

In addition to possessing masterful technical skills, Howe was a supremely accomplished artist. He had an unerring instinct for composition, a firm command of line and color, and a sure sense of what was essential—and nonessential—in a drawing. According to Childs, Howe possessed another important gift: "He had a talent for knowing what made a marvelous drawing."[12] As a comprehensive survey of his drawings reveals, Howe was among the finest architectural renderers of the twentieth century.

When it came to the manipulation of architectural space, Howe also had few equals. He found guidance and inspiration, as did Wright before him, in a question asked and answered by Chinese philosopher Lao Tzu: "What is the essence of a cup? It is the space within

VIEW FROM THE SOUTH

HOUSE FOR MR. AND MRS. NORMAN O. HILLEREN
NEAR BAY CITY, PIERCE COUNTY, WISCONSIN
JOHN H. HOWE, ARCHITECT

Howe enhanced the illusion of depth, as in this perspective
of the Norman O. and Ruth Hilleren House, near Bay
City, Wisconsin (1972), by anchoring one end of the frame
in a foreground element (at right) and the other end in
a background feature.

HOUSE FOR MR. AND MRS. KURT LYSNE   ISLAND G-252, RAINY LAKE, ONTARIO

JOHN H. HOWE, ARCHITECT

Lyrically beautiful perspective drawings, such as this one for an unexecuted house for Mr. and Mrs. Kurt Lysne, Rainy Lake, Ontario (1972), evoke Howe's belief in a harmonious relationship between architecture and nature.

Howe's design for Towerhouse, the Dr. Robert and Katherine Goodale House, Excelsior, Minnesota (1969), took inspiration from the hilly site and views of Lake Minnetonka.

that makes the cup useful."[13] Likewise, Howe shaped the space of each room in accordance with its purpose. He then related each room to other rooms based on how inhabitants would move between them. The eventual configuration of rooms generated the flow, size, and shape of the building. Stated another way, Howe designed his buildings from the inside out. As a result of this highly individualized process, he created singular houses of remarkable variety.

Because the land was the beginning of every Howe design, the horizontal or vertical character of an elevation was driven by the terrain. For example, his response to a hilly site (and he had many clients who owned them) might be to create multileveled plans that followed the contours of the land. One constant of most Howe-designed houses was a continuum of indoor to outdoor space often characterized by contrasting areas of prospect and refuge. Where a panoramic view of a lake was possible, Howe opened that aspect of the house to allow prospect, or expansive views. Where recess within the earth could provide a feeling of shelter or protection, he nestled a place of refuge within the contours of the land. The drama of many Howe houses derives from the juxtaposition of the two conditions; the experience of one enhances the awareness of the other.

Howe further underscored the unity between a house and its natural surroundings through a carefully selected—and limited—palette of materials, which he used on both interior and exterior surfaces, another principle he absorbed from Wright. Where possible (and if

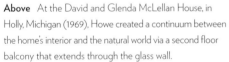

Above At the David and Glenda McLellan House, in Holly, Michigan (1969), Howe created a continuum between the home's interior and the natural world via a second floor balcony that extends through the glass wall.

Top right The Hilleren House, like many Howe designs, features a low-sloped, sheltering roof that almost touches the ground. This dramatic gesture heightens the sense of shelter and firmly roots the house to its site.

Bottom right The complexity of Howe's design for Sankaku and the dynamism of the spaces in the house are evident in this photograph from the second-floor loft.

Unity of design and the relationship of parts to the whole contribute to the sense of harmony and serenity at Redleaf, the house Howe designed for his friend William Krebes, in Lakeville, Minnesota (1978).

budget permitted), Howe specified stone and wood for construction materials. As a result, his houses appear to be an outgrowth of the land on which they are built. Another overarching concern was unity of design. He enhanced the feeling of harmony in his houses by complementing the architecture with furniture, cabinetry, lighting, and textiles of his own design.

If, to paraphrase Lao Tzu, the space within a Howe house is what is useful, it is also where the intangibles, such as serenity and timelessness, lie. In describing Howe's own home, Sankaku, Endo captured a few of its indefinable qualities: "Not at all large, it is a masterpiece of beauty, bewitching everyone with its charm and personality. During my life I have known profound emotion not very many times, and one was upon experiencing this house."[14]

Tranquil though they may be, Howe houses are also complex and cannot be fully grasped on first encounter. "It takes time to learn a new language," Marlene Schmidt wrote of her family's Howe-designed house. "We have lived here close to thirty years and are still excitedly, joyfully, thankfully learning the language of this house."[15]

William Krebes, Howe's lifelong friend, client, and fellow inmate at the Federal Correctional Institution in Sandstone, Minnesota (both served time there as conscientious objectors during World War II), used a musical analogy to describe the intricacies of Howe's architecture:

The strong, simple lines of Seagull, the Norma Johnson House near Grand Marais, Minnesota (1982), echo the timeless natural beauty of Lake Superior.

"Just as you can't fully experience a piece of music by looking at the notes, you can't fully experience these houses by walking around them or through them. . . . You have to live in them."

Ultimately, as Howe's character was shaped by his personal convictions, his buildings were born of his architectural beliefs. As Krebes explained, "John was very conscious of everything he did. His houses are more than beautiful; they have about them a feeling of principle. It's the latter that gives them their ageless quality, their real beauty, their 'sound.'"

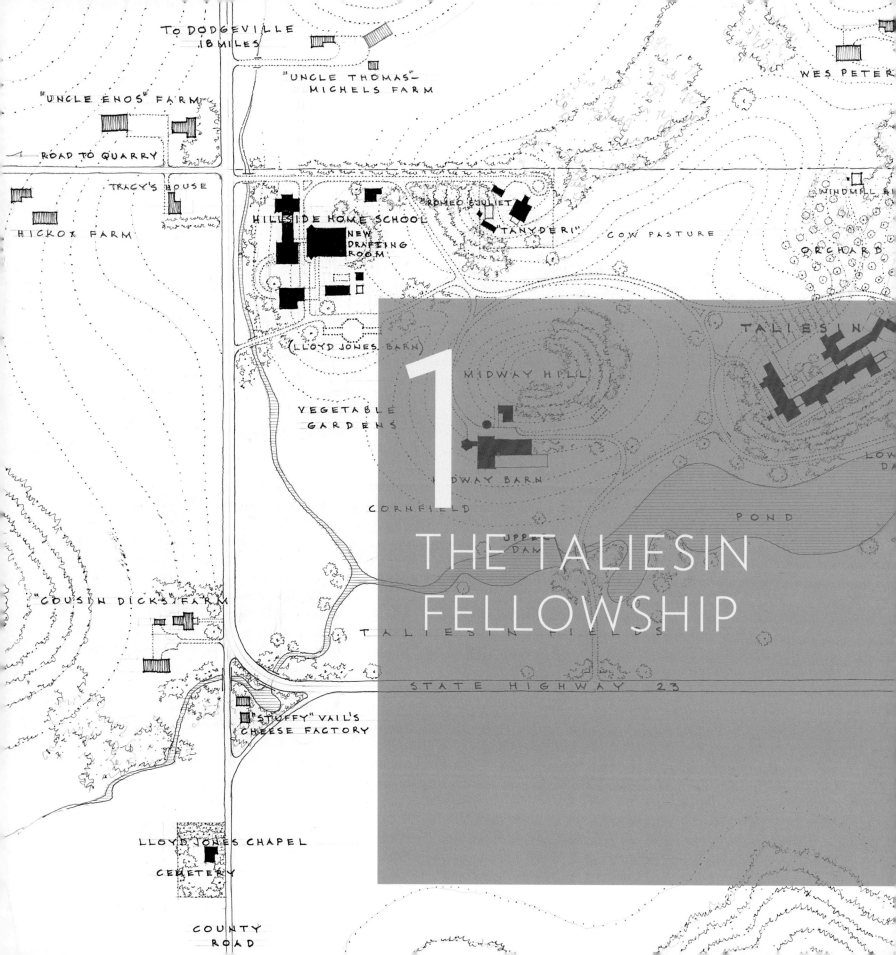

TO DODGEVILLE
.18 MILES

"UNCLE THOMAS-
MICHELS FARM

WES PETER

"UNCLE ENOS" FARM

ROAD TO QUARRY

TRACY'S HOUSE

HICKOX FARM

"ROMEO & JULIET"

"TANYDERI"

WINDMILL

COW PASTURE

ORCHARD

HILLSIDE HOME SCHOOL

NEW
DRAFTING
ROOM

(LLOYD JONES BARN)

TALIESIN

MIDWAY HILL

VEGETABLE
GARDENS

MIDWAY BARN

CORNFIELD

POND

LOW
DA

UPPER
DAM

"COUSIN DICK'S FARM

TALIESIN FIELDS

STATE HIGHWAY 23

"STUFFY" VAIL'S
CHEESE FACTORY

LLOYD JONES CHAPEL

CEMETERY

COUNTY
ROAD

1
THE TALIESIN
FELLOWSHIP

May 1932 was not an auspicious time to graduate from high school in the United States.
The Great Depression was nearing its nadir; the economy was reeling; the social fabric
was fraying. Yet John Henry Howe (or Jack, to friends and family) was completing his studies
at Evanston High School in that Chicago suburb.[1] His hope was to become an architect.
As the eldest of six children in a middle-class family, the challenge of raising tuition funds
imperiled his dream.

During Howe's senior year, architect Frank Lloyd Wright was formalizing plans to open
a school named the Taliesin Fellowship on his rural estate near Spring Green, Wisconsin.
This he publicized widely in newspaper interviews throughout the country. The stated goal
was to develop what Wright called "well-correlated human beings" at a "colony studying
modern life" and "developing Machine Age art." Wright declared a defining tenet of the
Fellowship: "To make the most of life in the Machine Age, a man's work and a man's life
must be a harmonized unit." Organizationally, Wright explained, the school would have
resident associates in sculpture, painting, and music, with special studies for building design
and building construction, typography, ceramics, woodwork, and textiles.[2]

An unstated goal of the educational endeavor was financial: Wright, his wife and partner
Olgivanna Lloyd Wright (Olgivanna Lazovich Hinzenberg, before they wed in 1928), and
his patron clients believed a Wright-led school of architecture could allow the renowned
architect a means of support during a time when architectural commissions were
almost nonexistent.

SERENDIPITOUS CONNECTION

As Wright's formulation of an arts school at his rural Wisconsin compound took shape,
Howe found a link to Wright by way of Charles Morgan, a prominent architectural renderer
in Chicago. Frequently lecturing to civic groups, Morgan, cartwheeling onto the stage,
gave a "chalk talk" lecture to Howe's high school architectural drawing class, inspiring the
aspiring architect.[3] More important, he mentioned that Wright was about to start a school.[4]

Taliesin, Wright's rural estate nestled in the hills of south-
western Wisconsin, as it looked when the Fellowship was
founded. This is one of many evocative images taken by
Howe shortly after he arrived at Taliesin as he immersed
himself in all aspects of Wright's work.

Charles Morgan was the premier architectural renderer in Chicago in the late 1920s and early 1930s, freelancing for many architects, including Wright, notably on the National Life Insurance Company project rendering, Chicago, Illinois (1924). He befriended the Howe family after taking Howe, a high school senior, to Taliesin for an interview with Wright.

Morgan, who worked for Wright rendering presentation perspectives on occasion, was listed in the initial Taliesin Fellowship prospectus as one of the resident associates.[5] Befriending the eager youngster, he showed Howe the skyscrapers of the downtown Loop from the backseat of his chauffeured Packard. He then invited Howe to accompany him on a visit to Taliesin in the spring of 1932.[6] Howe's application and acceptance into the Fellowship followed shortly thereafter. According to Howe, it was the fulfillment of an early desire. Prior to meeting Morgan, he assumed his only option would be enrolling at Armour Institute of Technology, which he later recalled as "a grim, dispiriting, Romanesque place on a soot-covered site on Chicago's west side."[7]

Howe had long wanted to pursue a career in architecture. For several years, he spent hours exploring the environs of suburban Chicago, often by bicycle, examining Wright's Prairie-era creations. His scrapbook from this period has photographs of Wright houses he took along with his sketches of details.[8] Howe's Evanston neighborhood was rife with progressive architecture by Wright, Walter Burley Griffin (a former Wright draftsman), George Washington Maher, and others. A maternal relative, Dr. Alfred W. Hebert, lived around the block in a house Griffin designed. So Howe was steeped in, and enamored of, Wright's work from early on. With his mother, he attended a Chicago Art Institute lecture by Wright in 1931 and even met his hero afterward.

Another connection to Wright came through Howe's mother, née Edith Hannah Hebert of Owasso, Illinois.[9] She had been educated at the Hillside Home School, near Spring Green, a progressive institution founded and run by Wright's maternal aunts, Ellen and Jane Lloyd Jones. Though Edith Hebert had been orphaned at a young age, her maternal uncle, Dr. Hebert, who served as the Lloyd Jones family dentist, enrolled her in the school in the early part of the century. She attended with Wright's son Lloyd, and had experienced Wright's architecture firsthand: he had added two structures to the school, starting with the Romeo and Juliet Windmill (1896) and the Hillside Home School II (1902).

Although Howe was admitted to Taliesin's inaugural class of apprentices, his parents could not afford the requisite $650 yearly tuition. Howe had a mere three hundred dollars, earned setting bowling pins at the Evanston Country Club.[10] He asked if some accommodation could be made. Wright responded, "Well, if you keep the fires going in the fireplaces, help with the housecleaning, and keep the hot water heater burning, why, I guess we can take you." Howe later joked that Wright never had a warm bath that entire winter at Taliesin, as the water heater leaked and the fire to heat the water tank kept going out. He was more successful with keeping the fires going in the fireplaces. Describing firewood hauling as backbreaking work, Howe recalled learning a trick: "After Mr. Wright had passed through a room, and gone on, I could take apart the fire and just leave the coals. Then I could put new wood on the coals when I knew he was coming back."[11]

THE TALIESIN COMMUNITY

By October 1932, Howe was enrolled in the Taliesin Fellowship along with twenty-nine other students and seven professional men long in Wright's employ (though they had long ceased being paid).[12] Notable among the latter were Henry Klumb, the chief draftsman, who was from Germany, and Karl Jensen, his secretary, from Denmark. Howe considered them "a cosmopolitan group, indeed." Suddenly surrounded by "the kids," as they called

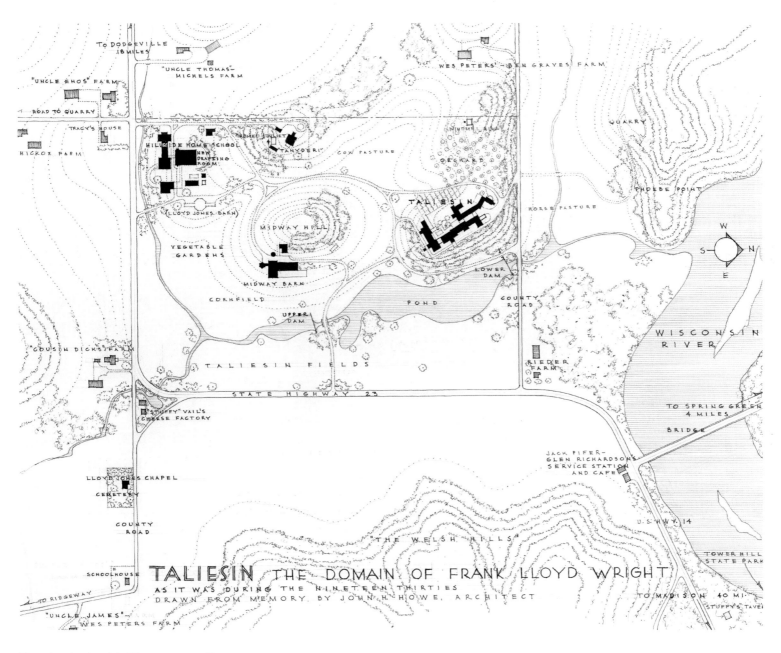

TALIESIN THE DOMAIN OF FRANK LLOYD WRIGHT
AS IT WAS DURING THE NINETEEN THIRTIES
DRAWN FROM MEMORY BY JOHN H. HOWE, ARCHITECT

Howe drew this plan of the Taliesin estate, near Spring Green, Wisconsin, from memory late in his life. It shows the relative locations of the main residence (Taliesin), the Hillside studio, Unity Chapel, and "Uncle James's"—later Wes Peters's—farm, Aldebaran, where the Howe Cottage, Inwood, is located.

the new arrivals, they didn't appreciate having been thrust into de facto teaching roles. Howe recollected, "When we apprentices began coming, they began leaving."[13]

Rounding out the community were the "devoted retainers," to quote Howe: farm helpers, carpenters, a plumber, and masons, who assisted with whatever project was at hand. At the center of it all was Wright, acting as patriarch of a large family with his wife, Olgivanna Lloyd Wright, "who kept things running as smoothly as possible," according to Howe, and their two daughters, Svetlana Hinzenberg Wright (Wright's stepdaughter from Olgivanna's previous marriage to Latvian architect Valdemar Hinzenberg) and Iovanna Wright. In practice, Olgivanna was the managing partner, administrator, work assignment list maker, and taskmaster for the day-to-day chores at the Fellowship.[14] She had as profound an impact on the Fellowship as Wright, structuring almost all nonarchitectural "cultural" endeavors over the years. Indeed, according to apprentice Kamal Amin, "The Taliesin community was uniquely her own creation."[15] Wright's primary concern was architecture; hers was the personal development of the lives of the apprentices, which she considered central to her work.

The class roll included several notables in future Taliesin lore: William Wesley "Wes" Peters, Edgar Tafel, Robert Mosher, Abe Dombar, John Lautner, Blaine and Hulda Drake, Yen Liang, William Bernoudy, and Alden Dow, among others.[16] Many of these individuals had some formal collegiate, architectural education, in the Beaux-Arts teaching method of the day. Typically, they had heard Wright lecture at their institutions, only to follow his subversive suggestion to leave those schools for a *real* education, meaning with him! Several hailed from overseas. None came directly from high school, as had Howe. He was a mere nineteen; only Svetlana Wright was younger.[17]

The Taliesin studio, circa 1935. Wright in his element, surrounded by Gene Masselink, Abe Dombar, Edgar Tafel, and John Howe. This cramped facility served the Fellowship until 1942, when the long-delayed Hillside studio was completed. Many masterpieces were created here.

Frank Lloyd Wright, age sixty-five, as he led the media blitz to launch the Taliesin Fellowship, 1932. Numerous articles appeared in major newspapers throughout the year, often accompanied by this photograph.

The core of it all was Frank Lloyd Wright. Howe described him: "Mr. Wright was a dynamo of creative ability. We were drawn ever closer into his orbit by this magnetic force and felt privileged to share his exciting life. He was our center of inspiration, the master, and we apprentices were his followers."[18]

THE FELLOWSHIP IN PRINCIPLE

Like Wright's buildings, which he described as totally integrated works of art that united, inside and outside, and related all details to the whole, Wright's conception of the Fellowship had a similar underlying philosophy: that of uniting life and art by means of work. It was anything but a conventional school, with nary a structured curriculum or any formal classes.

Notable was the lack of any formal teaching component at Taliesin. "Learn by doing" was Wright's dictum.[19] All work, no matter how menial, was deemed creative. Fellows were considered workers and the education declared to be informal. According to Howe, no project was ever finished; all was in a state of constant change. Whatever Wright deemed his next priority became the Fellowship's next priority. "Everything seemed to be in an agreeable state of flux," Taliesin apprentice Curtis Besinger explained.[20] Early on, everyone helped with everything: chopping wood, milking cows, making meals, and formally entertaining one another through choral performances, music recitals, and theater productions.

One might assume that in founding a school Wright was dedicating himself to a teaching role. In fact, Wright's various formulations of a school throughout the previous decade (i.e., the Hillside Home School of the Allied Arts) involved others in the primary teaching role. Wright's initial concept for the Taliesin Fellowship, in 1931, involved partnering with Dutch architect Hendricus Theodorus Wijdeveld, publisher of the journal *Wendingen,* who also had published a book on Wright's work.[21] The idea was for Wijdeveld to manage the school, while Wright acted in a consulting role and maintained his architectural practice. Ultimately, the partnership foundered, and Wright forged on alone.

Similarly, the proposed teaching force of the Taliesin Fellowship, three resident associates in sculpture, painting, and music, never materialized. Consequently, Wright started the Fellowship with himself as the only teacher and a reluctant one at that. Wright always insisted he was neither a preacher nor a teacher. Howe disagreed, stating emphatically that he was both. Indeed, once the professional men departed Taliesin, Wright was the only one left to teach the apprentices.[22]

Wright believed education to be a lifelong process whereby culture and the development of character were more important than formal academic training. As with plants in nature, Wright believed all living things to be the result of cultivation and environment. Life at Taliesin, which inextricably linked work and culture, built on this notion. Wright's goal was not to educate practicing architects but rather to develop complete men and women steeped in creative work. A major part of developing well-rounded, creative people involved the performing arts and the sharing of those arts with the wider Spring Green community. Thus, the Taliesin theater was conceived by Wright and Olgivanna as an essential component of the Fellowship.[23] Music, too, was an integral part of Taliesin life, recalled Howe. So much so that the words to Bach's "Jesu, Joy of Man's Desiring" were changed to "Joy in work is man's desiring," thus becoming the Fellowship hymn.[24]

THE FELLOWSHIP IN PRACTICE

The first year of the Fellowship was consumed by the task of establishing itself physically at Taliesin and Hillside. The name Taliesin refers to Wright's sprawling residence situated on his ancestors' farmlands. Originally constructed in 1911, it was rebuilt twice after disastrous fires, in 1914 and 1926. The property included the Taliesin studio and attached apprentice sleeping quarters reconstructed from former farm and service buildings. Hillside refers to several buildings nearly one mile distant across the estate, built for the Hillside Home School from 1886 on.

A concurrent task was to develop a community: establishing a system for allocating work, feeding itself, heating the premises, and building institutions for cultural expression. Everyone was feeling his or her way.[25] The routine was one of no routine, just as Wright preferred. There were "no rules, no regulations, no one told us anything," Tafel wrote about the early years. Olgivanna, intelligent, strong willed, and manipulative, was the force that kept the Fellowship in working order from the very start, he noted.[26]

When the incoming class gathered that first October, its members were put to work transforming the former Hillside Home School, boarded up since 1915, into a home for the Fellowship. New buildings, among them a drafting studio, a theater, a dining space, and living quarters, were on the drawing boards and needed translating into built reality. The brunt of the work fell to the new apprentices. Training was provided by the devoted retainers, who otherwise would have been on federal relief.

Howe (left) and the other fellows dine during a break from chores. Much of the activity in the first years of the Taliesin Fellowship focused on manual labor: building or renovating the facilities, doing farming chores, or cutting firewood.

Farm chores and construction activity were balanced with cultural enrichment, including the formation of a choir (seen here informally practicing), a Taliesin printing press, film presentations, music recitals, and training in the architectural studio. Howe is in the second row, left of center.

Lumber was acquired only by felling oak trees and milling the green lumber themselves. Stone was quarried on-site in the Wyoming Valley. Cement mortar was not bought but made, in a manner common since Roman times: limestone from the quarry was burned in a kiln for days at a time by crews tending the fire around the clock.

Farm chores were a priority, too, as the planting, weeding, and harvesting of crops (potatoes, apples, and vegetables) were necessary for sustenance. Corn, harvested by hand, provided income for essential purchases. Cows and goats, too, had to be milked, pigs tended, eggs gathered, and chickens fed and butchered.

Howe was exempted from much of this construction and farming duty from the outset, due to his responsibilities keeping fires burning in the fireplaces. He recounted his good fortune: "Keeping the fires going in the Taliesin studio allowed me to *be* there. While others were all out rebuilding the dams or bringing in the corn crop, or whatever else Mr. Wright had sent them to do, I more than had a foot in the door, you see. And so since I was there, I was the one to whom Mr. Wright said 'Lay this out, do this,' or whatever he had to do."[27] So Howe "really learned to draw," as he put it. Wright taught him colored pencil techniques and how to lay out three-point perspectives. Klumb instructed him on orthographic drawings: plans, sections, and elevations. Robert Goodall, another of the professional men, taught him working drawing techniques and sheet layout. Despite his youth and relative inexperience, Howe soon became a key contributor in the drafting studio at Taliesin, which, for Wright, was the center of everything.

Howe was inspired by the Prairie-era renderings from Wright's Oak Park studio. This view of the Kersey C. and Laura DeRhodes House, South Bend, Indiana (1906), was drawn by Marion Mahony, the master renderer from that phase of Wright's career. Howe regretted that he never met her.

Another reason for the predominance of farm chores, construction work, and firewood gathering in the daily routine was the reality that there was next to no architectural work to be done. There was none on the horizon, either. Howe and the others learned quickly that Taliesin was operating on a subsistence basis. "We were always in a state of emergency," recalled Howe. Wright was able to stay solvent with a smattering of income provided by a cadre of patron clients, the publication of Wright's *An Autobiography* in early 1932, occasional lectures, and the periodic sale of Asian art treasures from his vast collection, acquired during his years in Japan.[28] Paying architectural commissions were so sparse that between 1924 and 1933 Wright managed to get only two built: a house for a previous client and one for a Lloyd Jones relative.[29]

For most apprentices other than Howe, architectural education was not much in evidence. What *was* in evidence was Frank Lloyd Wright's force of character. "He thought of himself as a living legend and loved acting out the role," recounted apprentice Tafel. Wright believed each day was for new enjoyment, embracing each enthusiastically, never letting things go stale. Tafel added: "Wright felt time was pushing him, trying to overtake him. As a result he projected a kind of frenzy onto us. Always."[30] Howe also recalled Wright's enthusiasm for life and his welcoming of change.

IN THE DRAFTING STUDIO

During that first winter, the apprentices finally took turns working in the drafting studio. While half the group was outside in the bitter cold, cutting wood for the boilers and fireplaces, the other half would alternate between stoking the boilers and working in the drafting room. This was partly because the studio at Taliesin had only eight drafting tables. The much larger Hillside studio was only beginning a long construction campaign. Since Wright had no projects to speak of, retracing and redrawing older projects sufficed. The

Imperial Hotel, Tokyo, (1913–23), was a favorite teaching tool. As a didactic exercise, the apprentices drew and redrew plans and rooms from the hotel to learn their craft.[31]

In the studio, Wright also inculcated in his apprentices his core value: the seeking of beauty and harmony in everything. He achieved this by showing, describing, and explaining examples from his Japanese print collection. He had long revered Japanese prints, for he believed them to be all about the presentation and depiction of beauty and harmony. Wright explained to the apprentices that the prints "were an interpretation of space; a moment in space in another dimension." They "intensified his awareness of the elimination of the insignificant," a key component of his own design process.[32]

No one was a more eager student of Wright than John Howe. He was like a sponge, recalled Tafel.[33] Howe remembered learning by copying an earlier generation of Wright drawings, notably those from the Wasmuth Portfolio, *Ausgeführte Bauten und Entwürfe von Frank Lloyd Wright* of 1910 emulating essential techniques as well as Wrightian drawing styles. Years later Howe recollected he was more inspired by Wright's presentation drawings from the early Prairie work, with their lush coloration, than by the more recent, stark black-and-white perspectival plans favored by Klumb.[34]

Howe's fascination with these early drawings and built works led to his efforts to catalog the old drawings found throughout nooks and crannies of the studio, many scattered in rolls in an unheated, unfinished attic area. In a very real sense, Howe became the first Taliesin archivist and the foremost student of Wright's earlier projects.

Howe's devotion to the studio was clear from the start. His increasing skill was compounded by hard work and incredible dedication. Others described him as a true workaholic in the studio. "One would see him long after dinnertime, bent over his drawing board, where he remained until midnight," noted one observer.[35] Whenever not explicitly assigned to some other task, Howe could be found in the drafting studio at all hours, practicing and perfecting his craft.

One early measure of Howe's position in the drafting studio was his assignment to sharpen Wright's pencils. This was no menial task, performed with a mechanical device. Wright taught him how to use a mat knife to get the points just so.[36] Wright revered his pencils, as they were the tools of his trade, along with his T-square and triangle.

Howe and Tafel recounted similar recollections of the early Fellowship studio. Both reported that Wright had an infectious enthusiasm and was always good-natured when there. He sauntered in with a bounce in his step, and "he would hum a tune or give the punch line to one of his favorite jokes on entering the studio in the morning." His sense of mission permeated his thinking. His pursuit of perfection led him to revise drawings constantly. As he reworked designs, he would tell the apprentices, "That was alright yesterday, but it is not right today."[37]

Tafel astutely observed that the Fellowship was Wright's springboard back to creativity. In the studio environment, Wright reveled in the opportunity to show young people how clever he was and how fast he could draw.[38] Ever the optimist, he believed the dismal economy would improve, building would resume, and he would have created architects to revitalize the nation. His apprentices became "pencils in his hand," much as Wright had been to Louis Sullivan nearly fifty years previously. Howe was one of the select few who became serious about architecture.

A typical Sunday night formal event at Taliesin, with the Wrights presiding over a gathering of the Fellowship and invited guests. Choral or chamber music was performed by the apprentices.

DAILY LIFE AS A FELLOW

As was made clear in the *Fellowship Prospectus,* Taliesin was organized as a community of participants. Each individual was expected to give his or her all to the creation of a self-sufficient life. This meant participants devised their own rules, customs, and cultural entertainment, in addition to the work of construction, farming, meal chores, and architecture. One of these customs, afternoon tea at four, became an important daily ritual. All were expected to attend. Wright would lead the conversation about daily news items or relate something he was writing at the moment. Howe typically returned to the studio after the sessions, often accompanied by Wright.

Weekends at Taliesin had their own rhythm. Saturday was cleaning day but featured mandatory picnic excursions by car caravans to locales chosen by Wright—frequently to his favorite limestone outcroppings along the nearby Wisconsin River. Saturday evenings meant dinner at the theater, typically followed by a foreign film, as Wright was an enthusiast of the medium. Sunday morning brought a special breakfast and gathering either in the Lloyd Jones's family Unity Chapel or, in later years, in the Fellowship dining room at Hillside. At either venue, Wright talked to the assembled group, instilling in them his zest for architecture and love of principle.[39]

Sunday evening brought the weekend's pinnacle: a formal dress affair in the Wright family's Taliesin living room. This included dinner served at small tables and music recitals with a choir, string quartet, harp, or Wright's Bechstein concert grand piano. Fellows provided most of the entertainment for the Wrights and their invited guests. Wright often concluded the evening by reading his favorite passages from Ralph Waldo Emerson or

Walt Whitman. Notable guests who attended evening soirees in Howe's first decade in the Fellowship included author Alexander Woollcott, artist Thomas Hart Benton, singer and political activist Paul Robeson, critic Lewis Mumford, architectural historian Henry-Russell Hitchcock, and architects Edward Durell Stone, Willem Dudok, Eliel Saarinen, Philip Johnson, and Ludwig Mies van der Rohe. Mies came for lunch and stayed four days.[40] Contact with many of these luminaries greatly enriched Howe's cultural development.

Howe made his mark on the communal life of the Fellowship as a choir member and gardener. Early on, he resented that choir practice was in the late morning, taking time away from the drafting studio and the work he loved. Long after leaving Taliesin, however, he remarked that these choir sessions were among his favorite memories of that communal life. He also meticulously tended the semicircular garden just outside the drafting room and commented that he cleared his head as he weeded the flower gardens he had developed outside the studio.[41]

Howe had a keen photographic eye. His curiosity and study of Wright's work included a thorough photographic documentation of Taliesin, particularly during the early years. Those images reveal his interest in its architectural composition, with Taliesin shown from a great many vantage points. Once Taliesin West was constructed in Paradise Valley, Arizona, Howe also photographed that compound in the same manner, meticulously chronicling Wright's creation in the desert landscape.

Howe started his career in the drafting studio at Taliesin drawing the gallery bookshelves and fireplace hardware of the Malcolm and Nancy Willey House, Minneapolis, Minnesota (1934). Wright commissioned this photograph for publication in a 1935 *Architectural Forum* issue featuring the house.

FIRST PROJECTS

Concurrent with the arrival of the first apprentices of the Taliesin Fellowship came a letter from prospective client Nancy Willey of Minneapolis. She had just read Wright's autobiography and was inspired by his call for America's architects to provide affordable housing for America's middle class. She inquired if Wright might consider making that ideal a reality for her and her husband, Malcolm, a recently tenured professor of sociology at the University of Minnesota.

"I have little hope that you would take on anything so trivial, that was also not near you," she wrote. Unbeknown to her, Wright was without work and ready to design almost anything for anybody. He responded, "Nothing is trivial because it is not 'big'" and set the project in motion. He scrawled "Eureka, a client!" on her letter and posted it in the drafting room for all to see.[42] With that, the Fellowship had at least some architectural work, not just older drawings to copy. For Howe, it meant his first contribution to Wright's architecture.

The Willey House, both in its unexecuted form and in the second built version, is among the smaller yet more important works in Wright's residential canon. Not only is it the first project designed and completed after the formation of the Fellowship, it also represented a new focus for Wright's work: the affordable dwelling for middle-class American citizens. It is significant as a bridge between Wright's earlier Prairie work and the Usonian houses soon to come.[43]

Howe and Abe Dombar assisted on the working drawing set, which largely Klumb produced.[44] Howe drew interior elevations of the gallery, kitchen cabinets, and fireplace grate and apparatus. "[The Willey House] is where I first learned to draw," Howe later proclaimed. He credited Klumb with a primary teaching role on this project and, for that reason, always remained fond of him ("he was wonderful") and of the Willey House.[45]

Shortly after the production of the final Willey House drawings in early 1934, Wright secured funds from Edgar Kaufmann Sr. for the realization of an important project. The

As the Wisconsin winter set in, members of the Fellowship packed a truck and cars and wound their way south and west to Arizona. Traveling on a shoestring budget meant eating makeshift meals by the side of the road and many nights sleeping in the open or crowded into motel rooms or borrowed accommodations. Howe is shown standing next to the car.

Aerial view of La Hacienda courtyard with work ongoing on the Broadacre City model, Chandler, Arizona, winter 1935. The model, built in multiple segments, was moved under cover overnight and brought into the sunlight by day. Howe stands next to Wright (who is wearing a hat) and helped bring to life Wright's decentralized vision of the future.

Pittsburgh department store magnate, whose son was enrolled in the Fellowship, donated funds for the production of a large-scale exhibition model of Wright's idealized American place: Broadacre City. *The Disappearing City,* Wright's second publication of 1932, put forth the seminal idea of a city at once "everywhere and nowhere" that resulted from the decentralizing promise of the automobile. The proposed model showed a limited-access freeway (none yet existed), lined with factories and distribution warehouses, scattered tall buildings, and Usonian houses sitting on one-acre plots, among other building types. It was meant to bring into tangible form Wright's thesis about the future development of the country due to the sweeping changes brought about by the automobile. Wright had a contract to display the model at the Industrial Arts Exposition in New York City's Rockefeller Center, in the spring of 1935, with hopes for it to tour nationally.[46] Its design and construction became the main focus of the Fellowship during the winter of 1934–35.

To produce it, Wright took his doctor's advice to leave the Wisconsin winter behind and find a more salubrious climate to thwart his recurring bouts of pneumonia. So Wright embarked on a great adventure: leading the Fellowship, thirty-some people strong, on an automotive trek to Chandler, Arizona. There they could avoid the travails of another

Opposite top Perspective rendering of the Herbert and Katherine Jacobs House I, Madison, Wisconsin (1936), the first Usonian house to be constructed. Howe and Wright collaborated on this drawing, Wright adding a great deal of the vegetation.

Opposite bottom Paul and Jean Hanna, Honeycomb House, Palo Alto, California (1936). Howe not only drew this presentation rendering but also prepared his first set of working drawings for this early Usonian house.

Wisconsin winter, and the Broadacre model would take shape. Wright had secured lodging and a workplace for the entire Fellowship at La Hacienda, a quaint inn situated at the edge of town owned by Wright's good friend and patron Dr. Alexander Chandler. He was also affiliated with the prestigious San Marcos Hotel, an entrepreneur and powerful landowner, and had commissioned Wright's San Marcos-in-the-Desert, near Chandler, Arizona (1927), a project doomed by the stock market crash of 1929.[47]

The 1,500-mile journey relocated the entire Fellowship by car and truck caravan. The group ventured from Spring Green across the frozen midwestern prairie, the Great Plains, and the Rocky Mountains to Chandler.[48] This trip was undertaken in early January 1935, as winter settled in, on two-lane roads, long before the Interstate highway system made travel easier.

The expedition greatly expanded the horizons of the twenty-one-year-old Howe, who had not previously traveled beyond the Midwest. According to Howe, the seven-day journey south and west included sleeping in the attic of a college building in Lawrence, Kansas. Then came lunch with the eminent journalist and Progressive movement leader William Allen White in Emporia, Kansas. Later, they dined with former governor Henry Allen, a Wright client, at his 1917 Prairie house in Wichita, Kansas.[49] The next night was spent in sleeping bags on the floor of Wright's recently constructed Richard and Georgia Jones House in Tulsa, Oklahoma, 1929. Finally, they made the long haul across Texas, New Mexico, and half of Arizona.

La Hacienda, with its open courtyard, adjacent service sheds, and polo stables, allowed ample workshop space for constructing the ambitious model: almost thirteen feet by thirteen feet, made of many separate pieces. Howe was in the thick of the model-making effort, as photographs attest. He worked alongside Wright, "who changed things constantly," recalled Howe.[50] They usually worked on the model under the sun in the open courtyard, bringing it under the roof at night and when rain threatened. To work out specific components of the model prior to crafting them, Wright, Howe, and others drew the freeway overpass, the arena, and a dozen or so other elements. To accomplish this, drafting tables were set up under the roofs of the adjacent sheds. Howe recalls being amused by two or three mules at the fence at one edge of the courtyard, "wiggling their ears in a most comical way" as work progressed.[51] By the end of March, the model was pronounced complete and several apprentices drove it to New York City by pickup truck for installation and display at Rockefeller Center. As the truck departed, Wright, hoping the exposure would lead to further commissions, wryly commented about having all the Fellowship "eggs" in one basket.[52]

With the model completed, by April 1 the spring pilgrimage north and east back to Taliesin was on. The Wright family returned by train. For members of the Fellowship, the return trip was not a caravan; instead, cars filled with apprentices took the opportunity to explore their own routes back to Wisconsin. Howe and his traveling companions ventured to the Grand Canyon, then north through the mountains of Colorado, where a blizzard interrupted their journey.[53]

In early 1935 the pattern of the annual seasonal migration of the Fellowship was set. This continued throughout the rest of Wright's life and beyond; only the fuel rationing of World War II interrupted it. While Wright led the first caravan, "looking like gypsies," according to one participant, in subsequent years the Wright family traveled both directions

HOUSE FOR HERBERT JACOBS
MADISON, WISCONSIN

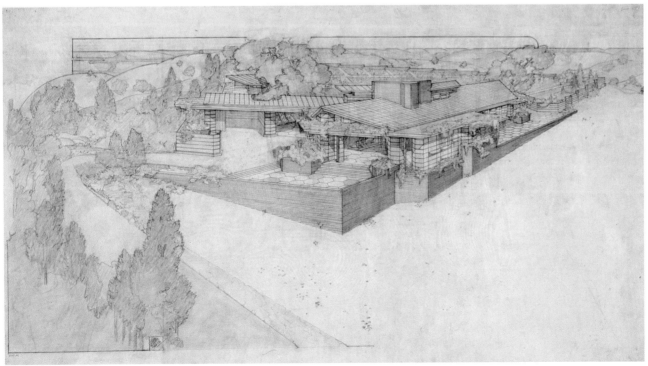

THE TALIESIN FELLOWSHIP

by train. Wes Peters, always the leader among the apprentices, led the caravans on the organized journeys south.[54]

A side trip to California punctuated the first Arizona stay.[55] The focus was visiting Wright's built work in Los Angeles (Aline Barnsdall's Hollyhock House [1917] and the four textile block houses) and touring Lloyd Wright's built work and studio.[56] A visit to winter recreation facilities at snowy Lake Arrowhead in the San Bernardino National Forest rounded out the trip.

THE FIRST USONIAN HOUSES

Wright's architectural fortunes remained tenuous in the mid-1930s and income was intermittent. Although the darkest days of the Depression had passed, the architectural profession had not rebounded in any meaningful way. Economically, Wright and the Fellowship still struggled to get by.

The publication of *An Autobiography* brought requests for modest dwellings from a number of middle-class individuals like the Willeys. Charles and Louise Hoult of Wichita, Kansas, commissioned the first of the Usonian houses in 1935. Though unbuilt, it was quickly followed by commissions for similar houses for Robert and Jeannette Lusk of Huron, South Dakota (1935, also unbuilt), and the Herbert Jacobs family of Madison, Wisconsin, the first to be constructed in 1936. Usonian was Wright's distinctive name for small, low-cost residences meant to house the middle class in a dignified democratic architecture. They relied heavily on prefabrication concepts and unit system modules. He thought of these innovative, experimental houses as key building blocks of Broadacre City.

Wright systematized the architectural production of the Usonians, with the houses built on standard units or dimensional modules. In plan the modules were typically four-foot squares, two-by-four-foot rectangles, diamonds, triangles, or hexagons. In section and elevation, vertical unit modules related to brick and board dimensions. Standard details for connections, window fabrication, roof overhangs, wall construction, and the like were developed and utilized again and again. With time, Howe became so adept at producing Usonian house working drawing sets that he could produce one in a week.[57]

S. C. Johnson & Son Administration Building, Racine, Wisconsin (1936). Howe occasionally stayed on the construction site for days at a time, drawing essential details for the ongoing construction and working in a temporary shed.

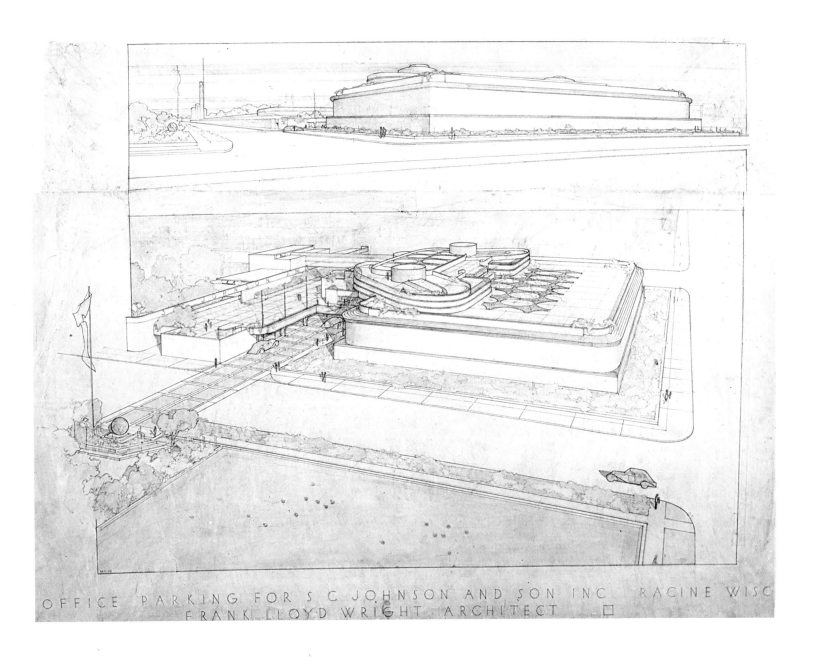

OFFICE PARKING FOR S C JOHNSON AND SON INC RACINE WISC
FRANK LLOYD WRIGHT ARCHITECT □

Howe played a major role in the team effort in the Taliesin
studio on the S. C. Johnson & Son Administration Building.
He drew numerous perspectives, as well as plans and
elevations for the original presentation. Many, many details
followed as the final building was realized.

THE TALIESIN FELLOWSHIP

Howe considered this tour de force of perspective drawing for the S. C. Johnson & Son Administration Building to be one of his toughest drawing challenges. Laying out three-point perspectives is an exacting chore; doing so with curves greatly heightens the degree of difficulty.

Howe had considerable involvement in these projects, typically assisting with plan and elevation drawings or laying out perspectives. However, for the next Usonian, that for Paul and Jean Hanna, of Palo Alto, California (1936), he was tasked with producing the working drawings, with Goodall acting as mentor. During the winter of 1935–36, again at La Hacienda, Howe learned from the more experienced Goodall how to produce the roughly ten-page set to guide the builders through construction.[58] Many of the details were drawn at one-half full size, so the carpenters would better understand how to put Wright's intricate geometric puzzle together. A heightened degree of difficulty was introduced with the Hanna House, also known as the Honeycomb House, due to the unit system of hexagonal modules that guided the plan. Wright was enamored of "the geometry of the bees" because he felt it was more sympathetic to human movement. Proudly, Howe recalled, "I had great sheets," meaning "I produced great pages of drawings for the construction set."[59] Howe also drew the presentation perspective, but Wright added most of the landscape features and vegetation, loosening up Howe's tighter, more precise drawing style, as he was to do on countless occasions in the future.

ECONOMIC RECOVERY AT LAST

Economic and architectural fortunes brightened considerably for the Fellowship when Wright secured two commissions in quick succession. One was a vacation home for Edgar Kaufmann Sr. and his wife, Liliane, in Mill Run, Pennsylvania (1935). It has been known since its design as Fallingwater. The second was for the S. C. Johnson & Son Administration Building in Racine, Wisconsin (1936). When fully realized, they catapulted Wright back into the architectural limelight, even landing him on the cover of *Time*, considered the most coveted honor in American life at the time.[60]

The ensuing publicity, in both the professional and popular press, resulted in a renewed flow of commissions for Wright as the economy recovered in the later 1930s. A great many Usonian residences followed, as young, adventurous, middle-class clients sought Wright's services. The incoming work also filled the coffers at Taliesin for the first time in ages. Within a five-year period, the growing Fellowship was transformed from a subsistence farming and construction brigade to a thriving architectural enterprise that produced a prodigious number of significant structures. By decade's end, architectural activity had "intensified," to use Howe's term. The trickle of new work from the early 1930s (four new projects in 1934 and five in 1935) ballooned to twenty-three in 1939 and thirty-two in 1940.

Creation of the S. C. Johnson & Son Administration Building became an epic undertaking for the Fellowship. It involved hundreds of drawings produced over several years, a contentious construction campaign, and huge cost overruns. It yielded the building that helped reestablish Wright as a preeminent architect at the forefront of the profession and a resurgent force on the American cultural landscape. Tafel aptly called it "Mr. Wright's Ninth Symphony."[61]

By 1935 Herbert F. Johnson Jr., the son in S. C. Johnson & Son Company, needed a new headquarters office building for his company, the sales of which were rising, despite the Depression, thanks to their Glo-Coat product.[62] Wright was recommended as architect; the two men bonded over their shared taste in streamlined Lincoln Zephyrs. The radical new office design responded to its industrial setting with a streamlined brick enclosure daylit from above and devoid of conventional windows. The monumental great hall promised the drama of a Gothic cathedral with its soaring spatial volume animated by filtered light from above. It soared in cost but immediately upon completion became a symbol of the possibilities of the modern age.

Recalling the design of the S. C. Johnson & Son Administration Building, Howe made it clear that this was a team effort in the drafting studio. In fact, the entire group of apprentice architects worked to meet the tight schedule for the ambitious project.[63] Peters and Mendel Glickman, Wright's engineer at the Fellowship, performed the complex engineering required for the daring columns that supported the roof of the great hall. Tafel monitored the on-site construction, interacting constantly with the contractor and addressing issue after issue as architectural intermediary between Wright back at Taliesin and the general contracting team at the site.

Howe indicated he played a central role in producing the plans, sections, and elevations of the building, as well as the numerous presentation perspectives. Eventually, he drew a great many construction details of the complicated structure, with its innovative materials, exposed concrete columns, heated and colored concrete floors, brick with cork insulation between the inside and outside wythes, Kasota stone, and bundled Pyrex glass tubing for roof skylights and horizontal illuminating bands. He produced what he considered to be one of his finest drawings, which also happened to be one of the hardest drawing challenges of his Taliesin career.[64] This is the section perspective of the great hall: the central, monumental room with its slender, dendriform columns supporting a glass roof. Howe recollected that he spent over a week on this one drawing, challenged by the tapered, circular forms of the columnar structures and the ubiquitous rounded corners.

Most often, the presentation drawings at Taliesin were produced with a combination of ink and Wright's favored colored pencils (the German Koh-I-Noor brand) on high-quality white tracing cloth.[65] For the S. C. Johnson & Son Administration Building, a Cherokee red pencil, Wright's favorite color, was utilized, alone, to simulate the brick coloration of the actual building. This gives these drawings a monochromatic presence, which Wright favored during this period.[66]

Right Wright never sat at the drawing board seeking inspiration. Instead, he took to the outdoors and nature, often grading the roads at Taliesin in the early morning (which were constantly washing out) or going for walks in the surrounding hills.

Opposite John Henry Howe, chief of the drafting studio at Taliesin when still in his mid-twenties. His singular dedication to working in the drafting studio allowed him to realize his boyhood dream: working at Wright's side, making organic architecture.

HOWE AND WRIGHT IN THE DRAFTING STUDIO

In later interviews, Howe described the pattern of his working relationship with Wright. He had already impressed Wright enough with his talent and dedication that his drafting table was adjacent to Wright's office in the Taliesin studio. In fact, as space was so tight in the studio, they shared this drafting table by the windows overlooking the dramatic vista to the Wisconsin River valley to the north.[67] In a natural but remarkably quick progression, Howe emerged as the most skillful of the apprentices in the studio and the quickest at producing finished work. With Klumb's departure in 1936, Howe took on the role of Wright's chief draftsman.

According to Howe, a typical morning at Taliesin began quite early when Wright knocked at Howe's door, saying, "Ho, Jack," urging him to join him in the drafting studio. The two men would review a sketch that Wright had just done so that Howe could further develop it.

After this early morning session in the studio, Wright often went for a walk or a horseback ride, or graded the gravel roads at Taliesin—one of his favorite pastimes. While engaged in these activities, Howe believed, Wright was really designing in his head. In Wright's absence, Howe drew at top speed: translating these rough-idea sketches into more finished plans, sections, and elevations to be used for presentation to clients. When Wright returned later, they would review Howe's progress.[68]

THE TALIESIN FELLOWSHIP

Wright's resurgent career led to a *Life* residential competition (September 26, 1938, issue) with traditional architect Royal Barry Wills for the Blackbourn family of Minneapolis, Minnesota. A local bank would fund only the Colonial, not the more radical Wright design rendered by Howe.

After Wright approved Howe's work, Howe painstakingly laid out three-dimensional perspectives in pencil or ink line work. These provided the armature, or underlay, for the final drawing. Either Howe or another apprentice would bring the presentation perspective to life by precisely filling in detail after detail. Next, the drawings were colored using colored pencils. The rendering process also included adding shade and shadow to simulate daylighting conditions. This was often done by a stipple (dots) or hatch (lines) technique. Through this laborious process, Howe transformed the perspectives from line drawings to lush representations of reality. Rendering also included adding entourage elements: landforms or adjacent buildings, people, cars, trees, vegetation, and clouds to achieve a greater sense of reality.

Most often, Howe produced the vast majority of final presentation drawings, with Wright adding even more vegetation to heighten the integration of the building with the natural setting. By careful examination, one can distinguish Howe's precise line work from Wright's looser additions. On select drawings, of which Howe was proudest, Wright added nothing whatsoever to his depiction. To meet deadlines on a project, others might pitch in to do the lettering or add people or cars. In interviews, Howe made it clear he hated drawing both.[69] Yet his notoriously frumpy streamlined red cars are as much a hallmark of his renderings as his distinctive lettering. This is how literally hundreds of projects were conceived and developed throughout their twenty-seven years working together.

Howe was the draftsman doing these perspectives for a simple reason: he, among the Fellowship members, was the most adept at this notoriously difficult architectural task. Thanks to his unrivaled talent, his drawings became real works of art. He was most skilled at bringing the proposed building to life in its recognizable setting. Another consideration was speed. Howe was legendary in the drafting room for the speed at which he could produce a finished drawing. He was virtually unmatched by anyone else in his rate of production. He commented that he needed this skill: "One had to move fast to keep ahead of Mr. Wright."[70] It gained Howe tremendous fame and respect within the ever-changing group of apprentices.

ARCHITECTURAL FORUM ISSUE OF JANUARY 1938

With the realization of the S. C. Johnson & Son Administration Building, Fallingwater, and the first Usonians, Wright was again at the forefront of his profession. In an unprecedented gesture, *Architectural Forum,* the leading American architecture magazine of the day, which was published by Wright's friend Howard Myers, asked Wright to guest-edit an issue dedicated to his revitalized career and recent work.[71] Editor Paul Grozt and an assistant were dispatched to Taliesin to work with Wright on the unique issue.

The format of the issue paired major Prairie-era Wright buildings with some of his more recent work. Wright's most famous early dwelling, the Frederick and Lora Robie House, Chicago (1909), was paired with Fallingwater. Similarly, the Larkin Company Administration Building, Buffalo, New York (1903), was paired with its recent counterpart, the newly completed S. C. Johnson & Son Administration Building. Wright assigned Howe the major responsibility of preparing schematic plans and other presentation drawings for both the more recent projects and the earlier Prairie creations.[72] Howe recalled being tremendously excited by the assignment and the virtual conversion of the studio into a magazine production facility.[73] The resulting issue remains a classic for Wright enthusiasts and scholars, for it neatly summarizes two major phases of his career with the comparative, didactic pairings of Wright's choosing.

TALIESIN-IN-THE-DESERT

With the sizable fees generated by the S. C. Johnson & Son Administration Building, Fallingwater, and Wingspread, the Herbert and Jane Johnson House, Racine, Wisconsin (1937), Wright was able to purchase land in Arizona in 1937 to escape Wisconsin winters for good. After an extensive search, he acquired a remote desert tract northeast of Phoenix, in Paradise Valley, near the little crossroads town of Scottsdale. Quickly, Wright set to work designing a winter compound for the expanding Fellowship, now numbering some forty members.

Howe helped with the few drawings for the Arizona Desert Camp, or Taliesin-in-the-Desert, or Taliesin West, as finally it came to be known. The real importance for him was in what Taliesin West meant for him personally and for the other apprentices. Now the Fellowship would have a second venue, one its members built themselves from the ground up.

The building of Taliesin West was another epic chapter in the history of the Fellowship, with myriad unanticipated hardships. A camp kitchen/dining area/drafting studio was established in a ravine or wash during the winter of 1937–38. This temporary shelter was built largely of wood and canvas. Wright hid the shelter in the wash because he deemed it unsightly and only an expedient until the permanent buildings were habitable. Not fully understood was the potential of washes to fill with water during and after the seasonal rains of November and December. So it was a vulnerable place and certainly not a dry one. Howe later commented that the drawings for Florida Southern College, Lakeland, Florida (1938), were produced in that camp and looked antiqued because they kept getting wet.[74] Clustered nearby, a series of tent shelters housed the apprentices that first winter.

The major construction activity that winter was building the access road to the future building site. The next winter, of 1938–39, a more ambitious construction campaign was undertaken by all in the Fellowship. Taliesin West was built of desert rubble masonry: loose boulders and rocks found on-site, mixed with concrete in slip forms of redwood boards

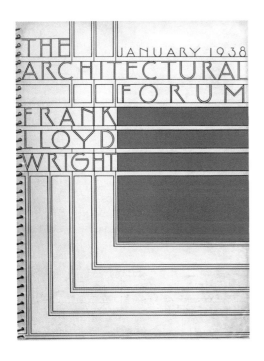

The cover of *Architectural Forum,* January 1938. The issue was devoted to Wright's resurgence and designed by him. It was produced in the Taliesin studio with Howe participating greatly by drawing presentation plans of buildings from all periods of Wright's career.

Above The Fellowship's temporary camp kitchen/studio built in a ravine at the Desert Camp, Paradise Valley, Arizona, winter 1937–38. Howe recalled preparing the Florida Southern College aerial perspective in this leaky tent, plagued by rain, which, he said, gave the drawings an antiqued look.

Left Wright's Taliesin West under construction, winter 1938. This intentionally primitive architectural creation was constructed with boulders from the desert floor set in concrete (known as desert rubble masonry), with a redwood frame above and canvas infill.

THE TALIESIN FELLOWSHIP

Discovering the American Southwest broadened Howe's horizons beyond the familiar landscape of his native Midwest. Here, Wright, Howe, and Peters examine the locally produced wares of an itinerant merchant who made routine visits to Taliesin West.

Above left "Cowboy Jack" Howe in an outfit of the desert Southwest, circa 1937. The change of scenery from Wisconsin to Arizona stimulated Wright's creativity and that of the Fellowship.

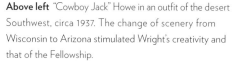

Above right Apprentices were encouraged to build their own shelters in the harsh desert environment. Sheepherder tents, built over a low desert rubble masonry foundation and concrete slab, served as the models for most. Overnight cold and winter rain made for unexpectedly severe challenges.

to construct bearing walls. Redwood beams, acting as overhead framework armatures, provided support for a canvas roof to keep the harsh sun and rain at bay, or so the theory went; in practice things were more problematic.[75] Cherokee red–tinted concrete was poured for the floors, inside and out. Peters led apprentice work parties in constructing the desert rubble masonry walls and placing redwood beams. The women installed the canvas covering for the tent-like enclosures. Most architectural work was suspended for the season as Wright's office, the drafting studio, kitchen and dining room, and kiva were constructed. The kiva, as the gathering space was named, was important for storing the drafting tables so they could be left behind, under lock and key, when the Fellowship returned to Wisconsin and not hauled across country any longer.

Wright considered the early result to be "a rough charcoal sketch for a building."[76] Construction activity continued during the winter of 1939–40, when the garden room (the great residential gathering space), suntrap (the Wrights' private living quarters), and the apprentice court were built. The next winter brought completion of the guest deck, utilizing the roof, and completion of the apprentices' quarters. As with Taliesin in Wisconsin, due to Wright's restless spirit, changes to the Taliesins were a constant until his death in 1959.

With growing numbers of apprentices, many in the Fellowship lived in sheepherder tents built on scattered concrete slab sites in the desert. These were even rougher accommodations than the apprentices were accustomed to in Wisconsin, where many slept in rooms in converted farm buildings. The early days at Taliesin West were primitive in the extreme: a generator for minimal electricity, only one radio telephone to the outside world, a rudimentary hand-dug latrine, cold water from hoses, and hot water available only in Scottsdale (a thirteen-mile drive on rutted, unpaved roads).

Howe documented the newly created Taliesin West in a series of photographs that complement those he made in Wisconsin shortly after arriving at Taliesin 1932. While Howe participated in its construction, he was also the first to be excused when the pressure to meet deadlines proved too great to ignore.

A rare early view of the newly completed studio at Taliesin West, circa 1940. The many buildings at the compound, which was meant to be a primitive camp, were constructed entirely by the apprentices and transformed over the years to better suit the climatic extremes of the desert.

AN EXPANDING FELLOWSHIP

By 1940, both Howe and the Fellowship had matured considerably. Howe was ensconced in the studio as "head man," to quote Besinger.[77] In this position, he acted as the conduit between Wright and the others in the studio. He instructed others in what to produce for a given project. His organizational skills were utilized to efficiently produce the necessary working drawing sets. As for the Fellowship, what had started as a nebulous experiment was now succeeding, both in economic and architectural terms.

Howe was in charge of an architectural staff approaching twenty people. More commissions were on the boards (i.e., being worked on) than at any time since the founding of the Fellowship.[78] By the outbreak of World War II, seventy-five houses had been commissioned during the nine years of the Fellowship in addition to larger nonresidential commissions. In Wisconsin, the studio was no longer in the original Taliesin but at the new, more spacious Hillside. The nodal point of Taliesin had shifted over the hill and with it the center of activity and of Howe's world.

Another perceptible shift was in the Fellowship itself. A hierarchy had developed, with the newcomers now cognizant of the senior apprentices and their somewhat privileged positions.[79] This hurt the morale of the newcomers and fostered resentment. New apprentices came with "preconceptions that were misconceptions," said Besinger, meaning they assumed they would start immediately in the drafting studio, which was seldom the case. Moreover, they were expected to provide the physical labor at the Taliesins. It was notable that by this time, many of the senior apprentices were not contributing much physical labor. Howe was in this latter group, to be sure, always needed in the drafting studio, by Wright's side.

The studio was dominated at this point by the senior apprentices (Peters, Howe, Tafel, Bob Mosher, Benjamin Dombar, Cornelia Brierly, Peter Berndtson, Blaine and Hulda Drake, and John deKoven Hill), making it hard for new apprentices to contribute there. This was made manifest in a poorly received skit, performed in the autumn of 1938, at the sixth anniversary celebration of the Fellowship's founding, by a quartet of newer apprentices who sang (to the tune of the "On, Wisconsin" fight song):

Taliesin, Taliesin

Dear old Shining Brow

Push the pencil 'round the paper,

Try to please Jack Howe.

Hail the red square and the T-square

And the long hair too.

Fight freshmen, but the stu-de-oo

Is not for you.[80]

In practice, each year brought new arrivals and departures, a revolving door of newcomers, few of whom stayed long. One of these was film director Nicholas Ray, who wrote to a friend, "I have felt the hand of genius, and it is a heavy hand."[81] On the positive side, the core group of seniors, mentioned above, now made up a seasoned architectural team. Most had come in the earliest years and had proved themselves with selfless contributions to the Fellowship and to the architectural effort in the studio.

PROSPERITY AND DISSATISFACTION

The increase in architectural activity meant the years of subsistence living were over, at least for the Wrights. Now necessities were augmented by luxuries, particularly for the family. Lectures were now given not to survive but to procure those luxuries, such as Wright's magnificent 1940 Lincoln Continental.

In addition to the discontents facing incoming apprentices, many of the seniors had issues that led to tensions and animosities. At the center of it was the outside work that several were able to garner. Simply put, Wright wanted apprentices to attend to his work, not their own. Accordingly, he changed the previous arrangement whereby apprentices could keep half of their fees for outside work. He declared during the summer of 1941 that an apprentice could keep one-third of the fee, with the Fellowship and Wright each receiving one-third. Naturally, this did not sit well with the senior apprentices who were bringing

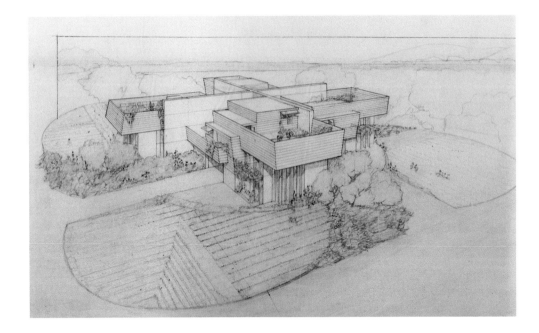

Aerial perspective by Howe of Wright's Cloverleaf Quadruple Housing, Pittsfield, Massachusetts (1942, unexecuted). As World War II loomed and architectural work waned, Wright sought federal commissions, ironically while actively opposing America's entry into the conflict.

in outside work. Many agreed they could not continue under the changed circumstances. Not in anger nor in protest, six seniors departed serially in the following months.[82]

This shift did not have a direct impact on Howe. As head of the studio, he was exactly where he wanted to be: at Wright's side, daily, helping the master create architecture. As such, he was far too busy to concern himself with outside commissions. Nevertheless, the team he led was greatly reduced to only Peters and Mosher as the remaining seniors in the studio.

The second source of discontent was not internal but external. By 1941, war clouds loomed worldwide and could no longer be ignored. The deteriorating situation in Europe had erupted into combat in September 1939; so, too, conflict threatened in the Pacific. Wright had espoused pacifism generally and disdain for all war as a solution to nationalistic concerns and urged America to stay out of any armed conflict. Many in the Fellowship "felt it was other people's war."[83]

Not so others. Many apprentices believed it their duty to serve their country in time of need and left to volunteer for, or were drafted into, the armed services. Several chose to resist the war effort and induction into service. All realized that little new architectural work would be forthcoming with the likely onset of war. Commissions had already fallen off dramatically. Increasingly, the Fellowship seemed in disarray. Suddenly, its very survival was in doubt and a sense of doom took over.[84] After the Japanese attack on Pearl Harbor and America's entry into the war in December 1941, the seasonal migration to Arizona was made impossible by wartime gas rationing. A sense of marking time set in as architectural work dried up.

The subsequent implementation of the draft for all eligible men meant each apprentice had to wrestle with the decision to serve (usually advocated by family) or to resist conscription (advocated by Wright). As a result, the war came close to Taliesin in a way that disrupted the work of the Fellowship. John Howe would be greatly affected.

2

A SANDSTONE EXILE

Frank Lloyd Wright was a born proselytizer, a trait he likely inherited from his outspoken Welsh clergymen ancestors. Not one to keep his opinions to himself, Wright freely and frequently expounded on a vast array of subjects, architectural or otherwise. No audience was more familiar with his views than the Taliesin Fellowship. One of Wright's most devoutly held convictions was an abiding commitment to pacifism. As he succinctly stated during a September 1, 1957, segment of *The Mike Wallace Interview,* "I'm against war, always have been and always will be, and everything connected with it is anathema to me."

Wright's pacifist views were challenged in the late 1930s and early 1940s as Nazi aggression escalated in Europe and the United States entered World War II. In 1941 he became estranged from one longtime friend and colleague when he and the cultural critic Lewis Mumford clashed over the issue of the country's involvement in the war. Mumford, who equated Wright's antiwar convictions with cowardice, vilified his friend for failing to "characterize Hitler and his followers" as the "gangsters" they were.[1] Wright in turn defended his patriotism and accused Mumford of being a hypocritical warmonger. "The Chinese say it well," he wrote. "He who runs out of ideas first strikes the first blow." Following the bitter exchange, the two men did not speak for ten years.[2]

John Howe and Wright's other young apprentices were forced to confront their beliefs in the early 1940s as draft-eligible American men were called to serve in World War II. Although ultimately nineteen Fellowship members were drafted or enlisted, others echoed Wright's pacifist stance and resisted induction.[3] "The apprentices were far from unanimous in their attitude toward the war," fellow Curtis Besinger wrote.[4] In the aftermath of the Japanese bombing of Pearl Harbor on December 7, 1941, several apprentices, including Edgar Tafel, James Charlton, Benjamin Dombar, and Robert May, reversed their antiwar stances and

Frank Lloyd Wright (with back to camera) addresses Fellowship members at Taliesin West in Scottsdale, Arizona, in 1941. Pictured from left are Ted Bower, Davy Davison, John Howe, Kenneth Lockhart, Peter Berndtson, Svetlana Peters, Wes Peters, Cornelia Brierly, and Kay Davison.

enlisted or were inducted into the military. May later explained, "Following the attack on Pearl Harbor, I realized that I could and willingly would fight in the armed forces of the United States."[5]

THE PETITION

On March 25, 1941, nine months prior to the attack on Pearl Harbor, Howe and twenty-five other members of the Taliesin Fellowship signed a petition that expressed their intention to "go on record as Objectors to the Compulsory Military Draft which threatens not only to destroy us as a group but violates the deepest concern of our individual consciences."[6] The petition made clear that Fellowship members believed—as a group—they were already serving their country with work that could "honestly be called a national objective." That work was "building better buildings for America, buildings more truly expressive of the land we live in and of the people of our great Democracy."[7] The petition ended with a plea: "We ask that our services in preparing for war be used in the constructive field in which we are already engaged . . . Compulsory conscription will only scatter us and render us impotent."

The petition was sent to Local Draft Board number 1 in Dodgeville, Wisconsin. The fellows' request for collective exemption was denied, but the report was kept on file.[8] Although the apprentices believed solidarity made their petition more persuasive, state and federal officials viewed the united action by "the youth of the Taliesin Fellowship" in another light.[9] They suspected Wright had unduly influenced the group's antidraft resolve and conduct, which some authorities regarded as subversive. The serious nature of the accusation would lead to government scrutiny of Wright and the Taliesin Fellowship in the coming years.

Although Besinger assumed that Wright had "read and perhaps edited" the document, he ascribed its authorship to senior apprentices.[10] Likewise, the signees rebutted any suggestion that Wright had written the communiqué or encouraged them to generate it. Wright also denied any ownership of the document but stood behind the fellows' stance. In December 1942 he was quoted in the *New York Herald Tribune* as saying, "As for conscription, I think it has deprived the young men in America of the honor and privilege of dedicating themselves as freeman to the service of their country. Were I born forty years later than 1869, I, too, would be a conscientious objector."[11]

While there is no question that Wright's empathy was ideologically sincere, he also had a practical reason to support the fellows' resistance to induction. In addition to counting on his stable of apprentices to provide fundamental architectural services, Wright also depended on them to perform a full range of chores necessary to sustain daily life—for him, his family, and the Fellowship—on the two large Taliesin properties in Spring Green, Wisconsin, and Scottsdale, Arizona. The wartime absence of many talented, productive, and able-bodied apprentices significantly decreased Fellowship numbers and substantially increased work-loads for those who remained behind. By May 1944 Fellowship numbers had dwindled to a mere few, but the list of essential tasks was as long as ever. It was a formidable challenge, as Wright's secretary Eugene "Gene" Masselink described: "After all, there are only Wes, Cornelia, Peter, Svet, Del, Bert, Johnnie, and me to do it all—and get the gardens and farms going—plus upkeep of the carcass," "carcass" meaning the Taliesin compound.[12] The task became even more daunting when wartime rationing of gasoline curtailed the Fellowship's annual winter migration from Wisconsin to Arizona. When the weather turned cold, the skeletal roster of members had to labor diligently to heat and keep habitable the sprawling complex in Spring Green.

CONSCIENTIOUS OBJECTION

At least five Fellowship members who claimed to be conscientious objectors (COs), including Howe, Besinger, Allen Lape "Davy" Davison, Howard Ten Brink, and Marcus Weston, received 1-A classifications, meaning they were available and fit for general military service. Although the men believed they could not serve in good conscience, to resist induction was to risk arrest and imprisonment. When 1-A status was conferred on them, "it started Wright to busying around," Howe wrote in an April 1942 letter to his parents. "He has seen every general or person of importance in Arizona, written to those in Wisconsin and Washington, and is going to see the President when in Washington." Wright also secured the services of Washington, D.C.-based attorney Robert Scher to represent the apprentices in court and to handle appeals.[13]

Besinger and Ten Brink successfully appealed for reclassification as COs. They spent the war years in a series of Civilian Public Service (CPS) camps, alternatives to military service for COs during World War II, where they performed a variety of civilian jobs. However, the appeals board rejected petitions requesting the same reclassification from Howe, Davison, and Weston.[14] By June 1943 the three men had been arrested, tried, and convicted for failure to report for military service. Judge Patrick T. Stone of Madison, Wisconsin, imposed a three-year sentence on Weston. Davison and Howe were given four-year sentences and hundred-dollar fines. All three men were sent to the Federal Correctional Institution in Sandstone, Minnesota, to serve their time.[15] Apprentice Aaron Green also faced prosecution for failure to report for induction. In 1942 he was arraigned in federal court and "given the opportunity to enlist in the Air Corps." He did so on October 6, 1942.[16]

Several factors may have resulted in the failure of Howe's appeal and his harsher sentence. Although he knew the majority of men who had been granted CO classification were Quakers, Mennonites, or members of similar religious sects known for nonviolent credos, Howe argued his objection to induction was rooted in personal and experiential—not religious—beliefs. He contended his convictions stemmed from "intelligence," not "blind faith," and in a "developed sense of values," not "childhood training." His bottom line was "I refuse to kill."[17]

With regard to reclassification, laws at the time permitted "a separate classification for war objectors only if it is found that their objection is based upon religious training and belief."[18] A March 1943 communication from U.S. Department of Justice assistant attorney general Wendell Berge stated that although Howe was an Episcopalian, "The Board thought that his beliefs were the result of the teachings of Frank Lloyd Wright, rather than any religious training and belief." Lacking the required religious inculcation, Howe did not qualify for classification as a CO. The board was also of the opinion that "no Presidential appeal was warranted."[19]

This was not the first time government representatives had questioned the origin of Howe's beliefs or raised the issue of undue influence by Wright on Fellowship members. Howe, Weston, and Davison were among the signers of the aforementioned 1941 petition received by the Dodgeville draft board, a pronouncement that was interpreted by some as being politically motivated. Believing Wright to be responsible for inciting the fellows' united action, in December 1942 Judge Stone requested an FBI investigation be launched into the architect and the

This Howe family portrait was taken in 1943 shortly before Howe's June 16 trial and conviction for refusing conscription into the military during World War II. John Howe is at far left.

Taliesin Fellowship, in essence suggesting Wright was flirting with sedition. In response to being accused of a subversive act, Wright publicly blasted the judge as "another one of the things that is wrong about America," called for his removal from the bench "for the safety of the nation," and assailed the government's "arrogant prejudice raised against any man who refuses to run with the pack."[20] None of the remarks was likely to sway Judge Stone's future rulings in favor of Howe's—or any other apprentice's—draft exemption.

That same month, on the order of Director J. Edgar Hoover, the FBI launched an investigation into possible "violation of the Sedition Statutes," by Wright. The following spring Berge, who had been asked by Hoover to evaluate the lengthy report, ruled no further action was warranted.[21]

Ultimately it is probable that Howe's father (and other members of his family) dealt the final blow to Howe's reclassification efforts by failing to endorse his son's convictions. Prior to his arrest, Howe traveled to Dodgeville to review his draft file.[22] "Almost everything was favorable . . . and in the F.B.I. report all of the neighbors or informants came to my support beautifully," he wrote to his parents. "The only hitch was the fact that my family did not seem to be in accord with my *beliefs,* which is of course not true, and supported the Hearing Officer's claim that I had been coerced by Mr. Wright. All I ask of you both is to believe in me and any decisions I may make and be willing to back me up. I feel so strongly about the whole business that words cannot express it." Howe closed the letter with a sober assessment of his position: "After all, I will live with myself and my work more than with anyone else; and there is no middle road, much as we may idly wish for one."[23]

INMATE NUMBER 1818

Immediately following conviction and sentencing on June 16 in Wausau, Wisconsin, Howe and Davison were sent to the Dane County jail in Madison. A week later they were transferred to the Federal Correctional Institution, Sandstone, a low-security prison in Pine County, Minnesota, about one hundred miles north of Minneapolis; Weston was already serving time at Sandstone.[24] There, as inmate number 1818, Howe joined other COs and political prisoners in confinement. Four weeks of quarantine followed.

"We are located in a large pine clearing alongside the Kettle River, which flows below in a deep, red, sandstone gorge and which, I regret to say, cannot be seen from the buildings," Howe reported to his mother.[25] He assured her, however, that the dormitory accommodations were comfortable, that the food was good, that sports facilities abounded, and that the atmosphere was restful. He looked forward to working in the garden or doing finish carpentry. "All of these things are possible here," he wrote.[26] Howe soon settled into a routine. In the mornings he was "free to be unfree in the dormitory."[27] Afternoons brought work in the prison library as a draftsman for the institution. He devoted evenings to teaching drawing and furniture design to inmates. "I was not only given pencil and paper but a three-year opportunity to have an architectural atelier in which others who were so minded could spend a couple of pleasant creative hours each evening."[28] The arrangement also provided Howe with a nook in the library in which to design his own work.

Although compared to penitentiary standards daily life at Sandstone was somewhat relaxed, contact with the outside world (and those with whom contact was permitted) was restricted and regimented. Incoming and outgoing letters had to adhere to a specified format and could not exceed a single sheet of paper. The size and weight of packages were strictly policed, as were the number and frequency of visitors.

As a rule, COs were assigned indoor work—a plus in the Minnesota winter months—but Howe yearned to be outdoors beyond the confines of "the barren courtyard where not a blade of grass could grow."[29] Occasionally he was assigned surveying duties along the Kettle River. There he would "stand alone among the birch trees and rocks contemplating my solitude, my presence there." Although the prison whistle inevitably wrenched him from communing with nature, his reveries remained potent: "The image of the birch trees and rocks would stay with me for several weeks and I would include them in my drawings of houses."

Howe maintained communication with members of his family while in prison. Wright also wrote and, occasionally, visited him and the other incarcerated Taliesin apprentices. In his notes, Wright often expressed frustration at the imprisonment of his "boys" and their removal from active work in the drafting room: "What a shame that such man-power as this is wasted while the nations quarrel like a pack of dogs . . . and my boys have to go out where they do not belong for crimes they did not commit, unless having a conscience is a crime."[30] He repeatedly assured Howe and Davison that he was actively pursuing appeals for them. Beyond his rants about the government's lack of wisdom and principles, Wright's letters could be informational and, every so often, included a candid admission. For example, in an August

1944 letter to Howe he wrote, "I've never needed my own 'Fellows' as much as I need them now. And I know how much you Fellows need your Fellowship. My impotence in connection with your imprisonment is hard to bear."[31]

THE MASSELINK–HOWE CORRESPONDENCE

Gene Masselink was Howe's most faithful and prolific correspondent during the Sandstone years; the two men, who were close friends, regularly exchanged letters over the thirty-three-month period. Only Masselink's half of the correspondence—approximately three hundred letters—exists today, but the extant letters provide insight into life and activities at Sandstone and Taliesin during Howe's confinement.

Masselink was a key figure at Taliesin. Trained as an artist and graphic designer, he served as Wright's secretary. In that capacity, he handled the architect's voluminous correspondence, typed his numerous manuscripts, and personally designed, typeset, and duplicated Taliesin publications—to enumerate but a few of his responsibilities. With Fellowship numbers at an all-time low during World War II—and with Howe confined at Sandstone—Masselink's responsibilities exponentially expanded. Yet, as busy as he was at Taliesin, he unfailingly found time to compose long, newsy letters to his imprisoned friend. In his very first note to Howe, dated July 18, 1943, Masselink proposed a mutual agreement by which "these letters are distinctly *not* reserved for posterity *nor* publication *nor* our grandchildren's children to tie in Cherokee red ribbons," alluding to Wright's favored color.[32] Fortunately, for history and historians, the pact was not enforced. The correspondence provides a valuable, personal account of the war years at Taliesin.

Masselink kept Howe apprised of new clients, the most significant of the period being the philanthropist Solomon R. Guggenheim and Baroness Hilla Rebay, who approached Wright in 1943 to design the museum of nonobjective art in New York City that would eventually bear Guggenheim's name. The letters also detailed Wright's activities, visitors to, and social events at Taliesin, as well as the everyday affairs of apprentices, friends, and family. Masselink kept Howe informed about the status of ongoing projects and the work flow in the drafting room, as a November 19, 1944, letter conveys: "How your heart would have warmed to hear

Wes telling the draughting room in general the other day (Ted and Johnnie—Kenn and the new boys all present) that if YOU were here, all this preliminary study work would have been up and out long ago."[33]

Masselink also confessed to the extraordinary pressure he felt due to a crushing workload at Taliesin. He often vented frustrations to Howe and, occasionally, sought his advice. In turn, he offered similar solace to Howe when needed. He sent cigarettes, candy bars, and books to Sandstone to lift his friend's spirits. Howe was also capable of cajoling his friend out of the occasional funk, as a witty Masselink comeback reveals: "I am so glad my recent suicide notes have been giving you pleasure. . . . Going on the well founded theory that Misery Loves Company—I thought they might."[34] Unquestionably, Masselink's letters were a lifeline for Howe and conduit of communication between him and the Fellowship during the Sandstone years. Masselink spent many late hours writing letters to assure his colleague that he had not been forgotten, had not been replaced, that his services were needed, and his return to Taliesin eagerly anticipated.

THE BOX PROJECTS

Despite being physically removed from Taliesin during his incarceration, Howe continued to participate (with Masselink's assistance) in the box projects, a semiannual Fellowship tradition. Each year, on Christmas and Wright's birthday (June 8), apprentices were invited to create projects of their own design to be presented to Wright as a gesture of appreciation. For Wright, the box projects afforded the opportunity to focus on each apprentice's individual skills and artistic development—a useful evaluation tool in the absence of a structured curriculum or grading system at the school.

All manner of artistic offerings, including drawings, paintings, poems, textiles, and nature studies, were collected and placed in a presentation box, designed and fabricated on each occasion by an apprentice or team of apprentices. The boxes were generally about eighteen

A Taliesin fellow explains his contribution to a box project in this photograph, circa 1950. The box projects, presented to Wright on Christmas and his birthday, were collections of drawings, designs, and creative efforts made by the fellows. Howe is standing in the back row, fourth from right.

While at Sandstone, Howe honed the sophistication of his graphic techniques as shown by these perspectives for a series of Six Cinder Block and Plywood Houses. The closely packed lines and stippling, or dots, that he used to render vegetation and convey texture and shadow would become a signature of his style.

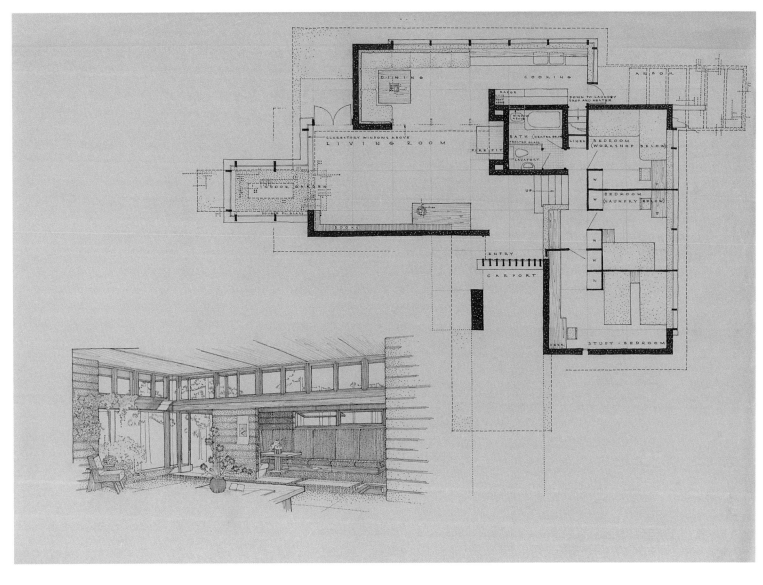

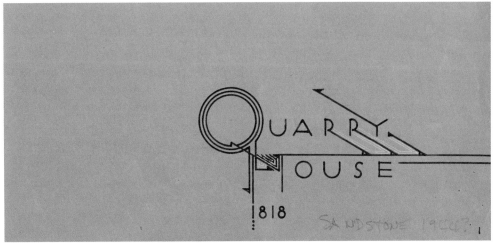

Above Most of Howe's Sandstone projects were fully developed, as this floor plan and interior perspective (companion drawings to the perspectives in the previous illustration) demonstrate.

Left Howe signed his Sandstone drawings, like this title page for a set of Quarry House renderings, with his inmate number, 1818.

A SANDSTONE EXILE

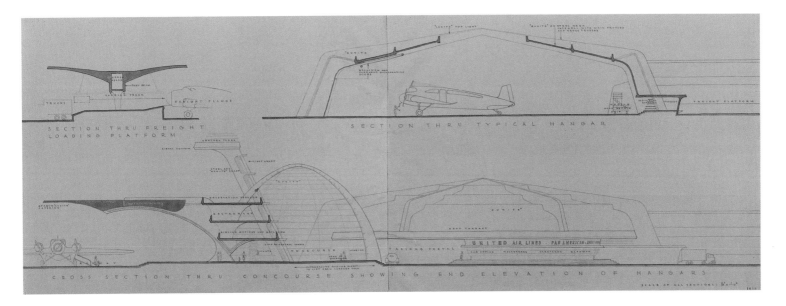

Opposite Drawing on his memory of a favorite Spring Green location and view, Howe placed his design for the Quarry House across the Wyoming Valley from Taliesin, which he depicted in the distance.

Above Howe created many visionary designs during his thirty-three months at Sandstone, including this one for an airport.

by twenty-four inches in dimension, or the size of a folded sheet of drafting paper.[35] On the appointed dates, with members of the Fellowship in attendance, Wright opened the box, listened to each apprentice's presentation, and critiqued his or her work. For Fellowship members, who spent the vast majority of their time laboring on projects designed by Wright, the box projects provided rare opportunities for creative expression. Howe, who had sometimes been too busy in the drafting room to be a regular contributor to the box projects, found plenty of time to participate during his imprisonment.[36]

Howe contributed at least half a dozen box projects in absentia. Among them were "Airport," "Community Cooperative," "Northern Nest," "Seven Brick Houses," "Six Cinder Block and Plywood Houses," "Quarry House," and a four-house collection he called "Variations of Usonian Type." Of Howe's drawings, Wright said (in his inimitable, if obtuse, style), "Say! Jack has 'em like rabbits." He praised the airport renderings as "the best and most beautiful" but came close to paying the ultimate compliment to Howe's Usonian designs: "I could build them just as they are—almost."[37] Wright generally wrote directly to Howe and Davison to thank them for their contributions. But on occasion, Masselink related Wright's praise in a letter. Of the "Quarry House," he wrote, "[Mr. Wright] went through the brown drawings of your house on the hill almost in wonder—I have never seen him like that. . . . [He] ended up saying you were without doubt the 'greatest draughtsman in the world.' "[38] If Wright had worried that incarceration might dull Howe's talent, the Sandstone drawings allayed his fears. "Well, I guess Jail is no bar to the growth of imagination," he observed.[39]

Howe's drawings for the box projects were consistently masterful. But some of the projects he conceived, such as "Airport," were also architecturally innovative. His proposed use of reinforced concrete to create sculptural, curvilinear forms and deep, wing-like cantilevers predated, by nearly two decades, Eero Saarinen's cutting-edge designs for the TWA terminal at John F. Kennedy International Airport (formerly Idlewild Airport) in New York City and Dulles International Airport in Sterling, Virginia. The Lucite-domed concourse and integrated control tower were imaginative—and prescient—visions for airport design.

BOUNDLESS CREATIVITY

The box projects were merely one aspect of Howe's creative output during his time at Sandstone. It was in the projects he conceived in his idle time—for no one's satisfaction but his own—that his imagination and talent shone most brilliantly. There were several reasons for this. At Sandstone, architecturally speaking, Howe was his own boss. With no clients (or Wright) to please, no budgets to constrain him, no deadlines to race toward, and lots of time on his hands, he was free to explore any and all creative impulses. For most of his career, Howe derived architectural inspiration from the dictum "the land is the beginning." Many of his most remarkable Sandstone projects, however, lacked site specificity and associated zoning or code requirements and restrictions; they were architectural fantasies. They were also therapeutic exercises. Howe believed his profession gave him an edge when it came to coping with incarceration. "Being an architect, I was better able to create a world within which to live," he later observed. "The confinements of prison not only need not be a barrier to the creative person, but given pencil and paper, can open wide vistas for him."[40] Howe signed the majority of the drawings he made at Sandstone with his inmate number, 1818.

Howe derived inspiration for his projects from various sources, including memories. For example, the semiannual journey the Fellowship took between Wisconsin and its winter haven in Arizona inspired him to conceive a twenty-eight-foot-long recreation vehicle—a cross between an automobile and a motor home. The prototype was equipped with a kitchen, bathroom with shower, heated seating area, writing desk, and sleeping accommodations for two. Flexible roof joints, with embedded lighting elements, allowed the living space to expand comfortably to a width of twelve feet. The vehicle provided amenities that would have improved the quality of life on any road trip in the 1940s.

For "House of Fabric," Howe explored similar themes of spatial economies while considering possible applications of new materials. He proposed a living area framed by lightweight ply-

This prototype for a recreational vehicle was inspired by Howe's memories of the Fellowship's seasonal road trips between Wisconsin and Arizona.

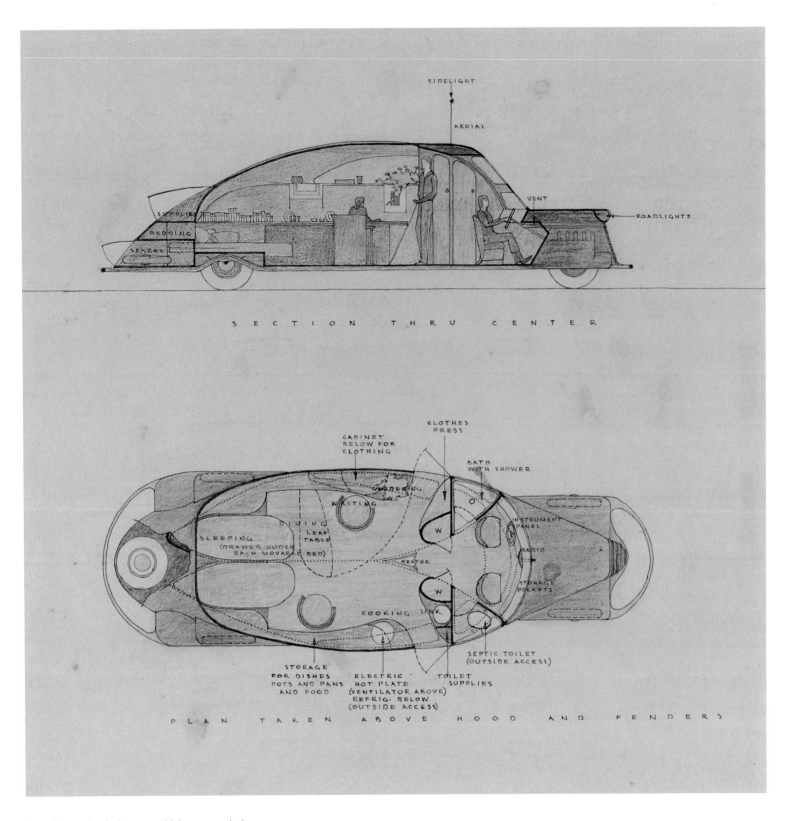

SIDELIGHT

AERIAL

SUPPLIES
BEDDING
SPARES

VENT
ROADLIGHTS

SECTION THRU CENTER

CLOTHES
PRESS

CABINET
BELOW FOR
CLOTHING

BATH
WITH SHOWER

GARDENING

WRITING

DINING
LEAF
TABLE

SLEEPING
(DRAWER UNDER
EACH MOVABLE BED)

W

INSTRUMENT
PANEL

RADIO

W

HEATER

STORAGE
POCKETS

COOKING   SINK

STORAGE
FOR DISHES
POTS AND PANS
AND FOOD

ELECTRIC
HOT PLATE
(VENTILATOR ABOVE)
REFRIG. BELOW
(OUTSIDE ACCESS)

TOILET
SUPPLIES

SEPTIC TOILET
(OUTSIDE ACCESS)

PLAN   TAKEN   ABOVE   HOOD   AND   FENDERS

According to Howe's plan, two could sleep, eat, and relax
in comfort in the expandable vehicle.

A SANDSTONE EXILE

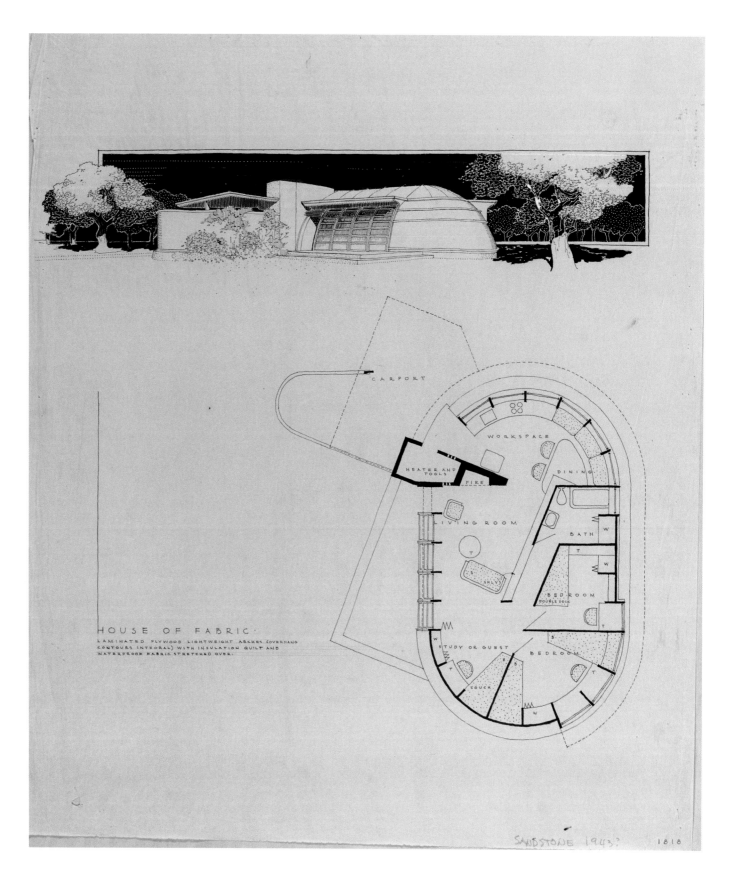

CARPORT

WORKSPACE

DINING

HEATER AND
TOOLS

FIRE

LIVING ROOM

BATH

W

T

S SHLV

T

W

BEDROOM
DOUBLE DECK

T

STUDY OR GUEST

BEDROOM

W

T

S

S

T

COUCH

W

HOUSE OF FABRIC:
LAMINATED PLYWOOD LIGHTWEIGHT ARCHES (OVERHANG
CONTOURS INTEGRAL) WITH INSULATION QUILT AND
WATERPROOF FABRIC STRETCHED OVER.

SANDSTONE 1943? 1818

A SANDSTONE EXILE

Opposite For his "House of Fabric," Howe considered waterproof, insulated fabric for the dwelling's walls.

Above Howe created this perspective for a building he envisioned as a church or a community center.

wood arches sheathed in waterproof, insulated fabric. The clever plan, created by colliding ovoid and rectilinear geometries, resulted in an efficient, spacious three-bedroom abode. As a veteran renderer of Wright's Usonian house plans, Howe may have taken inspiration from the spatial organization and innovative use of materials in these affordable homes for the American middle class. Wright's use of fabric in architecture, notably its early application in the desert compound at Taliesin West, may also have been in Howe's thoughts.

An amusing 1944 project, "A House for I. M. Timid," reveals Howe did not lose his sense of humor while incarcerated. As its title suggests, the design was not architecturally innovative, but the ordinary house was perfectly suited to its Caspar Milquetoast client, who lived at 1944 Middleovda Road. The street number was derived from the year the project was drawn. Although a lighthearted reading of "Middleovda Road" is possible, the drawing conveys a more thoughtful meaning. As previously mentioned, in a pre-arrest letter to his parents, Howe wrote that for a conscientious objector, "there is no middle road, much as we may idly wish for one." With a year of prison behind him and several yet to serve, Howe undoubtedly—more than idly—yearned for such an address.

Howe also created a number of projects for fellow Sandstone inmates who were serving time for their pacifist or political views. For the writer J. F. Powers, a conscientious objector who would win a National Book Award in 1963 for his novel *Morte d'Urban,* Howe envisioned "A Writer's Farm for Jim Powers."[41] Designed as a cooperative community (similar in concept to Taliesin), the large, multibuilding facility included a group kitchen, lounge, dining facilities, an eighty-seat amphitheater, pool, and a badminton court. The working-farm portion of the complex comprised a cow barn, silo, corncribs, milk and butter rooms, brooder, roosts, and three horse stalls.

For fellow Sandstone inmate Carlos Hudson, Howe designed an idyllic lakeside "Summer House for a Writer."

A wordsmith of a different kind inspired "Summer House for a Writer." For the Minneapolis labor reporter Carlos Hudson, who was serving time at Sandstone as the result of his involvement in a Teamsters dispute in Minneapolis in the early 1940s, Howe designed a small cottage on a sailboat-dotted lake.[42] A large brick fireplace, an asymmetrical chandelier, and expansive lake views dominated the intimate living quarters. The cottage was connected via a walkway to a freestanding, screened pavilion, which was conceived as a compact writer's studio complete with a desk on wheels, a fire pit, and inspirational vistas. A second walkway led to a floating pier on the lake. Howe realized the seductive charm of the idyllic retreat through skillful rendering and the sheer beauty of his evocative colored pencil perspectives.

THE BIG PROJECT

Howe's magnum opus at Sandstone was aptly named the "Big Project." A work of enormous size and scope, it prefigured America's ubiquitous large-scale, mixed-use complexes of later decades.[43] What set Howe's project apart from later examples was the inclusion of myriad community services and cultural offerings, in addition to a full range of retail stores. Although there were a few works in Wright's canon that might have provided some inspiration for the complex, particularly in terms of embracing the automobile, the conceptual and spatial organization of the project was Howe's alone.[44]

Above Howe's remarkable rendering skills are evident in this complex cutaway perspective of the main living areas of his design for Carlos Hudson.

Left This portion of a large aerial perspective of the "Big Project" shows how Howe divided the complex into multilevel units interconnected by pedestrian bridges.

A SANDSTONE EXILE

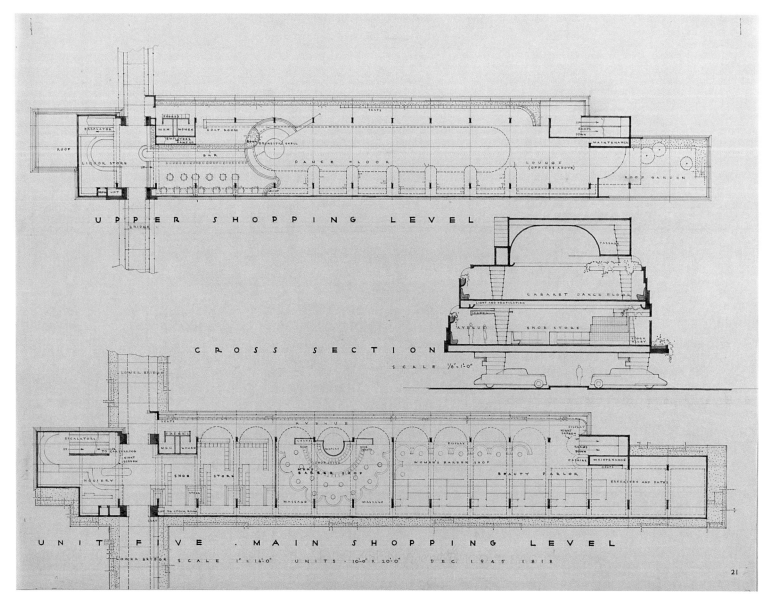

UPPER SHOPPING LEVEL

CROSS SECTION
SCALE 1/8" = 1'-0"

UNIT FIVE . MAIN SHOPPING LEVEL
SCALE 1" = 16'-0"   UNITS - 10'-0" X 20'-0"   DEC. 1945 1818

21

Above The floor plans and section of one of eight units of the Big Project detail a few of the diverse retail and recreational services Howe imagined for the vast, multiuse complex. Howe's vision prefigured the shopping centers and malls that began to proliferate in America in the mid-twentieth century.

Opposite top Howe's minutely detailed perspective, which he delicately rendered in Cherokee red pencil, helps evoke the experience of browsing in this Big Project retail shop.

Opposite bottom The vignette at upper left shows the Big Project's indoor swimming pool. The sketch at lower right depicts a restaurant.

As proposed, the multilevel, thirty-two-square-acre compound was divided into eight themed units that were interconnected by bridges and passageways. Whereas a dizzying array of retail merchants prevailed (including those selling men's, women's, and children's clothing, shoes, gowns, hosiery, sporting goods, gifts, books, cameras, hardware, tools, gadgets, novelties, dishes, silver, glassware, drapery, furniture, toys, games, baked goods, candy, and liquor, to name a few), Howe also allotted space for civic and community organizations (the Boy Scouts, Girl Scouts, and Daughters of the American Revolution were not forgotten) and provided such fundamental services as a bank, post office, barbershop, doctors' and dentists' offices, recreation facilities, and tourist services. The project also offered cultural amenities, including a library, museum, performance spaces, music practice rooms, and a movie theater. The film Howe (perhaps wistfully) chose to be "now playing" on the theater marquee was *À nous la liberté* (Freedom for us), a 1931 French left-wing comedy about an escaped convict. After-

A SANDSTONE EXILE

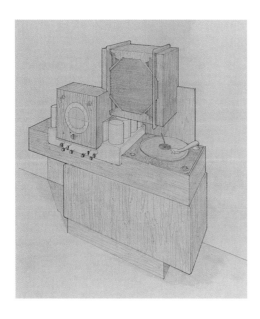

Howe designed this radio and phonograph console at Sandstone.

hour amenities, such as a roof garden, dance floor, bar, and cabaret with a revolving stage, were consigned to upper floors. For travelers, Howe incorporated tourist cabins, dining facilities, and a swimming pool. The complex provided ample parking, a gas station, and an auto repair shop. Ramped access and parking, as well as loading docks for delivery trucks, were included. In an introductory text panel, Howe explained that two innovative construction materials would be used to build the majority of the complex: "flexcore reinforced concrete tubing" for all floors and walls and " 'lucite' curved glazing" for showcases and fenestration.

Howe drew the massive project twice, the first time in colored pencil and the second in Cherokee red pencil. He retitled the second set "A Cooperative Community" and submitted it for inclusion in the 1945 Christmas box.

Howe's drawings for the Big Project demonstrate his total control over the complex elements of the project and intense focus on every aspect of it. The plans show masterful spatial organization, rational assemblage of parts, and efficient circulation patterns. In addition to detailing each element of every store and service, Howe brought life to the project through a series of engaging interior perspectives. The vignettes suggest the experience of inhabiting shops and venues. In size and vision, the Big Project was the unbuilt masterwork of Howe's career.

Not all of Howe's endeavors at Sandstone were architectural. Like Wright, he had a love of geometric patterns and a talent for abstraction. He put this aptitude to good use at Sandstone by designing stationery, Christmas cards, and other graphically inspired items, which he sent to Masselink for typesetting and printing. Howe also applied his love of pattern making to the design of textiles, creating weavings and loom pieces, including wall hangings, placemats, and pillow designs. He later recalled the textile projects "saved my sanity" when he was confined to the dormitory, where it was too noisy to read.[45] According to friend and fellow inmate William Krebes, Howe picked up the weaving technique from "something the Jehovah's Witnesses were doing." Although they created a square weaving frame using nails and wood, "John took it a few design steps further, making octagonal frames and geometric patterns."[46] Howe later reinterpreted or found other uses for many of the graphic designs he created at Sandstone.

Prior to his trial in 1943, Howe optimistically wrote his mother that if he were to be sentenced to prison, "I should not have to stay there more than several months at the longest."[47] He was wrong. In the end, Howe served thirty-three months of his four-year sentence. His release came in March 1946, six months after the end of the war.[48] In retrospect, he viewed his Sandstone confinement as "an education . . . and an opportunity for self cultivation," a large part of which was "a result of the absolute necessity of living an interior life. For the first time in my life I sought solitude and I reveled in it."[49]

Howe was welcomed back to Taliesin with open arms. As building activity in America resumed in the postwar years, he was also greeted with a full workload.

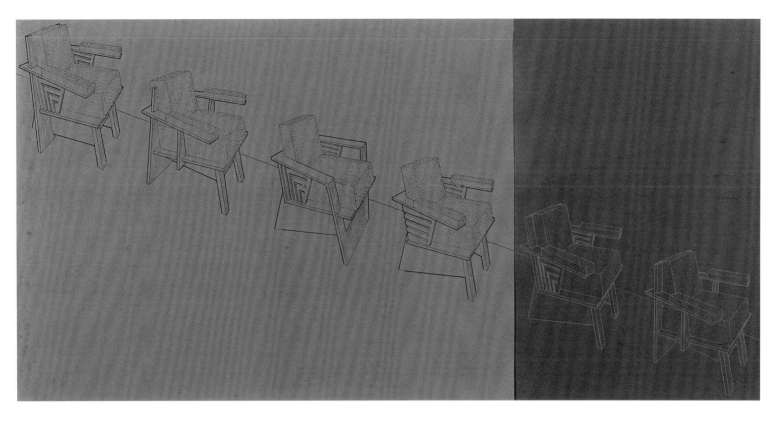

Above These variations on the theme of an armchair were designed by Howe at Sandstone.

Left At Sandstone, Howe indulged his talent for geometric abstraction to create graphics similar in spirit to this 1938 design for a holiday card for his parents.

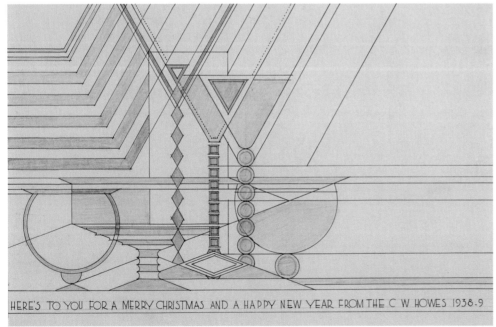

HERE'S TO YOU FOR A MERRY CHRISTMAS AND A HAPPY NEW YEAR FROM THE C W HOWES 1938-9

A SANDSTONE EXILE

3

RETURN TO TALIESIN

Howe (back row, second from right) practices Gurdjieffian movements, circa 1949, which were encouraged as part of Fellowship life by Olgivanna Lloyd Wright. In her twenties she was a pupil of Gurdjieff at his Institute for the Harmonious Development of Man and promoted his ideas within the Taliesin community.

When Howe returned to Taliesin in March 1946, it seemed a different place from the one he had left thirty-three months previously. Postwar prosperity had arrived and the Taliesin studios were busy again. A great many architectural projects were on the drafting boards, or at least queued up in the studio. Now that World War II had ended, many new apprentices were arriving, swelling the ranks to between fifty and sixty individuals. Most important, the spirit of the Fellowship was revived. Gone was the siege mentality that had prevailed in the lean years of the early 1940s. Optimism and a sense of renewal were in the air.

This positive energy was soon dashed in a tragic instant. A pregnant Svetlana Peters, Wright's stepdaughter, and her young son, Daniel, were killed when their Jeep crashed near Spring Green in September 1946. Her husband, Wes Peters, and all in the Fellowship were numb and grieved profoundly.

Svet, as she was known, had been the choir director and a key person in the musical life of the Fellowship. But she had been much more. She was a builder of bridges both within the Fellowship and toward the outside community. She was inclined by her nature to smooth over the sorts of factional rivalries, cliques, and divisions that occur in a tight-knit community.[1] Her death proved a major loss to the Fellowship and would be felt in many ways in future years.

The loss of Svetlana Peters became magnified over the years, particularly after Olgivanna, seeking spiritual renewal following her daughter's death, began a campaign to instill the spiritual teachings of her mentor, the Russian mystic George Gurdjieff, into the life of the Fellowship. Gradually, apprentices felt the tug of war between the architectural purpose of the Fellowship and the Gurdjieffian work, as it was called, championed with increasingly fervor by Olgivanna and her closest followers. This created a steadily increasing schism that underlay the last crowning decade of Wright's career. Eventually, many apprentices felt compelled to declare a primary loyalty to one or the other of the Wrights, at least by virtue of their actions. Olgivanna and her group of devotees became a kind of shadow organization within the Fellowship, according to apprentice Kamal Amin: "One of the tasks assigned her group of faithful followers was to report to her at all times what was said or done anywhere on the premises."[2] Naturally, Olgivanna's closest acolytes were seen as spies by those closest to Wright, which meant Howe and the other studio stalwarts.[3]

66

After returning to Taliesin from Sandstone, Howe made some of the most beautiful renderings of his career, as is evidenced by his magnificent perspective of the S. C. Johnson & Son Company Research Tower, designed in 1944 but stalled by the war. The tower's flare as it rose skyward proved too expensive to execute.

Oil tycoon Rogers Lacy commissioned a hotel for downtown Dallas, Texas (1946), that led to one of Howe's most powerful drawings. Howe captured the reflective nuances of the overlapping glass panels, set on the diagonal in this monumental cantilevered, concrete, and glass tower project.

RETURN TO THE STUDIO

Upon his return to the Fellowship, Howe was back at work, resuming his role as "the pencil in Wright's hand" and head of the drafting studio. With the pent-up demand from the construction hiatus of the war years, a multitude of major nonresidential commissions were under development. Simultaneously, work was proceeding on the working drawings for the Guggenheim Museum in New York City, a project begun in 1943; the Johnson Research Tower, Racine, Wisconsin (1944); and the Adelman Laundry in Milwaukee, Wisconsin (1945).[4] In addition, a great many new clients were requesting Usonian houses.

The studio architectural team reassembled again, with Howe and Peters now joined again by "Davy" Davison, also returning from the Federal Correctional Institution at Sandstone, and Curtis Besinger, returning from alternative service in a Civilian Public Service camp in California. In short order, Gordon Lee rejoined from Colorado. Augmenting them were several new apprentices, among them Ling Po, John Geiger, Peter Matthews, and Nils Schweizer.

ROGERS LACY HOTEL

In the summer of 1946, Wright's major focus was designing the Rogers Lacy Hotel for Dallas, Texas. This towering structure was intended to rise above an enclosed courtyard with street-level shops on a full block in the central business district. Lacy was a wealthy oilman

Opposite This detail of the streetscape at the base of the Rogers Lacy Hotel shows Howe's assured technique of stippled dots and repetitive lines. Interestingly, the cars and people were drawn by others; Howe hated drawing them.

Top Wright's Pittsburgh Point Park Civic Center #1, Pittsburgh, Pennsylvania (1947), commissioned by Edgar Kaufmann Sr., illustrates a reenvisioning of the downtown edge. Kaufmann thought Wright's vision far too grand, and it was abandoned.

Bottom A pioneering concept for 1949: the urban parking garage, as envisioned by Wright and seductively rendered by Howe for a city block opposite Kaufmann's department store in downtown Pittsburgh. The Self-Service Parking Garage was unexecuted, despite the monumental design and masterful rendering.

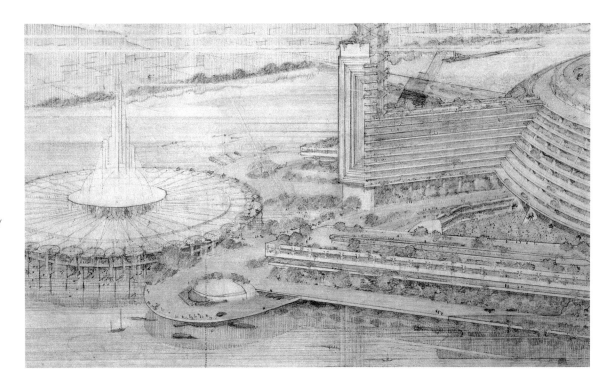

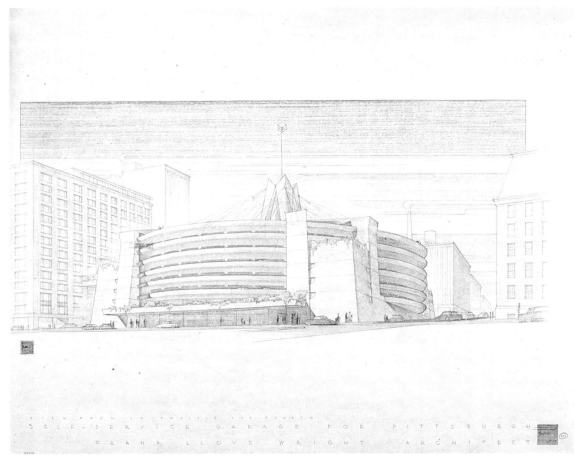

who was looking to diversify his holdings. Had the hotel been constructed, it would have been one of Wright's largest and tallest buildings. For the presentation of this innovative design, Howe produced one of the finest renderings of his career. Howe and Besinger teamed together on this endeavor, switching back to the Taliesin studio for the concentrated effort. They translated and developed Wright's sketches for an innovative glass "fish scale" skin, with fiberglass diffusers sandwiched between two glass layers. As conceived by Wright, the cantilevered concrete tower design featured a glass-roofed atrium, with lobby, shops, and services, prefiguring architect John Portman's mirror glass atrium hotel designs of the 1970s and 1980s.[5]

Howe's rendering of this design highlights the glass membrane that reflects the drama of the Texas sky. He used a technique of scribing hundreds of closely spaced horizontal lines to form the sky and composed curvilinear episodes of these lines to suggest moving clouds. The method is based on the compositional techniques of the Japanese prints of which Wright was so fond. "The Rogers Lacy exterior perspective was drawn on translucent twenty-four inch wide Japanese paper with imbedded silk fibers in brown ink. This meant erasing was not possible. In fact, the pen could barely touch the paper, lest it catch in the silk fibers and leave a blot. Colored pencil was then applied to the back or the front, or both to create a sense

Opposite The Vere C. and Lillian Morris House, Seacliff, San Francisco, California (1946). Howe recalled the Morrises were uninterested in this project, which they believed was far too grandiose. Nevertheless, it led to a sublime drawing by Howe, capturing the drama of the sentinel-like structure overlooking the Golden Gate.

Above Howe produced another image of Seacliff, the Morris House's initial scheme, shown from the landward approach on the streets of San Francisco. Here it seems like a completely different structure from the audacious one previously illustrated.

of depth and richness," wrote Besinger.[6] The animated streetscape, with pedestrians and the Cherokee red cars, helps integrate the building into the urban scene.

The twenty or so presentation drawings took nearly a month for Howe and Besinger to complete, with Howe producing the masterful exterior rendering as well as the plans. Besinger produced the sections and dramatic interior perspectives. All were then displayed at the Hillside studio for Wright's verbal presentation to Lacy. These sessions always excluded apprentices. The drawings were well received, per Besinger's account, but the project went no further as Lacy died suddenly before work could begin on construction drawings.[7] Howe had a somewhat different recollection about the presentation's reception. "Lacy was a very wealthy man whose only interest was in playing poker with his friends," he stated. "It was his lawyer who wanted him to put his money into something like this." Whatever the case, Howe was most proud that "Mr. Wright didn't change anything on this drawing."[8]

PITTSBURGH'S GOLDEN TRIANGLE PROJECTS

Shortly thereafter, in 1947 an urban design commission materialized, thanks to Edgar Kaufmann Sr., involving reenvisioning the downtown Pittsburgh waterfront. Kaufmann had no particular architectural program in mind, just an interest in redeveloping and revitalizing a derelict area of downtown Pittsburgh at the Golden Triangle where the three rivers meet. Wright was free to let his creativity run. The Pittsburgh Point Park Projects would yield a series of imaginative urban visions, complete with every conceivable civic component from courts to museums, sensational large-scale renderings by a number of apprentices, but ultimately no material realization. Howe led the team producing the detailed presentation perspectives. Kaufmann deemed the first scheme far too grand, calling it "overwhelming."[9]

Kaufmann's rejection led to the second scheme, focused on the bridges where the Monongahela and Allegheny Rivers meet to form the Ohio River.[10] Again the team, led by Howe, set to work. Howe and Lee translated Wright's vision by means of many presentation perspectives. The best of them, according to Howe, was the compelling night scene by Davison, who specialized in that dramatic technique. Nevertheless, this proposal was still far too grand for Kaufmann.

These efforts and further conversations did lead, in 1949, to a more feasible proposal for Kaufmann and downtown Pittsburgh: the Self-Service Parking Garage, covering an entire city block, situated across Fifth Avenue from Kaufmann's downtown department store. While these structures are ubiquitous in the urban landscape today, it was a pioneering idea when proposed. Like the earlier, more monumental visions for Pittsburgh, it was not built. Again, Howe produced a masterful rendering of the sculptural, spiraling concrete ramps, supported by steel suspension cables strung from a cluster of central masts. The rendering technique relies heavily on Howe's characteristic pointillist stipple technique, perfected at Sandstone, to subtly suggest shade and shadow.

RENDERING PERSPECTIVES

In an interview late in his life, Howe recounted how these perspective drawings were produced.[11] Most often he (but occasionally another apprentice skilled in three-point perspective

VIEW FROM SOUTHEAST
HOUSE FOR ZETA BETA TAU FRATERNITY
GAINESVILLE FLORIDA
FRANK LLOYD WRIGHT ARCHITECT

Opposite The Zeta Beta Tau Fraternity House for the University of Florida, Gainesville (1952), ranks among Howe's showiest drawings. He marshals all his talent and technique to portray what could be—or what might have been, as the lushly rendered project was never realized.

Right Typically, Wright drew an annotated plan and section to capture the essence of an architectural idea, to be translated by Howe into a full scheme. Here Wright included the elevations, one on each side of the sheet, for a desert house. From "How to Live in the Southwest," *Arizona Highways*, 1949.

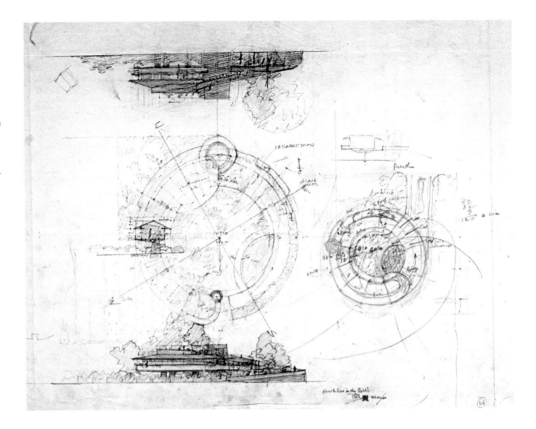

layout) would block out the preferred viewpoint view of the building in pencil. This factual outline would be the underlay for the subsequent drawing. If Wright approved the chosen vantage point, Howe or another would do an overlay drawing, first in lead pencil, with freehand lines, then rendered in colored pencil. As a next step, he would apply brown ink to provide "punch," or emphasis, to edges or details. This ink application could be guided by a straight-edge or stippled on, the latter Howe's preferred method, to suggest shade and shadow. Howe liked the freehand inking method best because it provided a more human touch. People and cars were often added, sometimes by another apprentice, as Howe notoriously hated drawing them. Last, the drawings would be lettered, with titles. This might be done by someone assisting on the drawing, as the entire presentation preparation often involved a team in the studio. Finally, Wright reviewed the drawing. In rare instances, he pronounced it ready for the client, initialing and dating the red signature square in the drawing's corner. More typically, Wright added more vegetation and landscape features until nature was more present in the drawing.[12] Occasionally, if warranted, multiple perspectives of the same project, including interiors, would be drawn. This was particularly true of major public commissions and of the grandest houses.

HOWE AND WRIGHT'S WORKING METHOD

By the late 1940s Howe had been at Wright's side in the studio for more than a decade, often sharing a drafting table. They had developed a comfortable working method whereby Wright first roughed out the essence of the scheme: "It was this central 'Idea' which constituted the soul of his buildings: parts being integrated with the whole," according to Howe.[13] Wright

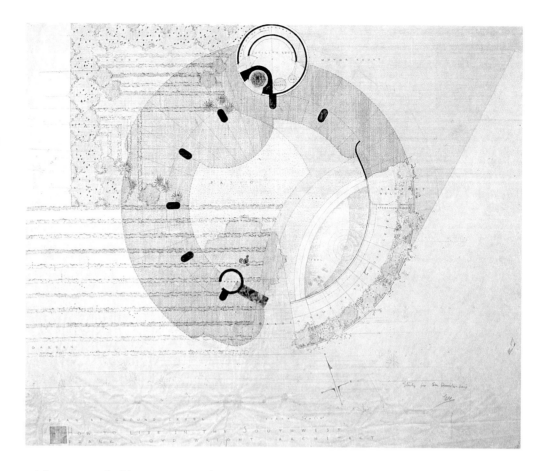

Right Howe's colored pencil plan rendering for "How to Live in the Southwest" reveals Wright's integration of landscape and building, even on a flat desert site.

Opposite top The desert house proposed in "How to Live in the Southwest" was built for Wright's son David and his wife, Gladys, in Phoenix, Arizona (1950). In this intimate portrait of the courtyard, with the concrete ramp of the house snaking around and above, Howe takes his presentational skills into the realm of fine art.

Opposite bottom The courtyard as executed: the David and Gladys Wright House, photographed by Pedro Guerrero.

might capture the idea on a scrap of paper at his bedside, directly on the survey supplied by the client, on tracing paper, or on thicker stock. Wright's drawings focused on the plan and section, with elevations occasionally included on the sides, bottom, and top of the sheet. He often drew freehand details and thumbnail perspectives on the sheet to test ideas as they occurred to him. Notes abounded, both to explain intentions and to guide Howe in the further architectural development.

Once Wright had committed the idea to paper, he typically moved on to answering his mail or to an outdoor activity, such as supervising the unending construction at the Taliesins. Howe then took the concept drawing and translated it into more fully developed plans, sections, and, finally, elevations. As Howe was quick to point out, the essence of Wright's idea was seldom conceived in an elevation, which derived from the inhabitable space inside.[14] After preparing these drawings, Howe started the presentation perspectives. These allowed the building to come to life from a variety of vantage points both inside and out; sometimes from above, sometimes, dramatically, from below, depending on the landscape. Howe preferred to produce both of these vantage points for a single project, giving the client "two for the price of one." Last came applying color using pencils, a technique Wright learned from Sullivan, which he, in turn, passed along to Howe. " 'The client likes color, Frank,' " Wright said to Howe, passing along verbatim the instruction Sullivan had given to Wright.[15]

This working method can be seen in several drawings for a residential project produced for a feature article titled "How to Live in the Southwest" (1949), Raymond Carlson's publication

RETURN TO TALIESIN

H O U S E   F O R   H U N T I N G T O N   H A R T F O R D
F R A N K   L L O Y D   W R I G H T   A R C H I T E C T
L L O Y D   W R I G H T   A S S O C I A T E

Above The multiple proposals for Huntington Hartford for a large tract in Hollywood, California (1947), resulted in flamboyant architectural fantasies, none of which were realized. This house is finely rendered by Howe, who was at the height of his graphic skills.

Opposite top The Play Resort for Huntington Hartford, Hollywood, California (1947), perched at the crest of the hill, was the culmination of the project. Its cantilevered disks recall the monument to the recently deceased Svetlana Wright Peters at Taliesin West.

Opposite bottom Howe considered this drawing of the Huntington Hartford Cottage Group, Hollywood, California (1947), among his showiest. He demonstrates all the techniques he perfected during his incarceration at Sandstone, taking his rendering abilities to new heights.

Arizona Highways.[16] Subsequently, this design was built in Phoenix, Arizona, for Wright's son David and his wife, Gladys. Howe translated Wright's conceptual work for this most unusual house—a concrete spiral rising above an orange grove, forming a shaded courtyard below. Like many conceptual plans, Wright worked out the essence of the project, "the Idea," on one sheet: initial conceptual plan, more developed plan, section, and two elevations.

Howe then took this raw material and transformed it into a fully rendered site plan, section, and elevation. Then two perspectives were prepared to depict the house more fully. The framed courtyard view is striking with its foreground and background elements. The curvilinear form heightened the degree of difficulty in constructing these perspectives accurately for this "coil of concrete," as the house was described in the contemporary press. Howe proudly stated of the courtyard perspective: "This is entirely my drawing; Mr. Wright didn't put a dot in this drawing."[17]

By the busy summer of 1947, Howe and Besinger had developed a close working relationship that became a pattern for the next eight years, until the latter left the Fellowship. Besinger became, in effect, an assistant to Howe, coordinating his activities on projects with Howe's efforts. This meant blocking out perspectives and drawing elevations while Howe concentrated on plans and sections. They became an effective team, whether working on large projects or producing the drawings for the myriad Usonian houses designed during those years. Ironically, Besinger recounts, Howe's determination to complete his own drawings

PLAY RESORT IN HOLLYWOOD HILLS FOR HUNTINGTON HARTFORD
FRANK LLOYD WRIGHT   LLOYD WRIGHT ASSOCIATE

COTTAGE GROUP CENTER
OF HUNTINGTON HARTFORD
FRANK LLOYD WRIGHT ARCHITECT
LLOYD WRIGHT ASSOCIATE

RETURN TO TALIESIN

by a self-imposed deadline meant he was disinclined to answer others' questions, which sometimes hindered the smooth working of the studio.[18]

HUNTINGTON HARTFORD PROJECTS

In early 1947 another ambitious, large-scale project emerged. A&P heir Huntington Hartford owned 130 acres of undeveloped land in the Hollywood Hills.[19] He planned to build a residence for himself, but much more ambitiously a Country Club/Play Resort/Sports Club and Resort Hotel, as they were variously labeled on the drawings. Although these, too, were never built (Hartford was as fickle and as disinterested as Lacy, according to Howe), Wright's designs resulted in a series of Howe's finest-quality renderings, with the hotel nestled in the shaded canyon down low and the sports club and residence crowning the flanking hills, up above to either side.[20] Howe considered his Sports Club rendering, of a design based on the memorial to Svetlana Peters at Taliesin West, among his best drawings. So too the Huntington Hartford Cottage Group rendering, also of 1947, of which Howe publicly said, "This is my showiest drawing, if I may say so. Mr. Wright didn't make any changes. It's really one of my best drawings."[21]

Notably, these extraordinary drawings were done in a remarkably short time frame, from summer 1946 to summer 1947. They reveal Howe at the height of his powers and reflect his enthusiasm at being back at Taliesin. As Howe emphasized, "All these years, I was doing what I wanted to do most."[22] These drawings also reflect the honing of Howe's drawing talents during his Sandstone stay. There he had developed a drawing technique consisting of ink lines of different weights and stipple dots of various densities.[23] Back at the Taliesins, he used this refined technique to vividly illustrate Wright's designs.

Howe spoke of the presentation renderings as something he did as a kind of play in between juggling working drawing campaigns on a multitude of buildings. He was always producing working drawing sets, either alone or with others whom he was supervising, "always carrying it forward."[24] By necessity, these campaigns involved keeping countless details in mind and coordinating plans, sections, elevations, and details on multiple projects at once.

A CHANGING FELLOWSHIP

The sheer size of the Fellowship in the postwar years meant it was no longer the intrepid, close-knit group of pioneering spirits it had been in the lean prewar years. Gone too was the sense of adventure and experimentation that characterized the years immediately after the Fellowship's beginning. Now, with fifty to sixty or more apprentices, both Taliesins were crowded, with housing accommodations strained.[25] The Fellowship was becoming impersonal and institutional.

An unstated but structured hierarchy had developed. At the innermost circle were the senior fellows, Peters, Howe, Masselink, Hill, Besinger, Davison, and others who had been in the Fellowship for a considerable time. Next was an intermediate group with less time invested but who had been there for several years. Last came the newcomers. The norm for them was a regimen related to the maintenance of the Fellowship life and constant physical labor: construction to accommodate the ever-expanding numbers. This had been a source of irritation in the founding years of the Fellowship, and before World War II as well. The problem at this point was the distinction between groups: some did construction work and chores, while others did not.

The economical Crosley Super Roadsters, purchased by Wright for the senior apprentices, were a decided contrast to his own preferred premium vehicles—Packards, Cords, and Lincolns. In this case, Wright's magnificent car of choice was a Cord L-29 Cabriolet.

With no orientation program or explanation of expectations, a practice of wholesome neglect characterized the newcomers' experience. In that context, it is no wonder so many new apprentices stayed only a short time. Former apprentice Carl Book, in attendance for eighteen months during 1955–56, recounted his experience: "It was a 'sad' educational experience. . . . It was just too weird."[26] And he had the good fortune of working in the drafting studio.

The senior fellows not only partook of studio activities and enjoyed direct access to Wright but were paid a monthly stipend of thirty dollars. This was called, somewhat derisively, "a pittance" by the seniors. Indeed, by Besinger's account, irritation was prevalent now that Wright was prospering and they were not.[27]

One sign of the prosperity after the end of World War II was the building activity at Taliesin West. Refinements to the living quarters were undertaken, making it less a primitive desert camp and providing a more finished interior space. The canvas roof was replaced with a more permanent panel system covered inside in canvas; window glass was added for the first time. New purchased furnishings and rugs made the interior less severe. In many areas, native desert plantings were replaced with more conventional nursery stock. These alterations markedly changed the character of the place. It was becoming "domesticated and civilized," to quote Besinger.[28]

Another sign of prosperity was the purchasing of cars for the senior apprentices. Wright favored a fleet of small, inexpensive cars for the seniors, bought in bulk at Smart Motors in Madison. Initially these were American Bantams, replaced during the summer of 1950, recalled Howe, with two-seat Crosley "Hotshots" that some likened to mechanized roller skates due to their unpredictable handling and small size.[29] By autumn 1952, British Hillman imports replaced the Crosleys, followed in turn by economical French Panhards. All these vehicle types were a far cry from the impressive Packards, Cords, and Lincoln Continentals favored by Wright, though he enjoyed driving around Taliesin in the apprentices' cars.[30]

ALL THOSE USONIAN HOUSES

In the thirteen years between Howe's return to Taliesin and Wright's death, "work in the drafting room focused on houses and more houses," in Besinger's words.[31] While Wright designed and Howe and the studio produced other large-scale projects, too, they also designed and produced houses by the dozens, both built and unbuilt. Wright, ever the restless pattern maker, explored different geometries in both their underlying compositional modules, or units, but also in their resulting architectural form. Some were based on square or rectangular

HOUSE FOR MR. AND MRS. ALFRED C. BERGMAN ST. PETERSBURG FLORIDA
FRANK LLOYD WRIGHT ARCHITECT

Above Howe produced yet another convincing rendering of a house completely integrated with its physical setting: the Alfred and Mary Bergman House, St. Petersburg, Florida (1948, unbuilt). Wright designed and Howe drew dozens of unexecuted houses between 1945 and 1959.

Opposite top Wright designed three iterations of this type of house. The first, for Robert and Ann Windfohr, Crownfield, Fort Worth, Texas (1948), was abandoned. Next, Wright brought it forth for Raúl Baillères, Acapulco, Mexico (1952). He redesigned this version for the Arthur Miller and Marilyn Monroe House, Roxbury, Connecticut (1957). None were constructed.

Opposite bottom The Howard and Helen Anthony House, Benton Harbor, Michigan (1949), was designed by apprentice Curtis Besinger and based on an unexecuted Wright design. Reputedly, Howe did the same on several late residential commissions, as Wright was often traveling or working on larger projects and the studio's production was chronically behind schedule.

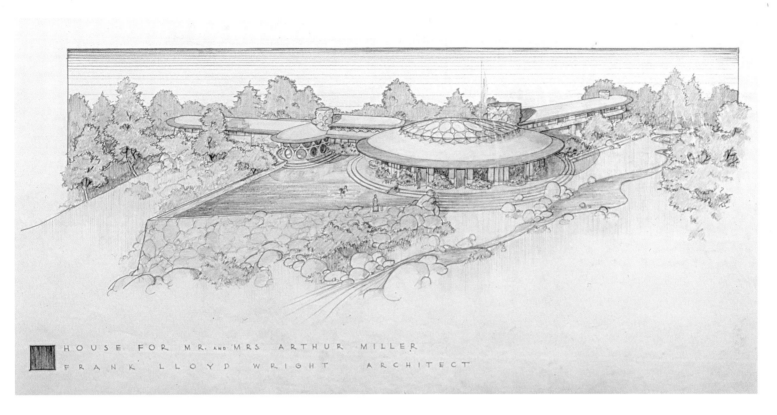

H O U S E   F O R   M R. AND M R S   A R T H U R   M I L L E R
F R A N K   L L O Y D   W R I G H T   A R C H I T E C T

modules, others on hexagonal, triangular, or parallelogram-based modules, and some on circular modules. The three unbuilt schemes for Maginel Wright Barney's Cottage (1948) at Taliesin each explored one of these different underlying geometries.

Reflecting on this plethora of Usonian houses, Besinger recalled three means by which these "came from nowhere into somewhere," as Howe described Wright's creativity.[32] For some, Wright explored a new idea or formal concept, and the resulting house was a totally novel creation. The Vere C. and Lillian Morris House, Seacliff, San Francisco, California (1946, unbuilt), is an example of this type in its dramatic integration into its setting. For others, Wright took a previous design as a starting point, perhaps at a client's suggestion. For example, the Ralph Jester House, Palos Verde, California (1938, unbuilt), was reworked three more times before a posthumous variant was built by Bruce Brooks Pfeiffer in 1974 at Taliesin West.

For the third way in which a Usonian house was designed, the pressure of time, Wright's frequent travels, or an impatient client meant Wright allowed Howe or Besinger or another apprentice to take the design lead on the scheme. These might then be reworked by Wright, but not always. Howe and the other apprentices were of course thoroughly immersed in the Wrightian grammar of the Usonians. Consequently, their designs tended to be variations on established themes. As an example of this method, Besinger described the creation of the

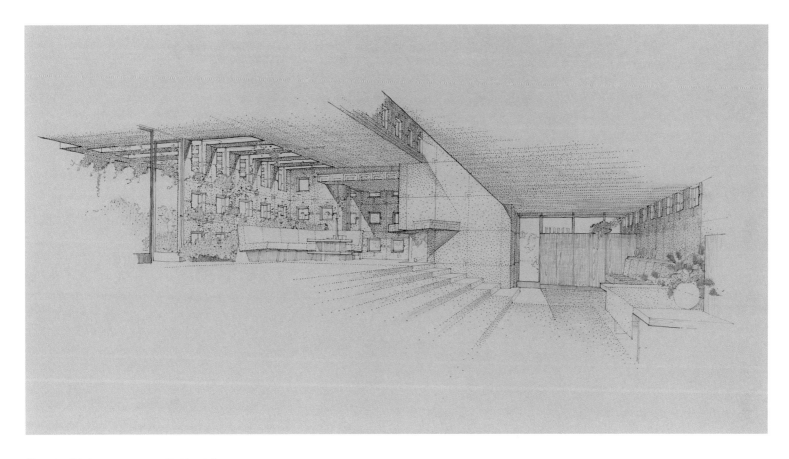

Opposite Wright was so impressed by Howe's fourteen-sheet presentation of this 1949 birthday box project, Concrete Block House, that he scrawled "special" on the cover sheet. Howe subsequently reprised the design for at least two clients but never managed to get it built.

Above Howe's magnificent rendering of the Concrete Block House interior shows his mastery of the stipple technique he favored. This interior perspective is one of the many sheets depicting the house presented to Wright at his eightieth birthday celebration, June 1949 (when he actually turned eighty-two).

Howard and Helen Anthony House, Benton Harbor, Michigan (1949). Howe asked him to prepare a preliminary design, based on an earlier scheme for a cottage by Wright.[33] It was approved largely as designed and subsequently built.

During the last few years of Wright's life, this latter method became more prevalent. In part this may be due to Wright's failing eyesight, clouded by cataracts, making detailed drawing work difficult for him. Wright was also busy with major institutional projects, the Marin County Civic Center, the Baghdad Project, and the construction of the Guggenheim Museum among them. Ever the consummate apprentice, Howe never took credit for designing a Usonian house.

Howe insisted that "Wright never looked to me or other apprentices for design ideas."[34] Yet, Wright did suggest the apprentices design concrete block houses for the Christmas box of 1949. Wright was interested in exploring further the concept of these Usonian Automatics, as he called them, as an economical means to house GIs and their families after the war. (His assumption was that owners would cast the concrete blocks themselves and construct much of the house without need of a contractor.) Wright's suggestion was stimulated by one of Howe's best box project submissions, prepared earlier in 1949. His Concrete Block House, prepared for Wright's eightieth birthday gala in June, was a fourteen-page set of drawings rendered in gold ink on tracing paper. Though purely line work and stipple, with no further coloration, it represents another pinnacle in his presentation work. Wright wrote "special" on the title sheet.[35]

HOWE IN THE FIELD

As much as Howe loved the excitement of his work at Wright's side in the studio, he longed to get into the field to supervise construction of a house. This he felt was an invaluable part of learning the craft of architecture: the back-and-forth of working out solutions to the inevitable issues that arise during the construction process. Yet Wright considered him so valuable in the studio, Howe said, "My job was working directly with Mr. Wright; he would never let me go out."[36] This is a slight exaggeration, since Howe was able to supervise one house under construction before World War II, the Clarence Sondern House in Kansas City, Missouri, in 1940. Nevertheless, Howe admitted that Wright's repeated refusals to consider him for site supervision duty aggravated him.

His next field opportunities did not come until 1949 and 1950, when he spent both summers in the Indiana/Michigan area, from South Bend and Kalamazoo to Benton Harbor and the Detroit area, supervising a number of nearby houses concurrently under construction. The Herman and Gertrude Mossberg House, South Bend, Indiana (1948), a large brick house with a grand living room and suspended staircase, was one of these. He also supervised the construction of the Robert and Rae Levin House (1948), in the Wright-planned community of Parkwyn Village, Kalamazoo, Michigan. Reputedly, he supervised the construction of all four Wright-designed houses in that community and the concurrent cluster of houses in Galesville, Michigan, as well as the Howard and Helen Anthony House, Benton Harbor, Michigan (1949); the Bradford and Ina Harper House in St. Joseph, Michigan (1950); and the Donald and Mary Lou Schaberg House, Okemos, Michigan (1950).[37] His presence in Michigan likewise meant supervisory trips to the William and Mary Palmer House in Ann Arbor, also under construction at that time. "I just drove an old Chevrolet from place to place," recounted Howe.[38]

Howe supervised the Herman and Gertrude Mossberg House, South Bend, Indiana (1948), and several southern Michigan houses during the summers of 1949 and 1950. Traveling in an old Chevrolet, he returned to Taliesin most weekends, rendering perspective drawings while there.

Howe and all supervising apprentices in the field were expected to return to Taliesin for the Saturday and Sunday gatherings. Wright wanted them to report back as he considered them his eyes and ears on-site. Frequently, after the brief weekend at Taliesin, they would return to the construction site with revisions and supplemental details. In Howe's case, he was also asked to produce presentation perspectives when back at Taliesin for the weekend; his rendering of the Pittsburgh Self-Service Parking Garage was done on one such weekend.[39] On at least one occasion, Howe did not return to Taliesin, weekending elsewhere. This prompted a characteristically laconic telegram from Wright: "Where are you and why?"[40]

Howe had upgraded from a simple tent to better living accommodations at Taliesin West, building the Desert Cabana in the late 1940s. He and Lu expanded it again shortly after their marriage in 1951.

LU MARIE SPARKS

Lu Marie Sparks, born in 1922, grew up in poverty in Holden, Missouri, a dirt farmer's daughter, by her own account. Adamant that she pursue an education, her parents, Leonard and Amy Sparks, sent her to Central Missouri State Teachers College in Warrensburg, Missouri. After graduation, in 1944, she became an English teacher in Santa Fe, New Mexico, and spent summers as a counselor at Cheley Summer Camp near Estes Park, Colorado.[41] She and Howe met at a dance in Scottsdale in 1949, where she taught English at the relocated Brownmoor School for Girls. They wed on November 7, 1951, in the Wright-designed Community Christian Church in Kansas City, Missouri (1940), not far from where Lu was raised. Howe helped superintend the building during its construction. A honeymoon in Mexico followed. They remained life partners to the end, forming a tight bond that proved most helpful in the ensuing years. Recalled by friends as "a flower in the desert," Lu was independent, resourceful, stubborn, and notoriously frugal.

Having married a senior apprentice, Lu joined the inner workings of the Fellowship, assisting in the office with secretarial work for Gene Masselink and others. She typed correspondence, building specification documents, Wright's lectures, weekly talks, and book manuscripts (even the manuscripts for Mrs. Wright's books). She also became involved in weaving activities, acted in the many periodic performances and celebrations, and served as a breakfast cook, once making eggs Benedict for seventy people for a Sunday breakfast.[42] When asked if she was particularly interested in architecture, she quipped she was just interested in one particular architect.

In 1948 Howe had designed and built a small desert cabana behind Taliesin West for himself. As newlyweds the Howes expanded the one-person dwelling into larger quarters, starting in winter 1951–52, completing much of the work themselves over several winters.

In Wisconsin, John and Lu settled into his bridge room at Taliesin but immediately made plans to live independently, as had Wes and Svet Peters previously. The couple acquired a portion of Peters's Aldebaran Farm (the Welsh name identifies a star following a constellation) across the Wyoming Valley east of Taliesin and Hillside.[43] Howe designed an intimate cottage, Inwood, and began a long construction campaign, executed in two phases lasting from 1953 until 1958.

Built of stone and wood and nestled into its hillside site, Inwood resembled a Wrightian version of an English cottage. Since, as Lu mentioned in interviews, "we had absolutely no money," the couple used "recycled barn timbers and stone" from the Taliesin quarry on-site.[44] Especially when the Wrights were traveling, friends in the Fellowship would assist in the construction activity.

Once built, Inwood allowed the Howes to have some semblance of a normal married life apart from the Fellowship and Olgivanna's watchful eyes. As one former apprentice recounted, "Mrs. Wright made life unbearable for married couples, particularly the women."[45] As a strong-willed manipulator, Olgivanna resented that Fellowship spouses, such as Lu, did not look to her for their primary loyalty. "She endeavored to be a third party to every relationship in the Fellowship," wrote Amin.[46] "She needed to be in total control of all situations," he continued, thriving on conflict she intentionally created and making sure that "everyone had to feel guilty about something."[47] Understanding this, the Howes formed a pact, vowing to each other that Olgivanna would never get between them.[48]

Top Lu Howe and Kay Davison at their looms in the apprentice court at Taliesin West, 1954.

Bottom Exterior view, Inwood, John and Lu Howe Cottage, Wyoming Valley, Wisconsin (circa 1955). The cottage was integrated into a wooded hillside opposite Taliesin and constructed fitfully over several years by the couple, with help from a cadre of apprentices.

Top Situated on the Wyoming Valley hillside directly east of Taliesin, Inwood had a panoramic view of the entire Taliesin estate. The window wall and vaulted ceiling allowed the small dwelling to feel much larger than its physical size.

Bottom From left to right: Allen Lape "Davy" Davison, John Howe, Lu Howe, and Kay Davison in the 1950s.

Top Howe and Wright in action at the Hillside studio, collaborating on the development of a schematic design. This was a familiar scene from 1942 (when the apprentices finally completed the studio) until Wright's death in 1959.

Bottom A familiar ritual at the Hillside studio: Wright reviewing plans Howe had developed. From early on Howe proved indispensable to the workings of the studio and quickly became Wright's closest assistant there. Wright acknowledged this in a note, "To Jack, my accomplice."

VIEW FROM THE SOUTH
BUILDING FOR THE H.C. PRICE CO.
BARTLESVILLE, OKLAHOMA
FRANK LLOYD WRIGHT, ARCHITECT

THE SOLOMON R. GUGGENHEIM MUSEUM
FRANK LLOYD WRIGHT ARCHITECT

Opposite Howe was in charge of juggling the work flow for producing Wright's major commissions, such as the Harold C. Price Company Tower, Bartlesville, Oklahoma (1952), along with a plethora of residential commissions throughout the 1950s, Wright's most productive decade by far in terms of commissions.

Above Howe produced this rendering of the Solomon Guggenheim Museum, New York, New York (circa 1953), after dozens of studies were created over the extended period of design and construction (1943–59).

MANIPULATING WRIGHT

As the 1950s progressed, Besinger noticed a tendency to manipulate Frank Lloyd Wright by various factions that had emerged within the Fellowship, "so much was done with the idea that Mr. Wright should not know."[49] Most of this intrigue involved keeping Wright in the dark about the increasing focus on Gurdjieffian activities, particularly the Movements, which took hours of group practice and considerable money and time to make elaborate costumes. In the studio, Howe, quite consciously, participated in some of this subterfuge.

Wright was notorious for making changes late in the production process and insisting those changes be made on the original working drawings. Howe objected to this for two reasons. He knew the changes could actually be made faster on a new sheet. Of greater concern was that when a portion of the drawing was erased, no record would remain of the changes; what remained was the result of the changes but not a record of the changes themselves, observed both Besinger and Howe. As time went on, Howe would surreptitiously make a second set of drawings. Doing so was simply easier than confronting Wright, for, as Howe noted candidly, "Mr. Wright could be impossible under any circumstances."[50]

In an effort to meet deadlines, Howe tried to rush Wright, or so Wright sensed, into signing drawings without the thorough review Wright preferred. Howe was trying to stave off last-minute changes in large measure to placate clients clamoring for their drawings. Wright enjoyed the signing ceremony, which allowed him to hold court in the studio, thereby bringing all work to a halt as he told stories. Howe explained, "The trouble was, Mr. Wright's time in the drafting room grew more precious and we had to make the most of it. And these sessions would go on too long; it was a real problem to cut them short, so that Mr. Wright would sign the drawings."[51]

AN EXPANDING WORKLOAD

Howe's sense of urgency was understandable, when considering the studio workload in the postwar period. Records show an average of thirty-three new projects came into the studio each year from 1946 through 1958, with a peak of fifty-nine new projects in 1957.[52] This was more than any year prior to the outbreak of World War II. This number accounts for just the new projects. A great many carried over from year to year. The houses, in particular, often required multiple schemes, owing to budget constraints or an assortment of other reasons, prior to getting built. Over 250 residential designs were produced during this frenetic postwar period.

As head of the studio, Howe was constantly juggling the production of these houses, "moving them along" for clients waiting for drawings, in addition to the more involved work required by significantly larger projects. During the early 1950s, these included renewed work on the Guggenheim Museum; more campus buildings for Florida Southern College in Lakeland; the H. C. Price Tower in Bartlesville, Oklahoma (1952); the Beth Sholom Synagogue in Elkins Park, Pennsylvania (1954); and the Monona Terrace Civic Center in Madison, Wisconsin (1956). All but the last was built. In the final few years, large-scale projects included the Kalita Humphreys Theater, Dallas, Texas (1955); the Marin County Civic Center, Marin County, California (1957); and the civic projects for Baghdad, Iraq. By the late 1950s, the drafting room numbered at least twenty-five apprentices working feverishly to bring these projects to fruition.

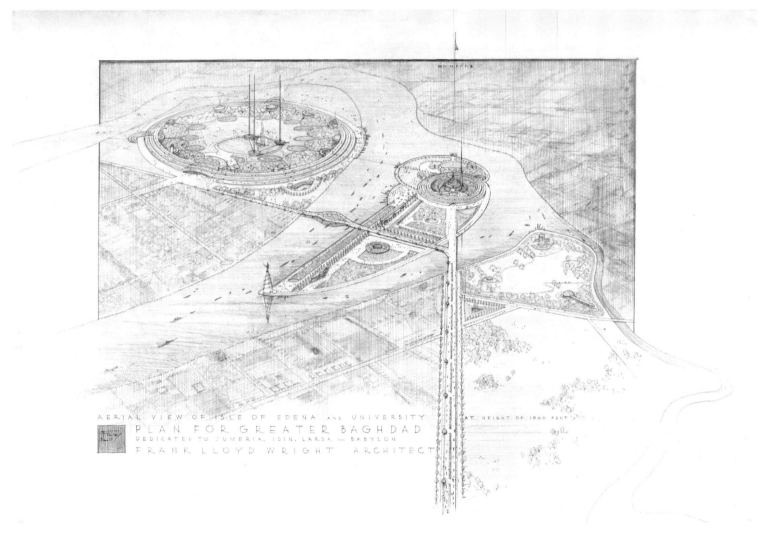

AERIAL VIEW OF ISLE OF EDENA AND UNIVERSITY AT HEIGHT OF 1000 FEET
PLAN FOR GREATER BAGHDAD
DEDICATED TO SUMERIA, ISIN, LARSA AND BABYLON
FRANK LLOYD WRIGHT ARCHITECT

With the aerial view for the Plan for Greater Baghdad, Iraq (1957), Howe illustrated Wright's urban design vision. The ambitious plans never came to be because of a political coup and the assassination of the client, King Faisal II, in July 1958.

Right With the presentation elevation for Haroun Al Rashid, Plan for Greater Baghdad, Howe turns an ordinary drawing into inspiration. Wes Peters drew the camels climbing the circular ziggurat.

Opposite In 1949 Wright designed and Howe produced renderings of many beautiful houses, including the Gerald Sussman Usonian Automatic, Pound Ridge, New York (1955, unbuilt). A number of these designs were built in the 1950s.

HAROUN AL RASHID
FRANK LLOYD WRIGHT ARCHITECT

HOUSE FOR MR AND MRS. GERALD SUSSMAN
POUNDRIDGE, WESTCHESTER COUNTY, NEW YORK
FRANK LLOYD WRIGHT   ARCHITECT

 SERIES
USONIAN Ⓒ
American Architecture

VIEW FROM THE SOUTH

The Howe-designed Bryant and Marjorie Denniston House, Newton, Iowa (1958), has affinities to Wright's Dr. Paul and Helen Olfelt House, St. Louis Park, Minnesota (1958). Both have lightness from a wrapping glass wall at the main living space.

Wright allowed Howe to do the Denniston House as an independent project. Howe created a Usonian design with a combination of grand and intimate spaces that pinwheel around the hearth.

THE DENNISTON HOUSE

In 1958 Wright permitted Howe to design a house for Lu's longtime friends Bryant and Marjorie Denniston in Newton, Iowa.[53] Since Wright frowned on independent work by apprentices, this was an unusual occurrence in the studio, perhaps a thank-you for all the years of sacrifice and dedication on Howe's part.

The Denniston House is a typical Wrightian, late-1950s Usonian in many respects, but a lightness and openness suggest Howe's designs of future years. The one-story brick, wood, and glass house has vaulted ceilings, ample expanses of glass, and an anchoring fireplace above a Cherokee red heated concrete floor. The roof drops nearly to the ground on one side, a favorite Howe compositional device. A trellis with patterned, perforated boards animates the exterior; a wood cutout geometric abstraction enlivens the entry. The triangular module on which the plan is based is another harbinger of things to come, as it was Howe's preferred geometry.

Opposite The vaulted ceiling and the delicate floor-to-ceiling glass wall of the Denniston House are characteristic of several very late Wright houses, many reputedly done without much involvement from the nonagenarian Wright.

Right Howe designed geometric wood cutout patterns for the trellis as well as an intricate wood abstraction for the entry to the Denniston House.

99

PREPARING FOR A CHANGE

The sense that Wright's time among them was short weighed on Howe and the studio regulars in the final years. It was another of the subtexts in the Fellowship throughout the crowning decade, despite Wright's energy and vigor. Consequently, several apprentices, Howe among them, pursued and received their architectural licenses in 1958 and 1959. They wanted and needed to become registered architects in order to practice their craft after Wright's passing and to carry on his architectural work.

And then the end came, rather suddenly, in April 1959 in Arizona. After working with Howe reviewing presentation drawings for the Donahoe Tryptic (as Helen Donahoe's Phoenix, Arizona [1959], cluster of three unbuilt houses was known), Wright took ill, was hospitalized, and died. For many in the Fellowship, the unimaginable had occurred. For Howe, the halcyon days at Taliesin had ended.

RETURN TO TALIESIN

DRIVEWAY

WALK

BATH

GALLEY

GUEST HOUSE

TERRACE

WALK

PARKING

FORECOURT

4

ART GALLERY

DOWN

AFTER WRIGHT

MASTER BEDROOM

BATH

UP

ENTR.

DOOR

BAR

UP

FIRE

LIVING ROOM

GALLEY

DINING

N

TERRACE

REFR.

W   E

S

1/8" = 1'-0"

RESIDENCE OF MRS. TOBY L. ROYSTON

WHITFORD ROAD, EXTON, PENNSYLVANIA

JOHN H. HOWE, ARCHITECT   1961-1972

Three years after her husband's death, Olgivanna Lloyd Wright, seen here in 1962, was firmly in control of the Taliesin Fellowship.

Frank Lloyd Wright died on April 6, 1959, in Phoenix, Arizona. He was ninety-one years old. At the time of his death, he had practiced architecture for more than seventy years, designed approximately one thousand projects (roughly half were built), and written nearly two dozen books. Both he and his work had been the subject of countless publications. His numerous late-life appearances on the popular new medium of television had allowed him to promote his work—and spread his iconoclastic views—to a broad American audience. In short, he was a giant in his field.

Wright also was a towering figure at the Fellowship, which he founded and led for twenty-seven years. During that time he received over six hundred commissions for which he and his apprentices produced thousands of drawings. Not one of them was signed or initialed by anyone other than Frank Lloyd Wright.

Wright remained active and involved with his work until the end of his life. As Howe later observed, "He retained to the end the same flexibility, quickness of mind, perception, and wit that were his during an entire lifetime."[1] Consequently, Wright's death was a shock to his family and those who were close to him. His loss was also a blow to members of the Fellowship, some of whom, including Howe, had come to Taliesin as teenagers. Not only were the fellows, a group of approximately sixty people, dependent on Wright for a livelihood, they (and their families) also relied on him for room, board, and other basic needs.[2] Wright's death left the Fellowship leaderless, in search of an identity, and in need of a plan to ensure the financial viability of the community and the two Taliesin properties that sustained their lives and work.

Following a period of mourning after Wright's death, Olgivanna Lloyd Wright took charge of affairs at Taliesin in what apprentice Louis Wiehle described as "a sea change."[3] Although Wright had been the undisputed head of architectural matters at the Fellowship since its inception in 1932, Olgivanna also exercised considerable administrative power.

Over the years, she escalated her direction of daily activities at Taliesin and, following Wright's death, seized sole control of the organization. She replaced her late husband as president of the Frank Lloyd Wright Foundation, established in 1940, and appointed two trusted senior apprentices, Wes Peters and Gene Masselink, as vice president and secretary, respectively.[4] Significantly, she did not give Howe, who had been Wright's right-hand man in the drafting room for almost three decades, any leadership role in the reorganized corporate structure, nor did she install him as chief architect of Taliesin Associated Architects (TAA), Wright's successor firm; she bestowed that honor on Peters, her son-in-law. "Jack was well aware that he was outranked for the top job," Wiehle said. But with regard to the founding of TAA, "he set aside his disappointment and moved right ahead in support of the new situation. He was a pragmatist," Wiehle recalled.[5] For the next five years Howe was a principal of TAA and remained in charge of the drafting room. Ultimately, however, Olgivanna's pointed rebuff would make Howe's decision to leave the Fellowship easier—and inevitable.

In the years following Wright's death, life in the Taliesin studio became more challenging, particularly for some of the fellows who had had a long-standing working relationship with Wright. According to Wiehle, "Daily routines went on much as before, but the involvement of Olgivanna in the architectural office was unprecedented." She required that all designs be presented to her for approval, and "there were frequent criticisms, rejections, and redesigns," he said.[6]

Howe had two major responsibilities at TAA. First, as head of the drafting room under chief architect Peters, he was in charge of work flow in the studio. That meant scheduling all

John Howe and Wes Peters sit at the center of this photograph of the core of the Fellowship from 1959. Front row, left to right: Gene Masselink, Tom Casey, Louis Wiehle, Cornelia Brierly, Howe, Peters, Davy Davison, Kenneth Lockhart. Back row: Joe Fabris, Charles Montooth, John Ottenheimer, James Pfefferkorn, Ling Po, Kamal Amin, John Rattenbury, Bruce Brooks Pfeiffer, David Dodge.

AFTER WRIGHT

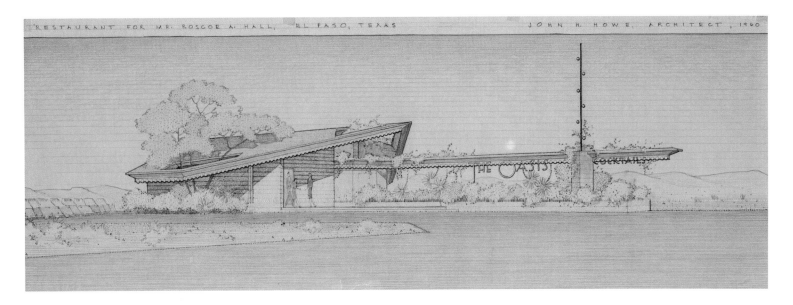

Howe lavished detail on the rendering for this unbuilt 1962 restaurant for Roscoe Hall in El Paso, Texas, one of thirty-eight Taliesin Associated Architects (TAA) projects credited to him.

projects for clients and sites across the country and beyond, and distributing work assignments to the roughly thirty architects, draftsmen, and draftswomen on staff. It was Howe's job to keep things moving—and to push projects forward—from initial design to the completion of working drawings. A master organizer, Howe kept meticulous records of "weekly work assignments," tracking who was working on which project. He also kept a careful eye on (and documentation of) daily attendance in the studio. Historically, Howe's records are useful in providing a chronology of studio projects of the period and insight into authorship of drawings.[7]

Second, Howe bore design responsibilities as a prominent TAA architect. During the five years he was with the TAA, the design of thirty-eight of the firm's projects were attributed to Howe.[8] As chief architect, Peters (like Wright before him) signed all drawings that left the studio, but Howe took credit for his design work by lettering his name under the commission title on his drawings.[9] By nearly all accounts, Howe and Peters were friends and worked well together. Howe later said, "Wes and I had a wonderful relationship because he admired me for what I could do and I admired him for what he could do."[10]

During his tenure at Taliesin, Howe became a superb renderer. Moreover, he developed a talent for intuiting Wright's architectural ideas and interpreting his conceptual sketches. He learned to master architectural detailing and to produce finely crafted sets of working drawings. It is also probable that Howe was responsible (but not credited) for the design of several of Wright's Usonian houses from the 1950s.[11]

Additionally, Howe designed dozens of houses, buildings, and site plans during his confinement in the Federal Correctional Institution, Sandstone, in the early 1940s. Over the years at Taliesin, he contributed fully developed schemes to Wright's birthday and Christmas boxes. Although the projects were not built, collectively the drawings demonstrate that Howe was an accomplished designer at the time of Wright's death.

By 1959 he had also assembled a small portfolio of built work. It included a 1945 cottage for Harvey Johnson in Genoa City, Wisconsin; a 1948 desert cabana (with a 1951 addition) for himself on the grounds of Taliesin West; and a cottage for himself and his wife, Lu, located across Wisconsin's Wyoming Valley from Taliesin.[12] The 845-square-foot stone structure,

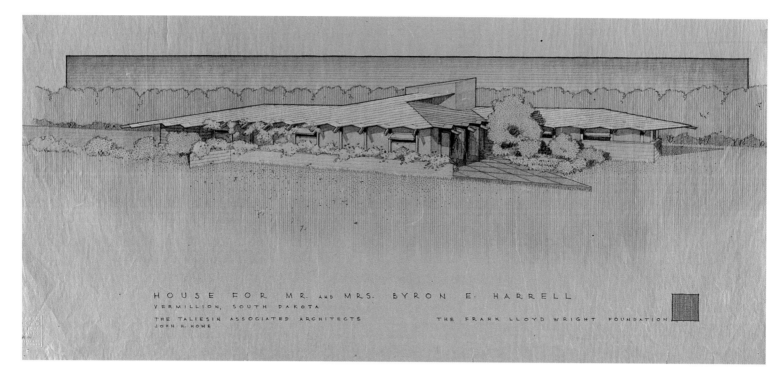

HOUSE FOR MR. AND MRS. BYRON E. HARRELL
VERMILLION, SOUTH DAKOTA
THE TALIESIN ASSOCIATED ARCHITECTS   THE FRANK LLOYD WRIGHT FOUNDATION
JOHN H. HOWE

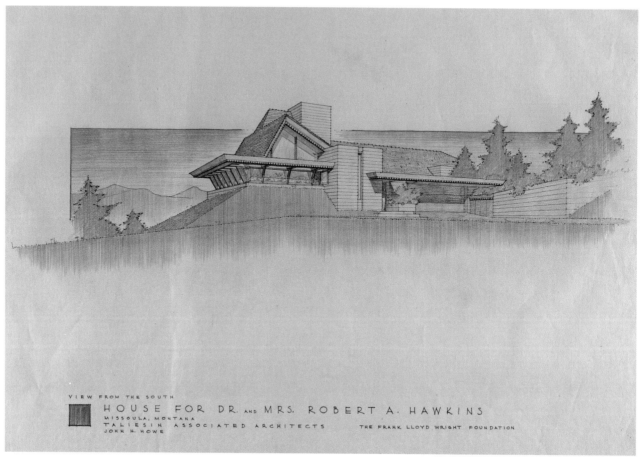

VIEW FROM THE SOUTH
HOUSE FOR DR. AND MRS. ROBERT A. HAWKINS
MISSOULA, MONTANA
TALIESIN ASSOCIATED ARCHITECTS   THE FRANK LLOYD WRIGHT FOUNDATION
JOHN H. HOWE

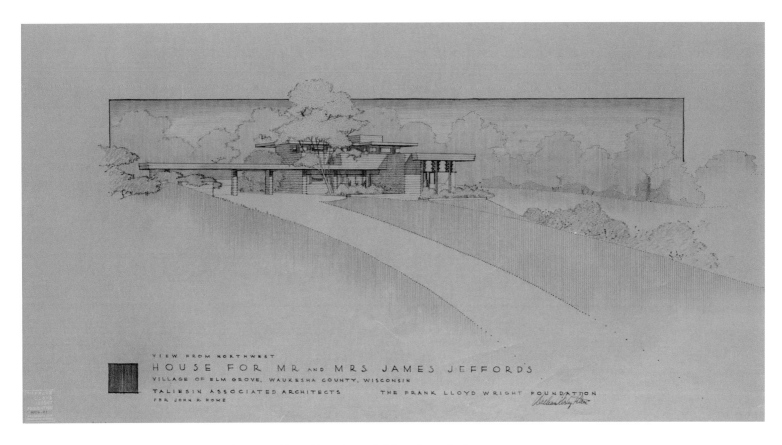

VIEW FROM NORTHWEST
HOUSE FOR MR. AND MRS. JAMES JEFFORDS
VILLAGE OF ELM GROVE, WAUKESHA COUNTY, WISCONSIN
TALIESIN ASSOCIATED ARCHITECTS   THE FRANK LLOYD WRIGHT FOUNDATION
PER JOHN H. HOWE

Opposite top For TAA, Howe designed this 1961 house in Vermillion, South Dakota, for Byron and Joyce Harrell, publishers of ornithological books. In plan, the roof with its unusually detailed eaves resembles a hawk in flight. In 1975 the Harrells, avid environmentalists, had Howe design a solar annex for the house.

Opposite bottom The Dr. Robert and Millicent Hawkins House in Missoula, Montana (1960), was another of Howe's TAA designs. The unbuilt house featured a two-story, asymmetrical living space.

Above Howe designed all four schemes for the James and Patricia Jeffords House, Elm Grove, Wisconsin (1960–61). But TAA chief architect William Wesley Peters signed them, as well as all drawings that left the studio.

In addition to commemorating the career of Frank Lloyd Wright, the October 1959 issue of *House Beautiful* featured work by Howe, other current TAA architects, and former members of the Taliesin Fellowship.

known as Inwood, was designed in 1953 and completed in 1958.[13] In 1958, Howe's design for a Usonian house for Bryant and Marjorie Denniston was under construction in Newton, Iowa. By the late 1950s, he had taken another important step to prepare for life after Wright: he became a registered architect in the state of Arizona on June 26, 1958.[14]

Although many TAA architects were competent designers and more than capable of completing Wright's unfinished commissions, few were known beyond Taliesin circles by name or professional reputation. For TAA to succeed, its architects needed national exposure and new clients.

NATIONAL EXPOSURE

One of the most adulatory posthumous tributes to Wright, "Your Heritage from Frank Lloyd Wright," appeared in the October 1959 issue of *House Beautiful* magazine. In the introductory essay to the commemorative issue, editor Elizabeth Gordon wrote, "The death of a great genius causes those of us who are left behind to stop short and try to assess what has been lost, as well as what has been left behind."

It was not surprising that Gordon, who once called Wright "the greatest architect who ever lived,"[15] would publish such a eulogy. Wright and *House Beautiful* had enjoyed a long, close, and mutually supportive relationship. Gordon was a steadfast promoter of Wright's work, and Wright appreciated her advocacy. In 1953, when Gordon needed a new architecture editor to replace the departing James Marston Fitch, Wright suggested Taliesin apprentice John deKoven Hill for the job. Hill worked for the magazine for a decade and eventually rose to the position of editorial director. Over time, at least three other Taliesin apprentices also served on the editorial team at *House Beautiful*. Of the close association between the two entities, Gordon later observed, the magazine's "architecture department was an extension of Taliesin."[16]

Although the stated goal of the October issue was to "evaluate what we all have gained from the creative genius," Gordon also endeavored to assure readers that Wright's architectural vision would not die with him. Instead, it would be carried on by TAA. In a sidebar titled "Work Continues in the Taliesin Studio," she wrote, "The experienced organization of 19 key men—registered architects, engineers, and designers—who worked closely with Wright for from 20 to 27 years, are continuing the work already in progress in the studio and are accepting many new projects of all types." The photograph accompanying the text showed TAA members at work in the drafting room—with Howe and Peters pictured front and center. For the reader's convenience, the issue printed a list of TAA members and other "architects who understand and use Wrightian principles."[17] To support these assertions, the issue prominently featured projects by current and former Taliesin apprentices. Gordon highlighted buildings by Howe, Aaron Green, Alden Dow, Lloyd Wright, Arthur Browning Parker, Charles Montooth, Fay Jones, and William Bernoudy, as well as decorative screens and panels by Masselink.

The magazine devoted a two-page spread to Inwood. The article, "Beyond the Functional—into the Poetic," spoke to the ways in which the house "everywhere turned necessity into poetry" and recognized that "architecture must nurture man's spirit as well as his body." Handsome black-and-white images by noted architectural photographer Maynard Parker captured the charms of the modest structure, including its "sense of spaciousness" and the

Above As published in the October 1959 issue of *House Beautiful*, this photograph shows the intimate and "poetic" relationship between Inwood and the surrounding landscape.

Left Views from Inwood (which is built into a hillside and almost indistinguishable from it) open across the Wyoming Valley to Taliesin.

AFTER WRIGHT

VIEW FROM NORTHEAST Looking Southwest
COTTAGE FOR MR. FREDERIC ROYSTON PHILADELPHIA, PEN
JOHN H. HOWE, ARCHITECT
TALIESIN ASSOCIATED ARCHITECTS THE FRANK LLOYD WRIGHT FOUNDATION

Opposite left This 1959 photograph of the bedroom at Inwood shows the massive stone fireplace that gives character to the room. The stone steps, at right, lead to living areas.

Opposite right Howe defined the (fold-down) desk nook, located in a corner of the bedroom at Inwood, by dropping the ceiling in that area.

Above Howe's perspective shows how the Frederic and Toby Royston Cottage, Exton, Pennsylvania (1961), was built into the contours of the land.

intimate connection between the house and its natural surroundings.[18] For those architects who had independent practices at the time of publication, the publicity was welcome national exposure. For Howe, it was the first time a building of his acknowledged design had been published.

FOLLY COTTAGE

One of Howe's earliest completed works as a TAA architect was a 1961 commission for Frederic and Toby Royston. Two years earlier, the couple met with Wright to discuss plans for a weekend cottage to be built on a wooded, twenty-acre site thirty-four miles west of their Society Hill residence in Philadelphia. When Wright died before the project could begin, the commission passed to TAA and Howe.

The Roystons were a socially prominent couple. Frederic was a leading U.S. importer of British sports cars, including Austins, Austin-Healeys, Morris Minors, and MGs.[19] He was well known in auto racing circles. Toby, a sports car driver herself, instigated the project.[20] Howe's design for Folly Cottage, as the country retreat was called, consisted of two companion structures, a cottage and a guesthouse. He used a triangular grid to generate the respective plans. Whereas the scheme for the cottage recalled his design for Inwood, the plan of the guesthouse was based on an unexecuted 1948 Wright design for a cottage for his sister Maginel Wright Barney, which was planned for a site near Taliesin.[21] Howe built the northeast sides of the low-profile cottage and guesthouse into the slope of a hill. On the southwest side of the structures, he opened views from interior rooms and contiguous terraces to the landscape beyond. The selection of Tennessee limestone and cypress for construction materials, and Howe's thoughtful integration of the buildings into the existing contours of the land, resulted in a harmonious composition inspired by Wright's principles of organic architecture.

The interiors of the cottage and guesthouse are animated by perforated, patterned boards, long a signature decorative element of Wright's Usonian house designs. Here, Howe used Honduran mahogany and a richly detailed pattern to create an elegant hallmark of the rooms. The deeply cantilevered, low-sloped roofs appear to float above glass expanses below, the panes of which meet in delicately mitered corners. The Roystons complemented Howe's architecture with numerous pieces of wood furniture designed by George Nakashima, an artisan based in New Hope, Pennsylvania.[22]

Culwell Construction Company built the cottage and guesthouse over a three-year period. The Oklahoma-based concern was responsible for the construction of the Wright-designed Price Tower in Bartlesville, Oklahoma (completed in 1956), and Beth Sholom Synagogue in Elkins Park, Pennsylvania (completed in 1959). Peters supervised the building of the cottage owing, in part, to his field involvement with the construction of the synagogue.

Opposite Deep overhanging eaves shelter both the
Royston guesthouse (foreground left) and the cottage.

Above Howe used Honduran mahogany for the built-in
furniture, bookshelves, and patterned, perforated-board
ceiling light in the Royston guesthouse.

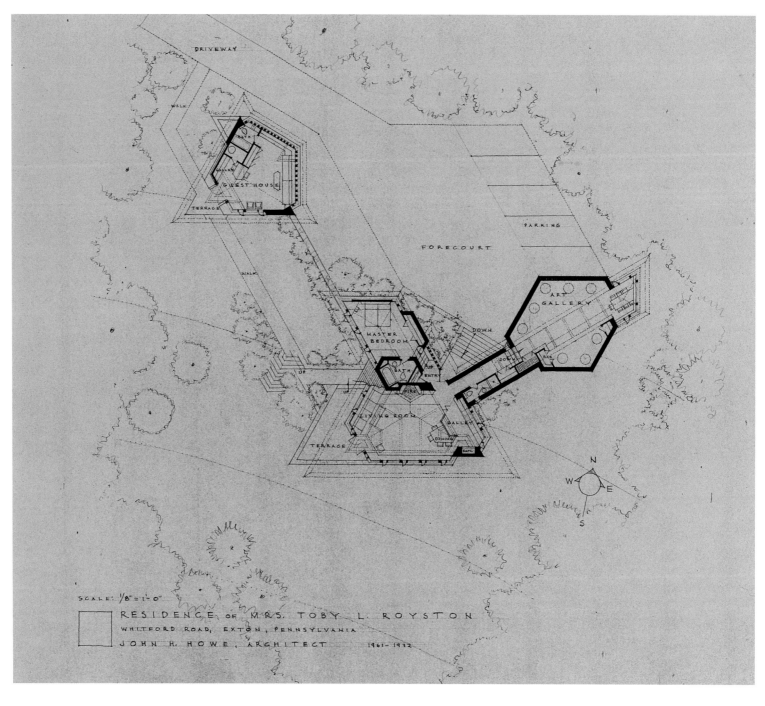

DRIVEWAY

WALK

BATH

GALLERY
GUEST HOUSE

TERRACE

PARKING

FORECOURT

WALK

ART
GALLERY

DOWN

MASTER
BEDROOM

UP
UP ENTRY

BATH

UP DOWN

BIKE

LIVING ROOM

GALLERY

TERRACE

DINING

REFR.

N
W E
S

SCALE: 1/8" = 1'-0"

RESIDENCE OF MRS. TOBY L. ROYSTON
WHITFORD ROAD, EXTON, PENNSYLVANIA
JOHN H. HOWE, ARCHITECT   1961-1972

This plan drawing shows the siting of the original Royston cottage and guesthouse, as well as the art gallery addition completed in 1974.

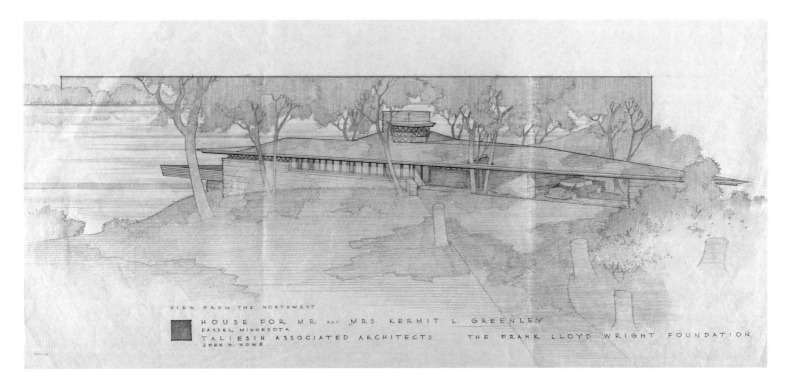

VIEW FROM THE NORTHWEST
HOUSE FOR MR. AND MRS. KERMIT L. GREENLEY
DASSEL, MINNESOTA
TALIESIN ASSOCIATED ARCHITECTS   THE FRANK LLOYD WRIGHT FOUNDATION
JOHN H. HOWE

As this perspective for the Kermit L. and Evelyn Greenley House, Dassel, Minnesota (1962), shows, Howe expressed corners and endpoints of roofs, balconies, and chimneys to give a full sense of the design. To prevent foliage from obscuring essential elements of the house, he "chopped" down foreground trees but still depicted their shadows on the ground.

The Roystons divorced not long after Folly Cottage was built, but Toby remained in residence until her death at age ninety-two in 2009.[23] In 1968, she approached Howe, who was then practicing independently in Minnesota, to design an art gallery addition on the lower level of the cottage. It was built in 1974.

DESIGNS FOR MINNESOTA

As a TAA architect Howe began to build a client base, particularly in Minnesota. His earliest project in the state was an unexecuted 1960 design for Mr. and Mrs. George Hovland in Duluth. A 1962 residence for Kermit L. and Evelyn Greenley in Dassel, Minnesota, also was not realized. Howe's first completed building in Minnesota was a 1961 residence for David and Jane Tilford LaBerge in Stillwater. At the time, David was a young associate professor of psychology at the University of Minnesota and the musical director and conductor of the Bach Society of Minnesota. Jane was a violinist.

Originally, David LaBerge wanted to build a house designed by Frank Lloyd Wright. In 1955, by chance, he met the architect in the Indianapolis airport where both men were awaiting flights. LaBerge, who was on his way to Chicago to purchase a new Bösendorfer piano, approached Wright. "We discussed the merits of his Bechstein and my Bösendorfer piano," he recalled. Although it was his only encounter with Wright, he later wrote, "that brief visit with the great man was etched in my mind."[24]

LaBerge said of his move to Minnesota in 1958, "My impression of the Minnesota landscape soon kindled a desire to build there a Frank Lloyd Wright house I had in my mind's eye ever since I was a high school student." A year later, when LaBerge had the opportunity to build a house on a small plot of University of Minnesota–owned land in the University Grove neighborhood of Falcon Heights, he learned of Wright's death. "I searched magazines and books to

113

find which of his associates at Taliesin had built houses that most closely matched the image I carried in my mind those many years," he said. LaBerge discovered the *House Beautiful* article about Inwood, the "delightful little stone, wood, and glass structure" Howe designed.

The LaBerges contacted Howe and met with him at Taliesin to discuss the house they desired. A few weeks later, they received a set of drawings. The couple approved of the siting of the house, and David was pleased that the plan provided ample room for his grand piano and adequate rehearsal space for "a string quartet and for my newly formed small chorus."[25] The couple particularly liked the "elongated points" of the roof's corners, which they felt kept the house from "seeming boxy." Unfortunately, that very feature, according to David, "mortally pierced" their plans to build in University Grove; the neighborhood's architectural review committee would not approve Howe's design because the roof ends extended beyond acceptable property boundaries.[26] Undaunted, the LaBerges set out to find a "site that would live up to John's design" and located one in Stillwater Township.[27] According to David, Howe sited the house "over the edge of the hill, making the house 'of the hill' instead of 'on the hill,'" a practice favored by Wright.[28] The spacious site allowed the roof ends to extend "freely in all directions," to the delight of the LaBerges.

After some effort, David LaBerge found a contractor who was willing to build a nontraditional house on a wooded site one-half mile from the nearest public road. Fortunately, the contractor

HOUSE FOR MR. AND MRS. DAVID LABERGE   MINNEAPOLIS, MINNESOTA
TALIESIN ASSOCIATED ARCHITECTS   THE FRANK LLOYD WRIGHT FOUNDATION
JOHN H. HOWE

Opposite The David and Jane Tilford LaBerge House, Stillwater, Minnesota (1961), was designed while Howe was with TAA and was his first house built in the state.

Right Howe included a skylight in the vaulted ceiling of the LaBerge House.

Opposite top The Philip and Sidney Wear House, Wayzata (1961), was one of Howe's earliest Minnesota houses. It was demolished in 2010.

Opposite bottom The living room of the Wear House featured a Kasota stone fireplace and built-in seating.

hired a carpenter who could "visualize in three, maybe even four or five dimensions," a gift LaBerge later stated was required "to put together the multi-angled roof that covered the splendid interior space" of the house. A skilled stonemason named "Snow-Ball" Thomsen rounded out the construction team. He was responsible for finely crafting the Kasota stone walls of the house in a manner similar to the stonework at Taliesin in Spring Green.

The LaBerges' recollections of living in the house resonated with Howe's personal architectural philosophy: the land is the beginning. During the six years they resided there, the couple came to appreciate how the house was "so much a part of the land into which it is built." For David LaBerge, the house and the land on which it stood were inseparable. More than one-half century after leaving the house, he claims his "mind is still flooded with memories of the special moments that the land remembers."

THE POET IN STONE

The coverage of the Howes' cottage in *House Beautiful* caught the attention of another Minnesota couple, Philip and Sidney Wear. Sidney was a longtime admirer of Frank Lloyd Wright; she wrote an honors thesis on his work when she was a student at Brown University.[29] When she and her husband acquired a seven-acre parcel of land near Lake Minnetonka, she resolved to ask Wright to design a house for the site, but his death precluded that plan. Instead, she contacted Taliesin to find an architect who shared Wright's principles of organic architecture and who could design a home for her family, which at the time included three sons. Prior to visiting Taliesin and meeting with Olgivanna Lloyd Wright, Sidney reviewed the October 1959 issue of *House Beautiful* and was captivated by the photographs of Inwood. In describing the qualities of the cottage, the article explained that Wright had been "a poet who wrote his sonnets in syllables of stone." It further noted that Howe had "grasped well the lesson of the poet-builder" in his design for the cottage. Sidney had found her architect. Olgivanna, who was now in charge at Taliesin, had other ideas. She put forth Peters as the man for the job. Sidney disagreed and instead requested the "poet in stone" whose work she admired in *House Beautiful*.[30] A call was placed to Howe, who was working in the Hillside studio. He received the commission and designed a modest house for the Wears in 1961. Howe built the one-level Kasota stone and wood dwelling, which had a partial basement, into a hilly slope. No garage or carport was provided. The heart of the house was a sunken living room dominated by a stone fireplace, the mass of which rose to meet the vaulted ceiling. Howe designed the intimate built-in seating that flanked one side of the fireplace, the cabinetry that lined the gallery leading to the bedrooms, the perforated wood panels between the master bedroom and living room, and a coffee table. Howe later designed an outbuilding for the property in 1967 and a patio addition in 1971.

Sidney Wear, a descendant of the influential Washburn family whose members included founders of the Minnesota Milling Company, which eventually became General Mills, was an advocate of Howe's work.[31] She spread the word of his architectural talents among her business associates and friends in the Lake Minnetonka area, resulting in additional clients and commissions for Howe. After her divorce from Philip, Sidney remained in the house until shortly before her death in 2010. That same year, the property was sold and the house torn down to make way for new residential construction.

AFTER WRIGHT

CLIENTS FOR LIFE

George R. Johnson, a prominent Minneapolis attorney, and his wife, Norma, were also among the many readers of the *House Beautiful* commemorative issue. Like the LaBerges and the Wears, they were inspired by the feature on Howe in the magazine. "They were great admirers of Mr. Wright's work and felt that because of my long and close association with Mr. Wright, I could give them a house that most closely followed his principles," Howe later wrote.[32] He also admitted to being "delighted for an opportunity to pursue my own architectural work after thirty-two years at Taliesin." The association between Howe and the Johnsons would prove to be a long-lasting and productive one. In total, Howe designed more than a dozen projects for the couple, the majority of which were built.[33] After her husband's death in 1981, Norma Johnson continued to commission Howe for additional architectural design work.

Wintertree (1963), as the first Johnson residence is known, is located above the North Arm of Lake Minnetonka, about fifteen miles from Minneapolis.[34] For maximum drama—and to capitalize on views of the lake—Howe placed the house atop a steep, wooded ridge between a rolling lawn to the east and the cascading lakeshore to the west. On the lake side of the house, the roof cantilevers from the two-story living room and hovers above south- and west-facing glass walls, which frame expansive views of the lake. In contrast, the sheltering roof of the original guesthouse terminates just above the ground. The plan of the guesthouse was based on the aforementioned unexecuted design for Maginel Wright Barney.

HOUSE FOR MR. AND MRS. GEORGE R. JOHNSON
WAYZATA, MINNESOTA
JOHN H. HOWE ARCHITECT   TALIESIN ASSOCIATED ARCHITECTS

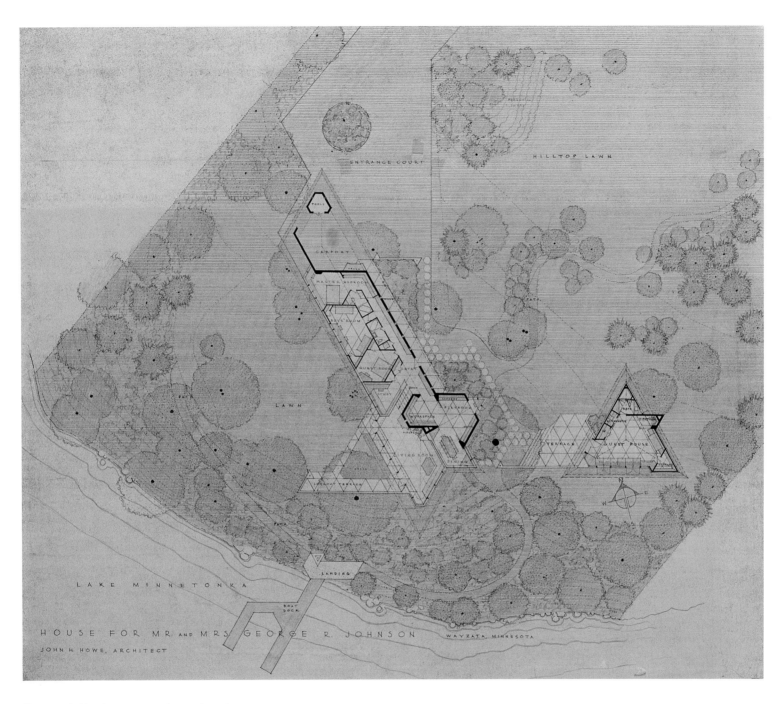

HOUSE FOR MR. AND MRS. GEORGE R. JOHNSON   WAYZATA, MINNESOTA
JOHN H. HOWE, ARCHITECT

Opposite As Howe's presentation drawing shows, he used the contours of the land to create a two-story glass living area on the Lake Minnetonka side of the George and Norma Johnson House I (1963).

Above Existing site conditions, such as contours and the water's edge, helped Howe determine the placement of the Johnson House I on the land. He developed the plan based on an equilateral triangular module.

AFTER WRIGHT

Above The triangular geometry of the plan of the Johnson House I is expressed in the shape of the fountain and walkway pavers. In 1988 Howe designed a family room addition to link the main part of the house to the guesthouse, which now functions as a master bedroom.

Opposite top The glass-walled living room of the Johnson House I offers expansive views of the North Arm of Lake Minnetonka.

Opposite bottom On the lake side of the Johnson House I, the two-story living room is dominated by a triangular roof.

AFTER WRIGHT

Howe designed the light fixture that illuminates the sidewalk leading to the entry of the Johnson House I.

Howe laid out the plan of the house on a unit system based on the module of an equilateral triangle. He believed a plan generated by triangular geometry was more flexible and allowed a greater flow of space than "could be obtained with conventional ninety-degree angles and the usual box-shaped rooms they produce."[35]

As Wright had done before him, Howe incorporated the fireplace and workspace in a single masonry mass. Responding to the Johnsons' request for a house that would be easy to maintain and suited to a family with two small boys, he clustered the workspace (or kitchen), dining room, playroom, and laundry together.

The exterior of the house is constructed of red brick and California redwood with Minnesota Kasota stone used for wall copings. Interior finish materials consist of red-tinted concrete, jointed along the unit lines, for floors, and Philippine mahogany and brick for interior walls. Howe also designed furniture for Wintertree and, four years after the house was completed, created an entrance gate, guesthouse, and storage building for the large property. He later reflected that the house had "the qualities of architecture that Mr. Wright adhered to," including "a sense of the ground . . . a sense of shelter . . . a sense of materials . . . a sense of space, and . . . a sense of proportion."[36]

The Johnsons lived in Wintertree until 1974, when they commissioned Howe to design a second home for them that would better accommodate a family with two teenage boys.

A DANCE CENTER IN THE DESERT

In 1963 Howe had the opportunity to design and build his first nonresidential project, the Tucson Creative Dance Center for dancer, author, educator, and filmmaker Barbara Mettler.[37] After studying dance in Germany and leading studios in New York City and New Hampshire, Mettler moved to Tucson, where she planned to establish a permanent studio. "I looked everywhere for a building which I could transform into a dance studio," she later wrote, "but I found nothing suitable, so I decided to build my own."[38] Mettler purchased a three-acre plot of land and went to nearby Taliesin to discuss her project. There, she found John Howe. According to dance historian Rob Dobson, in Howe she found a "compatible soul" who seemed to have "a remarkable grasp of Mettler's design needs."[39]

In many ways, Mettler, who was born and raised in Chicago, was an ideal client for Howe, as she would have been for Wright. Her avowed core principles of "beauty, freedom, and democracy" resonated closely with Wright's tenets as well as those of Howe and other Fellowship members.[40] She also had a deep respect for nature, preferred to live and work in close concert with it, and often staged dance performances outdoors. Mettler was captivated by the landscape of the Tucson area: "In the desert there is space to move and feel and think and be yourself," she observed. "To create has always meant to me tuning in to the ultimate beauty within and around us which is waiting to be revealed."[41]

The entry to the dance center is located between the building's two main parts: an arc-shaped workroom wing that houses the director's office, a small studio, and dressing rooms, and the main dance studio, which is circular in plan. Howe generated the plan of the studio in response to Mettler's request for a large circular dance floor with stepped seating on the perimeter. In lieu of structural columns that would have impeded the dancers' freedom of movement, Howe spanned the fifty-eight-foot diameter of the studio and supported its curved, turquoise-colored roof with a three-legged truss system supported on exterior piers. The

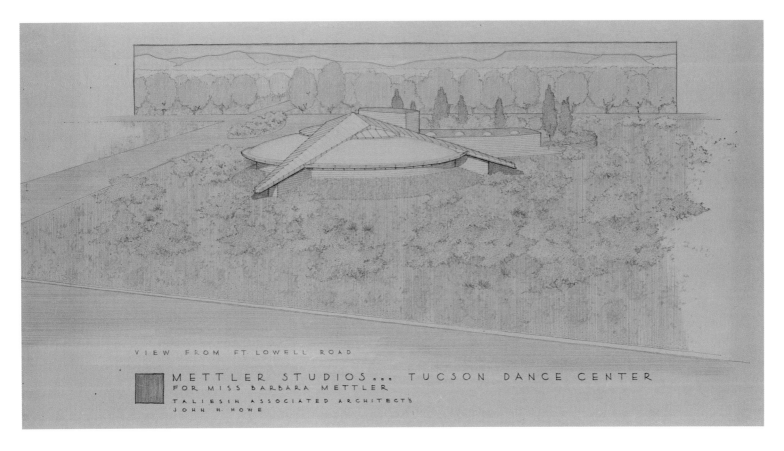

VIEW FROM FT. LOWELL ROAD

METTLER STUDIOS... TUCSON DANCE CENTER
FOR MISS BARBARA METTLER
TALIESIN ASSOCIATED ARCHITECTS
JOHN H. HOWE

This aerial perspective of the Tucson Creative Dance Center, Tucson, Arizona (1963), shows the circular dance studio and three-legged structural system that supports the roof.

Above left Workmen frame one leg of the truss system that supports the unusual clear-span roof of the Tucson Creative Dance Center.

Above right Howe placed the entrance to the Tucson Creative Dance Center between the administrative wing and the main studio.

Opposite Barbara Mettler, client for the Tucson Creative Dance Center commission, requested a circular dance studio with stepped seating on the perimeter.

outward thrust of the roof is contained by a steel cable perimeter tension ring that can be adjusted as necessary.[42] Walls of earth-colored concrete block, and the partial earth berming of the building, create an inwardly focused space and protect interiors from the extremes of the desert climate. Howe used the curved wall of the building's administrative wing, along with an arc-shaped bed of plantings, to define the second circular component of the design— a large dance garden for outdoor performances. As Mettler requested, a portion of the site's natural desert flora was left untouched.

The design of the building was so unorthodox that Mettler had difficulty securing a loan and finding someone to construct it, a dilemma previously experienced by some of Wright's clients.[43] According to Mettler, the building, particularly its colorful, unusually shaped roof, was an object of curiosity for many passersby, who asked, "What is it?" Unfazed by the queries, she explained, "Arizona is a territory where you can do as you please."[44] Mettler documented the building, and the creative dance performances staged within and around it, in several videos and films.[45]

While Mettler appreciated the building's functionality, she was most pleased that it, "like any living thing, expresses the life that goes on within it . . . all aspects of our dance life." She thanked Howe for designing a building that organically grew from "freedom of expression, art as activity, pure movement as the material of dance, [and] dance as a three-dimensional art."[46] In 1968 Mettler commissioned Howe to design a small house for her and her elderly mother, Mrs. Minnie Warner, on the grounds of the Tucson Creative Dance Center. Although the house was not built, the rectilinear geometry of Howe's design intriguingly counterpointed the curvilinear plan of the dance center.

AFTER WRIGHT

Right Dancers perform in the desert dance garden, a feature Barbara Mettler asked Howe to provide for the Tucson Creative Dance Center.

Opposite In 1964 Howe created a teahouse for the garden of the Frank Lloyd Wright–designed William and Mary Palmer House, Ann Arbor, Michigan (1950). The teahouse features a sunken area for tea ceremonies and gatherings.

WRIGHT REVISITED

In addition to having the opportunity to work on new projects during his years as a TAA architect, Howe planned additions for at least ten Wright-designed houses.[47] He also served as renovation architect for updates to two Wright buildings he knew well. In 1961 Howe and Peters directed interior repairs and painting at Unity Temple in Oak Park, Illinois (1905), a building Howe had first discovered as a teenager on bicycle excursions from his home in nearby Evanston.[48] In the late 1930s Howe produced drawings for Wingspread, the Herbert F. and Jane Johnson House in Wind Point, Wisconsin (1937), designed for the head of S. C. Johnson & Son. In 1959 the house was donated by the Johnson family to the Johnson Foundation and turned into an international conference center. Howe was renovation architect for the project.

In 1964 Howe designed a freestanding teahouse for the garden of the Wright-designed William and Mary Palmer House in Ann Arbor, Michigan (1950). According to historian Grant Hildebrand, the couple asked Howe, who had been on-site during the construction of the house, to design "a place of rest and tranquility that would shape the character of the garden around it."[49] Inspired by the gardens they studied during an extended trip to Japan, the Palmers requested Howe design a teahouse that would pay "homage to Kyoto" but also harmonize with the materials and geometries of their Wright-designed house. At the time the Palmers commissioned Howe to design the teahouse, he had not yet traveled to Japan. Soon, however, he would experience the country and culture that sparked the Palmers' interest in a garden structure and had profoundly influenced Frank Lloyd Wright.

Howe based the plan of the teahouse on the same equilateral triangle that generated the plan of the main house, a module he had used—and would continue to favor—in his design work. Beyond an "entry of unforgettably intimate breadth," the diminutive teahouse opens to a space with a raised ceiling, a sunken area for "tea, conversation, and contemplation," a fireplace, and carefully framed views. One vista extends beyond a juncture of glass planes

AFTER WRIGHT

that terminates in an angular prow—a dramatic gesture Howe used to great effect in several of his houses. Considered together, the Palmer House and Teahouse may well be the most evocative, sensitive, and harmonious architectural "collaboration" achieved between Wright and one of his fellows.

DEPARTURE FROM TALIESIN

On July 15, 1962, Gene Masselink died of a sudden heart attack. He was fifty-one years old. In addition to being an indefatigable worker, Masselink also could bridge gaps among factions at Taliesin and smooth differences with his diplomatic charm. Well liked and respected, he would be missed by all, but especially by Howe, who had been sustained by his friend's faithful correspondence during his nearly three-year imprisonment at Sandstone.

Life was changing in other ways at the Fellowship. By 1964 Olgivanna had assumed near-total control over architectural activities, making work and daily existence increasingly difficult for fellows. With Masselink gone, there was no one to mediate escalating tensions at Taliesin or to negotiate quarrels between disparate factions. As one observer noted, Howe "put up with a lot" during his last years at Taliesin but was able to block out distractions because of his "tubular focus" on work.[50] "Jack was overshadowed in the TAA structure by the ubiquitous presence of Wesley Peters. All major projects were diverted to [him]," recalled Wiehle.[51] For some time, Olgivanna had made it clear she did not consider Howe a member of her inner circle, but now she also—inexplicably—began to question his professional credentials.[52]

Howe realistically assessed the situation: "When Mrs. Wright said that she was an architect, and when she took charge of the drafting room and had to approve of anything that was sent out from the drafting room, I decided it was past time for me to leave and be starting

The geometry, materials, and details of the Palmers' teahouse were chosen by Howe to resonate with their Wright-designed residence.

Frank Lloyd Wright presented Howe with this 1770 print by the Japanese artist Shunshō and inscribed it "To Jack—the Senior True."

my own architectural practice."[53] Lu Howe later said the idea of departing from Taliesin kept "nibbling" at them over time.[54] In the summer of 1964, Howe advised Olgivanna that he and Lu would be leaving the Fellowship that fall. Prior to their departure, and with Olgivanna's halfhearted permission, they joined other apprentices on a planned, three-week driving tour of Europe. As Howe recalled, "Mrs. Wright said 'go ahead, you might as well.' Well, I felt that we had earned it and so we went on that wonderful trip."[55]

When they returned from Europe, Howe admitted, "I didn't know where to go to practice architecture. I had thought of Michigan, but there didn't seem to be any real encouragement there. And so I called Aaron Green and asked him if I could come and work for him as an interlude to my establishing my own practice someplace."[56] Green welcomed Howe to his practice and offered Lu a position as one of two secretaries in the office. In October the Howes embarked on new lives and careers in San Francisco. John Howe was fifty-one years old.

As challenging as the years before his departure might have been, Howe looked back on his life and work at Taliesin with pride and gratitude. As a longstanding member of the Taliesin Fellowship, he later wrote, "I had the delightful experience for many years starting in 1932 of participating in history as it was being made . . . and learning architecture from the ground up." He expressed appreciation for the principles of organic architecture he learned from Wright, noting, "The older I get the more grateful I feel for his architectural ethic because I find it provides both a keel and a rudder for my own architectural work."[57]

Of the roughly thirty men and women who were charter members of the Fellowship, only two were still at Taliesin at the time of Wright's death: Howe and Peters. Along with Masselink, who joined the Fellowship in 1933 and remained there until his death, Howe and Peters were, without question, the longest-serving and most senior members of the Fellowship. "Wright had with Howe a relationship of complete trust," Wiehle observed. "Wright had come to depend heavily on Jack, who never expressed the slightest doubt about Wright's architectural genius, while also protecting his architectural credibility. And Jack would firmly argue his case if there was a difference," he added.[58]

Howe possessed a deep respect for Wright—the man and his teachings. Likewise, Wright held Howe in high regard for his talents and his ability to run the studio efficiently and smoothly. On occasion, Wright let Howe know just how valuable he was to him. Prior to his death, Wright, a noted collector of Asian art, presented Howe with an eighteenth-century Japanese print from his collection, which he inscribed "To Jack—the Senior True."[59] It was among the possessions Howe took with him when he left Taliesin in 1964.

129

5
THE FREEDOM
OF CALIFORNIA

John and Lu Howe enjoyed the freedom of life away from the tense atmosphere at Taliesin during their three years in San Francisco, though Howe was bittersweet about having left his life's work. He recalled that living atop Russian Hill was an exhilarating experience.

After weathering five years with Olgivanna Lloyd Wright in charge of the Fellowship, enduring her "interference" and "outbursts," to quote apprentice Carl Book, the Howes left Taliesin in the autumn of 1964, bound for San Francisco and a new life.[1] As with Wright's sudden death five and a half years before, many in the Fellowship were unprepared for the news, given that John had been an apprentice for thirty-two years and Lu a highly regarded member of the community for over a dozen.

For Lu, this move represented the return to a normal existence after thirteen years as part of a larger community. The Taliesin Fellowship was one she had married into rather than sought out. For Howe, the move was both momentous and bittersweet. He had joined the Fellowship when he was just nineteen years old, directly from high school. He had spent virtually his entire adult life there, rising to a position of considerable authority and tremendous respect. Now fifty-one years old, he was leaving all that behind for an uncharted future in a place half a continent away, one with which he was unfamiliar.

Nevertheless, an adventure was at hand. "We were [our] own bosses, at last," recalled Lu. "It was like a second honeymoon . . . a fun time."[2] And before long, the Howes were relishing the experience. Howe was eager to see what the outside world was like.[3] After all, he had spent time away from the Fellowship only sporadically, either in the confines of the Federal Correctional Institution at Sandstone, Minnesota, when supervising the occasional project, or on seasonal treks between the two Taliesins. In San Francisco, Howe reported to client William Palmer, "We are enjoying life here *tremendously*. It is like living in Hong Kong, for we are surrounded by Chinese families and ocean-going ships pass the foot of our hill. We hear fog horns all night."[4] Later Howe recollected, "It was great, to live right on top of Russian Hill. . . . It was the center of the universe! [We had] panoramic views of San Francisco Bay from the Golden Gate Bridge to the Bay Bridge."[5]

Although San Francisco was new to them, they had contacts in the Bay Area, notably Howe's sister Betty and her husband, Paul Mobley, residing in Berkeley, plus Aaron Green and other former Taliesin apprentices. They found an apartment at 1655 Jones Street, near the center of downtown. Donald Brown, a friend and longtime Taliesin apprentice, lived in a unit beneath them.[6] Best of all, they both had secured architectural employment at Aaron Green Associates, a short cable car ride down the hill. Green's Wright-designed office interior provided a somewhat familiar setting, even though its address, 319 Grant Street, was in the heart of the business district—a far cry from the remote settings of the Taliesins.[7] Howe joined the drafting room staff of eight or so, while Lu resumed a role familiar to her: she typed specifications, helped the office run smoothly, and offered her dry wit and good spirit. They enjoyed the pleasure of walking to work, downhill all the way.

AARON GREEN ASSOCIATES

Howe and Green had become friends in 1940 when the latter joined the Taliesin Fellowship. They were split apart by the war years, when Green enlisted in the military during his arraignment for draft resistance; he served overseas as a bombardier. Their friendship resumed in the 1950s, when Green was the local architect assisting on Wright's northern California commissions. Green, whom Howe trusted, felt bad about Howe's unhappy situation at Taliesin and was pleased to be able to employ the Howes, though he did so only after securing Mrs. Wright's approval.[8]

Green had come to the Fellowship from his native Alabama. He supervised construction of the Wright-designed Stanley and Mildred Rosenbaum House, Florence, Alabama (1939), and Florida Southern College's E. T. Roux Library, Lakeland, Florida (1941). In the Taliesin studio, he produced the Detroit Auto Workers' Cooperative Homestead drawings in 1941, though the project remained unexecuted. After he returned from service in the Army Air Forces, he married Jean Haber, niece of Wright client Rose Pauson, and began a successful architectural practice in Los Angeles, specializing in residences designed in the Wrightian, organic manner.[9] He relocated north to the Bay Area in the early 1950s, when his wife inherited a large estate in Los Altos, south of San Francisco.[10]

Green's role as Frank Lloyd Wright's West Coast representative furthered his career and benefited both men. Most likely, a commission like the Marin County Civic Center would have gone to neither architect without the promised involvement of the other. Green also taught in the architecture school at Stanford University in Palo Alto, where he led design studio classes as an adjunct faculty member. Consequently, his office was staffed with two sorts of employees: bright young men plucked from Stanford and those from Taliesin who had migrated west.[11]

The younger men in Green's office welcomed their distinguished older colleague from Taliesin. To enhance their skills, he gave them all "Jack Howe Perspective Lessons," recalled Jan Novie, head of Aaron Green Associates.[12] He particularly impressed them with his calm, professional demeanor and no-nonsense approach in the office. They respected his insistence on being treated like a regular guy despite his vaunted credentials. They also liked the fact (though it surprised them) that he focused on present projects rather than on past accomplishments.[13] This, of course, was a lesson Howe had learned from Wright: the current project was the most important.

Aaron Green Associates doubled as Wright's West Coast Field Office, San Francisco, California, 1951. Wright's design of the reception area is signature organic architecture; the drafting studio was one floor above in the downtown office building.

THE FREEDOM OF CALIFORNIA

Aaron Green and Frank Lloyd Wright in 1957, after Wright had given a lecture to architecture students at the University of California, Berkeley. Green, a former Taliesin apprentice, acted as Wright's West Coast representative and assisted on many of his California projects.

As might be expected, Green was the firm's unquestioned design leader. Officially, Howe's role was much as it had been at Taliesin: to produce his unsurpassed renderings of schematic designs and to develop them through construction drawings. Together, Green and Howe forged a harmonious professional relationship during the three years they worked together, not unlike the one Wright and Howe had developed over nearly three decades. Several of Howe's San Francisco officemates remember him saying, "Green is just like Mr. Wright," referring to Green's outsized, outgoing personality. They also recalled that "it was magic" when they—Howe and Green—were together.[14]

CALIFORNIA PROJECTS

Among the most compelling drawings Howe did while in California are those for the Santa Clara County Peace Officers Association. This nonprofit group was dedicated to serving the educational, training, and recreational needs of the county's law enforcement community. Having acquired an undeveloped forty-two-acre tract in Cupertino, the group hired Green to design three distinct and ambitious projects for their campus. The renderings for the smallest of these, the Association Building, demonstrates a residential feel and an unmistakable Howe design sensibility. The Woelffel Youth Center, which featured a dining hall seating five hundred, was planned to be nearly twice as large as the Association Building. The proposed Police Officers Training Academy was larger still, containing a library, a lecture hall, and a dormitory with 120 beds, among other features.[15] Despite the lush presentation drawings, none of the structures were built, perhaps because of the ambitious nature of the program.

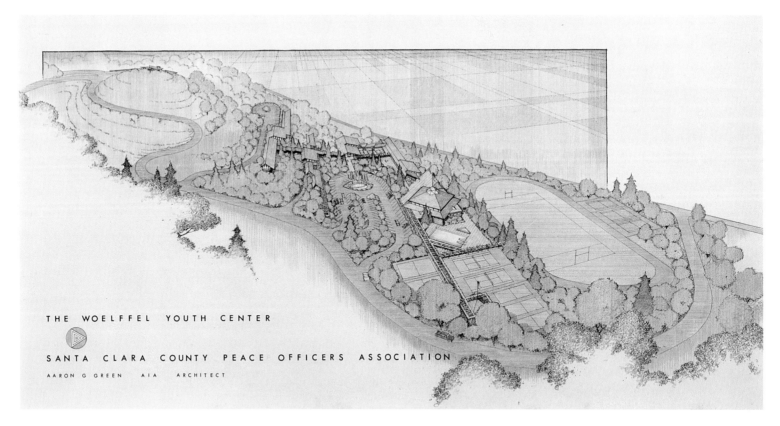

THE WOELFFEL YOUTH CENTER

SANTA CLARA COUNTY PEACE OFFICERS ASSOCIATION

AARON G GREEN   AIA   ARCHITECT

THE WOELFFEL YOUTH CENTER

SANTA CLARA COUNTY PEACE OFFICERS ASSOCIATION

AARON G GREEN • AIA • ARCHITECT

SANTA CLARA COUNTY PEACE OFFICERS ASSOCIATION
ASSOCIATION BUILDING
AARON G GREEN AIA ARCHITECT

Opposite top An aerial view of the Woelffel Youth Center facility, the Santa Clara County Peace Officers Association, Santa Clara, California (1966), designed by Aaron Green Associates on a rural site in today's Silicon Valley. Howe's three renderings for these unbuilt projects are among his finest.

Opposite bottom Howe's rendering of the automotive entry to the Woelffel Youth Center shows the organic architecture of Aaron Green Associates cascading down the hillside of the undulating site.

Above This presentation perspective of the Association Building of the Santa Clara Peace Officers Association, by Aaron Green Associates, demonstrates Howe's abilities. The framing of the drawing (particularly the handling of the redwoods) and the foreground vegetation are deftly rendered.

THE FREEDOM OF CALIFORNIA

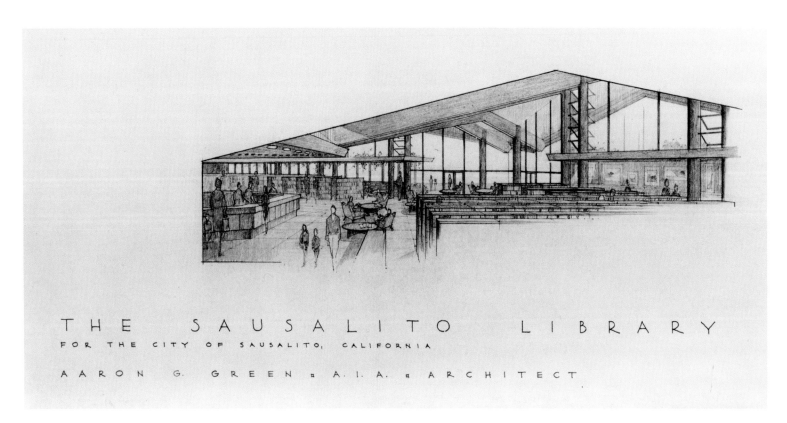

THE SAUSALITO LIBRARY
FOR THE CITY OF SAUSALITO, CALIFORNIA

AARON G. GREEN □ A.I.A. □ ARCHITECT

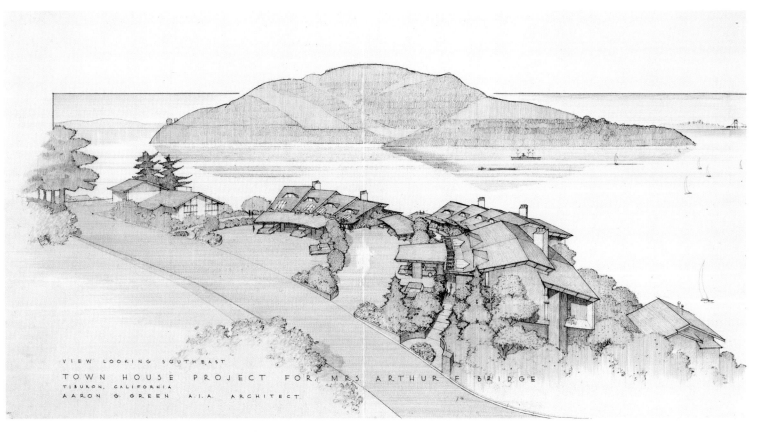

VIEW LOOKING SOUTHEAST

TOWN HOUSE PROJECT FOR MRS ARTHUR F BRIDGE
TIBURON, CALIFORNIA
AARON G GREEN A.I.A. ARCHITECT

THE FREEDOM OF CALIFORNIA

Opposite top The Sausalito Library, a waterfront project designed by Aaron Green Associates in 1965 in Sausalito, California, was not built.

Opposite bottom The Town House Project for Mrs. Arthur F. Bridge, Tiburon, California (1965), was rendered by Howe to show its siting along the shore of San Francisco Bay, with Angel Island in the background. This Aaron Green Associates project was never built, despite the seductive rendering.

Right Yum Kip Lee Office Building, Honolulu, Hawaii (1966, unexecuted), as rendered by Howe. Aaron Green Associates had a diversified practice with residential commissions and a variety of other building types during Howe's tenure (1964–67).

Another unbuilt project for which Howe prepared the presentation drawings was the Sausalito Library (1965). Intended for a prominent waterfront site, it was designed as a simple gabled form, with a glass infill wall to capture the stunning east-facing views across the bay. The Town House Project for Mrs. Arthur F. Bridge in Tiburon, California (1965), was another unbuilt project for which Howe contributed his rendering talents to the design presentation. Howe's colored pencil plans and aerial perspectives illustrate the strong geometry and sensitive scale of the Green design along the bay.[16]

Howe worked on one executed residence for Green during his three years in the office. This was for a dynamic physician, Dr. Victor Ohta and his wife, Virginia, who also commissioned a medical clinic, the Santa Cruz Medical Center, from Green, though it was never built. With a sensational ten-acre wilderness site, the Ohtas wrote an eloquent request to Green, characterizing the sort of environment in which they hoped to live. Mentioning views, intimacy, and sun patterns, they declared, "We want to feel glorious in the kitchen."[17]

218

Triangular variations from a basic
theme of disciplined rectangles give
this house a reflexive, free-flowing
shape that will allow it to fit easily
into the natural contours of the site.

THE FREEDOM OF CALIFORNIA

Opposite Howe's aerial perspective of the Victor and Virginia Ohta House, Soquel, California, published in *House Beautiful* (October 1965). The text described what the Ohtas requested in terms of design characteristics and how Aaron Green Associates' design met those expectations.

Above left The Ohta House, Soquel, California (1966), has a characteristic Wrightian fireplace as the core element of the plan, as well as intimate areas that complement the vaulted ceilings.

Above right The Ohta House has an expansive kitchen that opens to the living and dining areas of the house and captures views of Monterey Bay in the distance. Natural materials of redwood and stone complete the organic design.

The Victor and Virginia Ohta House, Soquel, California (1966), sits among redwoods on a ridge overlooking Monterey Bay, deftly wedded to its isolated site. The spacious 3,800-square-foot house of Arizona sandstone, teak, redwood, and glass features several juxtaposed, intersecting axes with multiple glass prows thrusting out from an anchoring stone fireplace. Each prow is further extended by a deck or terrace so that outdoor living spaces could also capture the views. Green designed exactly the sort of dwelling the couple requested: sun filled, with a kitchen totally integrated with the other gathering spaces. Outside, an intricate redwood and stone trellis frames a free-form swimming pool, linked to the kitchen and dining areas through floor-to-ceiling glass walls. A Japanese garden completes the tranquil setting. Sadly, the Ohta House was the site of a gruesome tragedy, which claimed the family's lives, just a few years after its completion.[18]

The largest commission Howe saw realized during his time with Green's office was the Newark Community Center (1966). The Parks Department of the city of Newark on the southeastern shore of San Francisco Bay envisioned creating a large community center that would be set within an expansive city park. Neighborhood concern over the size of the endeavor resulted in the decidedly residential character given to the structures. The center is one story with a low, hipped roof that minimizes its perceived size. Green designed a U-shaped plan that includes an array of gathering spaces clustered around a courtyard. A pergola that provides shading for walkways links the discrete elements. A freestanding park pavilion, which completed the scheme, acts as the gateway to the athletic fields beyond. Designed by Howe, the pavilion has a cantilevered roofline and intricate, triangular geometry in plan that is reminiscent of a number of Wright's Usonian houses.[19]

For the community center, Howe produced the kind of stunning presentation drawings that were his trademark, all rendered in colored pencil: plans, exterior perspectives, an intimate

THE NEWARK COMMUNITY CENTER □ CITY OF NEWARK □ CALIFORNIA

AARON G GREEN □ A.I.A □ ARCHITECT □ 319 GRANT AVENUE □ SAN FRANCISCO □ CALIFORNIA □ 94108

THE NEWARK COMMUNITY CENTER □ CITY OF NEWARK □ CALIFORNIA

AARON G GREEN □ A.I.A □ ARCHITECT □ 319 GRANT AVENUE □ SAN FRANCISCO □ CALIFORNIA □ 94108

THE FREEDOM OF CALIFORNIA

Opposite top Newark Community Center, Newark, California (1966), as rendered by Howe for Aaron Green Associates. Howe produced most of the working drawings for this major civic commission.

Opposite bottom Howe produced all four of the presentation perspective drawings for the Newark Community Center. This view of the courtyard, framed by the trellis above, accurately conveyed the sense of the domestic scale of the executed building.

Above Howe designed the Park Pavilion, a freestanding structure by the athletic fields within the park at the Newark Community Center. The pointed prow and extreme ends to the projecting hip roof overhangs are characteristic features of his designs.

THE FREEDOM OF CALIFORNIA

HOUSE FOR MR. AND MRS. PAUL C. MOBLEY
NOVATO, MARIN COUNTY, CALIFORNIA
JOHN H. HOWE

Howe's sepia rendering of his independent commission for the Paul C. and Betty Mobley House, Novato, California (1965), recalls the technique he used so often at Taliesin in the years after Sandstone. It depicts the unbuilt scheme, nestled amid the oak-studded, undulating grasslands of Marin County.

Above This compelling detail of the Mobley House, designed for Howe's sister and her family, shows Howe's fine-grained pointillist technique to full advantage. The unbuilt scheme proved too expensive and was abandoned in favor of a simpler design.

Right Exterior view, Mobley House, shortly after construction. The built version is a simple asymmetrical gable that climbs the hilly site from a tuck-under carport down low.

view into the courtyard, and an interior perspective view centered on the oversized Wrightian hearth. Without question the overall design was Green's, yet certain individual elements do suggest Howe's involvement. For example, on the courtyard side, the glass rising to the cantilevered soffit has no header and only minimal vertical wood supports: this is a signature Wright/Howe feature, seen in numerous projects, both previously and subsequently.

THE PAUL AND BETTY MOBLEY HOUSE

For Howe, a decided advantage of living in San Francisco was proximity to his younger sister Betty, a painter; her husband, Paul Mobley, a public school administrator; and their four children. Soon after moving west, Howe was working on a house for the family on a lot in Novato, among rolling hills in suburban Marin County. Howe produced a sepia perspective of the proposed dwelling that ranks among his finest drawings. Completed in autumn 1966, the house became his first fully realized independent commission since leaving Taliesin.

The steep, oak-covered Mobley lot necessitated a design that could skillfully accommodate the hilly terrain. Howe's initial design literally climbed the hill from a tuck-under carport to a cantilevered living room at the apex of the structure. A set of interior stairs navigated upward through four levels, culminating at the living room. In an all-too-familiar tale, however, the initial scheme proved too costly to build. A slightly revised scheme met the same fate. Undeterred, Howe simply started over and came up with a completely new scheme, as he had been compelled to do on many residential projects at Taliesin.[20]

John and Lu Howe traveled extensively in Japan in the autumn of 1966, including a stay at Wright's Imperial Hotel, Tokyo, completed in 1923 (demolished in 1968). The building had particular significance for Howe: when he first joined the Taliesin Fellowship, he honed his technique by copying its drawings.

The constructed version used the same basic strategy as the earlier one, but with simpler massing and geometry of the plan. The asymmetrical gable rises from the carport area to encompass and organize the facade: first the bedroom lineup, then rising to a ridge with the vaulted living room. The latter cantilevers forward, as part of the rectilinear grid, which organizes the plan. The living room windows join in mitered corners, set so that glass pane meets glass pane, as in many of Howe's best works. This motif intends to dematerialize the window wall and all but eliminate the distinction between inside and outside.

Resawn redwood, stucco, glass, and cedar shingles comprise the exterior material palette of the Mobley House. The interior is a combination of gypsum board and tongue-and-groove redwood paneling. This more economical approach, with manufactured windows and less wood, was a harbinger of things to come as construction practices evolved and became ever more standardized in postwar America. Later Howe commented that the materials and methods that were so economical in the prewar years were prohibitively expensive by the 1960s and subsequently were challenging him greatly.

THE CALIFORNIA HONEYMOON ENDS

The Howes' post-Taliesin adventures continued in 1966 with a trip to Japan to see firsthand the culture that had so captivated Wright and influenced their life at Taliesin. With his sister's house completed that October, the Howes departed on a six-week tour that included Kamakura, Nikko, Kyoto, Tokyo, Nara, and a return visit to Kyoto. Former Taliesin apprentice Raku Endo helped organize their itinerary and arranged for Howe to lecture on his career with Wright to students at two Tokyo educational institutions, Waseda University and the University of Fine Arts.[21]

While in Japan, the couple made pilgrimages to the several Wright buildings that had been constructed there between 1915 and 1923. Their visit to the Imperial Hotel in Tokyo, shortly before its demolition in 1968, must have been particularly poignant. Howe had traced its drawings over and over again while learning his craft as a neophyte at Taliesin more than thirty years earlier. His later comments reveal that he could discuss detailed particulars of the spaces and decorative details of the building from memory. The hotel management, understanding from Endo their visitors' special stature, arranged for the Howes to stay in the room where the Wrights had lodged; the room was decorated with signed photographs and other memorabilia.[22]

After returning to San Francisco from Japan, Howe suggested to Green "letting the kids go," as he phrased it, to form a two-person partnership. The presumed division of labor envisioned Green securing the project commissions, the projects designed by both, and the working drawings produced by Howe at his prodigious rate of speed. Green demurred, indicating he already had established the sort of office environment he preferred. They were men of different temperaments, despite their friendship—Green was an extrovert and Howe an introvert. As Howe discovered, they held differing opinions on the way the office should function.[23]

Rebuffed, the Howes took stock and decided it was time to start an independent practice. But where? Although they loved San Francisco, it was not home. Nor did they want to stay in a city where Howe would be competing directly with Green. They flirted briefly with an opportunity in Santa Cruz, California, but it didn't work out, Howe recollected.[24] They recognized the Midwest was their home; he was from Illinois and had lived for over thirty years in Wisconsin, she from Missouri. Besides, they still owned Inwood, the cottage they built

Above Howe brought the commission for the Richard and Carol Helstad House, Oconto Falls, Wisconsin (1966), with him to Aaron Green Associates. This perspective reveals Howe's unexecuted Usonian design.

with their own hands in the Wyoming Valley overlooking Taliesin, and longed to make use of it. Minneapolis became the obvious choice, thanks to numerous TAA client contacts and Bill Krebes's presence there, Howe's one ongoing friendship from his Sandstone incarceration.[25] By the autumn of 1967, the Howes were living in an apartment rented from Krebes just a few miles from Wright's Willey House, which Howe had helped draw as one of his first studio assignments as a young Taliesin apprentice thirty-three years previously.

Prior to leaving California, Howe took advantage of another opportunity afforded by urban life in San Francisco: to express his political beliefs on a large stage as America's involvement in the Vietnam War escalated. Given Howe's pacifism and imprisonment during World War II, it is not surprising that he was not a supporter of America's involvement in the Vietnam War. Rising domestic opposition to that conflict, particularly in centers of liberal thought like San Francisco and Berkeley, coincided with his time in California. Howe participated in several notable peace marches, according to his colleagues at Aaron Green Associates, who marched alongside him.[26] Surely the largest of these was the Spring Mobilization to End the War held on April 15, 1967. Howe was one of a hundred thousand marchers who progressed from Second and Market Street, near the Green office downtown, to Kezar Stadium in Golden Gate Park.[27]

Right Howe was able to realize a second house in California many years after departing from Aaron Green's office. The Edward and Rosemarie Edwards House, Healdsburg, California (1986), of redwood, brick, and glass, is set among the redwoods of Sonoma County.

Left Howe designed the Edward and Rosemarie Edwards House as a series of pavilions linked by raised walkways to lessen the impact on the redwood-sprinkled site.

Right The intricate redwood trellis of the Edwards House links two lobes of the main house and lessens the distinction between inside and outside. Glass overhead allows the redwood canopy to be seen through the geometric frame.

ONE LAST CALIFORNIA HOUSE

Eventually Howe's independent Minnesota architectural practice involved opportunities to design for sites all around the country, from Connecticut and Maine to North Carolina and Oregon. One commission even gave Howe the chance to build another house in northern California.

In 1983, now firmly established in his second career in Minneapolis, Howe received a commission from Edward and Rosemarie Edwards of Excelsior, Minnesota, for a vacation house set among the redwoods in Healdsburg, California, about seventy-five miles north of San Francisco. The house as completed is among his finer late works, with construction supervised by fellow Taliesin apprentice and Aaron Green Associates colleague Carl Book. It is composed of a series of four independent pavilions, linked by distinctive elevated walkways of brick on a seven-acre site. Each one-story pavilion, built of redwood, brick, and glass, is based on a hexagonal geometry. The main living and bedroom pavilions are linked by a unique, enclosed, solarium-like framework. This diamond trellis, as Howe labeled it, is a redwood-and-glass frame that allows maximum connection to the surrounding redwoods as it joins the two spaces. Howe's design response to the mild climate and lush landscape of coastal northern California is indicative of his prowess as an organic architect, always creatively responding to the land.

147

6
A NEW CAREER
IN MINNESOTA

By 1967 the Howes were ready to leave California and strike out on their own. No longer interested in working for someone else, and believing that San Francisco was "overstocked with architects," they set their sights on returning to the Midwest.[1] The Howes were both Midwesterners by birth, and, with the exception of the three years he spent in Aaron Green's employ in San Francisco and yearly winter stays at Taliesin West in Scottsdale, Arizona, John Howe had lived in the region all his life. Following some business trips to Minnesota, he said he "kind of got the message that [it] was the place to be."[2] The fact that the Howes' cottage in Spring Green, Wisconsin, was an easy drive from the Twin Cities was another plus.

There was also the promise of work in the state. By 1964, as a TAA architect, Howe had designed five projects for sites in Minnesota, three of which were built. His well-connected clients, who were pleased with their Howe-designed homes, spread the word of his architectural abilities among friends and colleagues. Although not known to Howe at the time, the clients for two of his early Minnesota commissions (Philip and Sidney Wear and George R. and Norma Johnson) would rehire him to design additional projects in the future. Howe also had friends of long standing in the area, including William Krebes, a fellow conscientious objector. The two men met when Krebes was a student in Howe's furniture design class for inmates at the Federal Correctional Institution in Sandstone, Minnesota. Between 1967 and 1990, Krebes commissioned Howe to design eleven projects for him, including Redleaf, his residence in Lakeville, Minnesota.[3] During those years Krebes also collaborated with his friend on a number of architectural projects, including the fabrication of Howe-designed furniture.

During his twenty-seven years with Wright, Howe worked on scores of the architect's projects for sites in the region, the first being the 1934 Malcolm and Nancy Willey house in

Above The Malcolm and Nancy Willey House, Minneapolis (1934), was one of the first projects Howe worked on at Taliesin. Forty years later, he remodeled the kitchen of the house for its third owner.

Right Redleaf, in Lakeville, Minnesota, designed in 1978, was one of eleven projects Howe designed for his friend William Krebes.

Minneapolis. Howe claimed to have "learned to draw" on the project when he assisted with a few interior elevations for the small pre-Usonian house in the Prospect Park neighborhood.[4] Despite his modest contributions to the commission, it remained memorable for him. The Howes "loved the house" and considered buying it from its second owners, Russell and Jane Burris.[5] Although they did not purchase it, John Howe never stopped feeling protective of the dwelling as its third owner, Harvey Glanzer, discovered in 1972: "Shortly after I bought the Willey House there was a knock at the kitchen door. I opened it and there stood a man. He said, 'I'm Jack Howe. I come with the house.' "[6] Two years later, Glanzer hired Howe to remodel the kitchen of the house.

JOHN H. HOWE, ARCHITECT

One of the ways Howe announced his arrival in the Twin Cities—and raised awareness of his talent—was by displaying his renderings in a number of public venues. "Drawings are the language of an architecture and I made my presence known by exhibiting my drawings in the Marquette skyway and in Northwestern banks," he said.[7] He was also the subject of several articles in the press. In 1967 *Twin Citian* magazine published companion articles on Wright and Howe. The first piece, which included a photo of the two men, made clear Howe's pedigree as the architect's chief draftsman. It explained: "John Howe spent much of his early career sharing a drawing board with Frank Lloyd Wright."[8] The second article assured readers that Wright's design sensibilities had not died with him, but instead had been "bequeathed" to members of the Taliesin Fellowship. It further advised: "One of the most distinguished alumni of the Fellowship, John Howe, is opening an office at 7601 Wayzata Boulevard."[9] Although Howe arrived in Minnesota as "the pencil in Wright's hand," he would soon earn solid credentials as "John H. Howe, Architect."

Howe once wrote that "the only valid architectural criterion is one based upon an understanding of fundamental principles," which he believed to be the tenets of organic architecture. He added, however: "The young architect does Mr. Wright a disservice by blindly imitating his buildings rather than following his principles."[10] Howe hoped his independent career would constitute "a continuity" with that of Wright, but he repeatedly stated he had no interest in merely imitating Wright's buildings.[11] As early as 1966, he wrote, "Imitators . . . always promote a 'style' where once meaningful forms become empty clichés. True followers search for new expressions, realizing that the solution for any problem must come from within the problem itself, not from without. . . . True art can never be a re-statement."[12] Because Howe was so thoroughly grounded in his architectural principles, he was able to use them without compromise to adapt his designs to the demands, constraints, opportunities, and new materials and technologies of the second half of the twentieth century. For that reason he created a body of work that was true to his ethic but also relevant in an ever-changing world.

Unquestionably, Howe's celebrated history as Wright's chief draftsman helped launch his practice in Minnesota. But that same history may also have initially contributed to a general underestimation of Howe's significant architectural skills and the perception that he was merely a disciple of Wright. The many Wright-centric articles that appeared in the press offered little insight into Howe's independence and integrity. When he arrived in Minnesota, few people knew that Howe had been willing to spend nearly three years in prison rather than compromise his unshakable beliefs. This same strength of character, coupled with Howe's incomparable talent and love of architecture, would help him establish a remarkably successful second career in Minnesota—one that was singularly and uniquely John Howe's alone.

INITIATING A DESIGN AND WORKING WITH THE CLIENT

Howe was a methodical and disciplined architect. Early in his career he developed a process for initiating a design and working with a client, one that was rooted in the principles of organic architecture. It began with a topographical map of the site. "Even more than Mr. Wright, I made my design on the topographical map, which shows the contours and the natural features of the land," he said.[13] Howe argued that this approach was particularly necessary in the Minneapolis area, a region characterized by hilly, wooded sites. Respect for nature was deeply ingrained in Howe, and his designs were predicated on understanding a site's specific conditions. This knowledge allowed him to design a plan that would best preserve a site's natural assets. "Of course there are trees to be saved . . . valuable trees. You feature the features of the land," he reasoned.

Next, came the list of the clients' requirements: "What their dreams are, what their basic needs are . . . how much they can afford," he explained. Many clients described Howe as a confident architect who had well-formed, firm opinions about his designs. Although he worked collegially with clients, he had strong views and resisted altering plans without adequate justification. For example, if a client did not like the location of a particular window, that was not reason enough for Howe to remove it. However, if a client did not like a window because it failed to capture a favorite view or admit morning sun, Howe would make a revision. "I listen to them . . . but I need a reason to change something," he said. Howe claimed he did not pressure his clients or insist they accept something that ultimately would not be right for them: "It's their design. . . . It isn't my design. I'm just the person doing it," he stated. The fact that several of his clients became repeat clients—and many became friends—would seem to support Howe's contention.

Finally Howe considered climate when initiating a design—particularly when the site was in Minnesota. "The severe Minnesota winters dictate a sun-seeking, cold-shunning design," he wrote.[14] Therefore, he favored buildings with southeast exposures that invited in sunlight and warmth, and offered passive solar advantages. In contrast, he blocked cold on the northwest side of a house by building walls into the earth or protecting them with low, sheltering roofs. Howe's former apprentice Geoffrey Childs believed that climate was one of the reasons Howe's residential architecture is "airier" and "lighter" than many of Wright's residences. "In Minnesota the sun is so important," he noted. "This is not the place to build dark buildings."[15]

A COTTAGE IN THE WOODS

The first clients of John H. Howe, Architect, were Walter and Marlene Schmidt. By 1967 the couple had tired of living in the flight path of the Minneapolis–St. Paul Airport and were looking for a new home. Walter, an electrical engineer for Univac, and Marlene, a photographer and writer employed by the University of Minnesota, yearned for a "cottage in the woods" and an architect to design it. After learning of Howe's connection with Wright, they decided to contact him. When the couple visited Howe in his Minneapolis office they were so impressed by his drawings for the Mr. and Mrs. Robert Chapman House in Old Lyme, Connecticut (1962, unbuilt), they resolved to have him design their new home in Credit River Township.[16]

HOUSE FOR MR. AND MRS. ROBERT CHAPMAN
OLD LYME, CONNECTICUT
TALIESIN ASSOCIATED ARCHITECTS   THE FRANK LLOYD WRIGHT FOUNDA
JOHN H. HOWE

Above Howe's perspective drawing of the unbuilt Mr. and Mrs. Robert Chapman House, Old Lyme, Connecticut, a 1962 Taliesin Associated Architects project, convinced prospective clients Walter and Marlene Schmidt of his talents.

Opposite left A massive fireplace dominates the living room of the Schmidt House.

Opposite top right The kitchen, living room, and dining room of the Walter and Marlene Schmidt House in Credit River Township, Minnesota (1968), nestle into the earth.

Opposite bottom right A balcony overlooks the lower level of the Schmidt House.

Beyond a desire for a forested cottage with "informal warmth," a "big fireplace," and the ability "to look down into the living room" from above, the Schmidts admittedly "had no concept what we wanted in a house."[17] Although Howe's idea of a "big fireplace" was dimensionally grander than their own, he did give the couple exactly what they hoped for in a house. "We needed John's ideas. We had faith in him," Marlene recalled.

The Schmidts anticipated their new house, which Howe dubbed "Walmar," would be constructed on a hilly prominence on their lot. But Howe urged them to build on the "least desirable part of the site. You want to be able to look at the most beautiful parts," he explained. When they saw the architectural drawings, the Schmidts deemed the project to be beyond their means to afford and asked Howe to scale down the size of the house. "But then we realized that we liked the original, so we went back to it and borrowed money to build it," said Walter.

The house, which was planned on a square module, is built of clear cedar, cedar plywood, and Minnesota Kasota stone. To keep costs down, the Schmidts supplied much of the labor; they insulated the house, did the electrical work, and built furniture from Howe's plans. Although Howe provided the generous fireplace the Schmidts desired, it did not work to anyone's satisfaction. "When the cushions on the banquette next to the fireplace caught on fire," explained Marlene, they installed a copper hood and fire screen.

The Schmidts remained lifelong friends with their architect and his wife, and the couples were frequent guests in each other's homes. In a 1989 interview Howe admitted that despite his fondness for his hosts, he sometimes succumbed to architectural distractions when he

visited Walmar: "I just sit there enjoying the house when I'm there. I don't pay attention to the conversation part of the time. I just look around."[18]

Although the Schmidts may have provided some construction labor, Marlene made clear that "the whole house is John." She ascribed many of the qualities they love in their home to the fact that "John was not a practical man. If he had to choose between beauty and practicality, he chose beauty, for which we are ever grateful."[19]

A HOUSE IN HOLLY, MICHIGAN

In 1968, when David and Glenda McLellan began to explore the idea of building a house for their young family that was reflective of Wright's principles of organic design, they first considered the work of former Taliesin apprentice and fellow Michigander Alden Dow. Although they admired the design of Dow's Midland studio, after meeting with him there they realized he was not the right architect for their project.[20]

Instead the quest led the couple to the Wright-designed Palmer House (1950) in Ann Arbor. David, who would later become the second chief engineer of the Corvette sports car, immediately bonded with Corvette owners William and Mary Palmer.[21] Mary suggested the McLellans contact Howe, who had been on-site during the construction of their house and had designed a teahouse for their garden in 1964.

On her advice, the McLellans visited Howe in Minneapolis. Upon seeing his work—and realizing Howe was the man who had drawn so many of the Wright renderings they had long admired—they "knew immediately, if we could possibly have him [design the house] it would be wonderful," said Glenda.[22] Some months later when they received the plans for the house, they were "more than satisfied."

The couple asked Howe to design a two-thousand-square-foot, three-bedroom house with an attached garage. They also asked him to generate the plan using a triangular module, as he had done in the Palmers' house, because "it gave the house a wonderful flowing character," explained David. The triangular geometry resulted in walls and windows that meet in

Opposite Howe provided a cozy seating nook on the second floor of the Schmidt House.

Above The David and Glenda McLellan House (1969) stands on a wooded, twenty-acre site in Holly, Michigan.

60-degree and 120-degree angles, which define and open the space in unique ways. Although the house was planned for a one-and-one-half-acre hilly site, it was eventually built on a twenty-acre wooded site in Holly, Michigan.[23]

The profile of the brick and redwood house is dominated by a broad, sheltering roof plane that extends low to the ground on the northwest side. On the southeast, the house rises to two stories, and one thousand square feet of window wall wraps the living spaces. According to David, it is a unique aspect of the house that "totally integrated the inside of the living and dining areas with the out of doors."[24] Howe further blurred the boundaries between inside and outside by extending a portion of the second-floor loft through the glass expanse, thereby creating a cantilevered balcony. He would repeat this gesture to equally dramatic effect in several houses that were built in Minnesota at about the same time.

Howe dynamically articulated the spaces of the light-filled interior of the house. He contrasted the soaring volume of the dining area with an intimate, sunken living room partially sheltered by a second-floor balcony. Beyond the living room, a staircase composed of a series of suspended steps rises to the second level of the house. Interior finish materials include blond mahogany, gypsum board, glass, and Cherokee red–tinted concrete floors in

Opposite left Glass meets roof in the soaring two-story dining room of the McLellan House.

Opposite top right A second-floor balcony, which penetrates the glass wall as it moves from indoors to outdoors, visually extends the playroom space of the McLellan House.

Opposite bottom right At the McLellan House, a suspended staircase provides access to the second-floor bedrooms.

noncarpeted areas. Howe designed revisions to the house in the 1970s. After he closed his practice in 1992, the McLellans contacted Howe's former apprentice Geoffrey Childs to design a garage, studio, and guest quarters, which were completed in 1996.[25]

The McLellans appreciated Howe's architectural talents, as David explained: "It's clear to me that John saw the three-dimensional spaces he was creating in much the same way as Mr. Wright did. It is a unique talent to be able to see space and also to see how to construct the building that gives you these spaces." Howe apparently also was pleased with his design for the house. Along with the schematic drawings he sent to the McLellans, he included a note in which he described the house as a "jewel." The McLellans believed they received Howe's best effort because they gave him "free [rein] to create architectural poetry."[26]

TOWERHOUSE

As Wright before him, Howe had the good fortune to have architecturally adventurous clients who owned spectacular building lots—attributes possessed by Dr. Robert and Katherine Goodale of Minneapolis. The demands of Dr. Goodale's professional responsibilities in the city precluded the building of a family cabin "up north." Instead, in 1969 the couple commissioned Howe to design a family vacation house close to home on Lake Minnetonka.

The Goodales planned to build a cabin on land that once was part of the Frederick C. Van Dusen estate in Excelsior. They purchased two of the subdivided estate lots, including one on which stood a circa 1900 water tower, one of three extant estate structures. Howe later nicknamed the cabin he designed for the Goodales "Towerhouse," a reference to the historic water tower on the site.

In keeping with his core principle "the land is the beginning," Howe began his design process by acquainting himself with the site, which boasted three hundred feet of shoreline. After walking the terrain, he proposed building the house into a hillside above the lake. He rooted the building to the sloping site with a rectangular mass comprising the entry, stairwell, and kitchen. A massive floor-to-ceiling stone fireplace in the living room further anchored the 2,500-square-foot structure to the incline. Howe specified that the stone be laid with a percentage of "random long stones projecting," to lend visual interest.[27] The positioning of the house on the hilly site necessitated placing the entrance on the upper level. In response to this condition, Howe created an entry sequence that proceeds from the driveway via a bridge to a mezzanine level in the house. From that vantage point, views unfold to living areas below and through the treetops to the lake beyond.

Howe's design for the "cabin" is a bold interpretation of a Minnesota vacation house. The heart of the dwelling is a double-prowed glass volume that contains the living and dining areas. The retreat's unusual curvilinear configuration resembles Wright's lozenge-shaped residential designs of the 1950s, for many of which Howe likely prepared drawings.[28] In the Goodale House, Howe heightened the drama by raising the height of the glass volume to two stories and delicately mitering window wall joints at the two prows. The cantilevered balcony (a rectangular extension of the second floor) penetrates the curved glass wall and reaches toward the lake, further blurring the distinction between inside and outside. To create the porch, Howe wrapped screening around slim steel tension rods to structure the room's corners, without sacrificing views of the lake to excess framing.[29] He also designed the built-in furniture and fireplace grate.

A NEW CAREER IN MINNESOTA

V I E W F R O M W E S T

Howe had originally planned to raise the roof of Towerhouse, the Dr. Robert and Katherine Goodale House in Excelsior, Minnesota (1969), as this perspective sketch shows.

Howe's exquisite drawings for the project, one of his most distinctive designs, show that he originally planned to raise the roof an additional story and build the house predominantly of Kasota stone. Due to budget constraints, he removed the upper level and reduced the amount of stone used in construction.

The Goodales provided Howe with a "desiderata" of the family's wants and needs for the house, but stressed that the final design was "totally Howe's." Although they found him "willing to compromise," they noted Howe could tactfully stand his ground. As a case in point, in response to a request for privacy drapes, they recalled, Howe "simply stalled until it was no longer an issue." The Goodales later conceded that even when they initially didn't agree with Howe, they inevitably came to realize he was right.[30]

BEYOND THE HOUSE

Sixty-five projects came Howe's way between 1968 and 1973. Although the vast majority were for houses, residential additions or renovations, and master plans for neighborhoods, eight were different building types. Only one of the nonresidential projects of the period was built.[31]

In 1968 Howe served on the Learning Resources Consultants committee, an advisory group to Macalester College in St. Paul, Minnesota.[32] The committee's task was to consult and advise on a master plan, library, and student union for the school, work that Howe found to be both interesting and challenging. His task involved traveling to California to study the ways in which various universities had addressed similar planning issues on their campuses. Because Howe served as architectural consultant, not project architect, he was expected to deliver a written report of his findings to the committee. Instead, he submitted plans because, he argued, architects spoke primarily through drawings and "words are only [meaningful] in reference to drawings."[33] Howe believed the project died, in part, when former U.S. vice president Hubert H. Humphrey returned to Minnesota in 1969 to teach at Macalester College and resisted the demolition of a campus building that stood in the way of a new master plan.[34]

Above The soaring vertical mass of the Kasota stone fireplace anchors the Goodale House to the sloping site.

Top right The two-story living room of the Goodale House is wrapped on all sides by walls of glass, allowing uninterrupted views of the woods and the lake.

Bottom right Howe blurred the boundary between indoors and outdoors by extending a second-floor balcony through the glass window wall to the outside of the Goodale House.

Glass walls meet in a mitered joint in this two-story prow of the Goodale House.

The Minnesota Outward Bound School presented a different design challenge for Howe. The project came to him in 1970 through Marshall Erdman, a former colleague of Wright, who suggested to Alan Hale, the school's director, that Howe be hired as architect for the project. The intended location of the complex was a hilly site on the Kawishiwi River in Ely, Minnesota, near the Boundary Waters Canoe Area Wilderness. In a letter to Erdman dated November 6, 1969, Howe wrote, "On Monday we flew by private plane to the camp. . . . It is indeed a beautiful site at the confluence of a fast-moving river with rapids and a serene lake."[35]

The architectural program called for two buildings to accommodate both summer and winter functions at the camp, one to house administrative services and the other to contain the main dining hall and lounge.[36] Correspondence reveals that the viability of the project depended on the school's ability to raise the necessary construction funds. Although Howe was assured that Hale and the trustees were "very impressed with your work on our behalf and have every intent of entering into a contract with you," the project did not advance beyond the initial planning phase.[37] Nonetheless, Howe created a pair of perspectives and a site plan for the project. They are notable not only for the way they reveal his understanding of the features of the land and his sensitive integration of design elements within it but also for the evocative beauty of the drawings.

The school was not built, but that same year the project led to a realized residential commission for Edward Dayton, a trustee of Minnesota Outward Bound and a member of the philanthropically active family that founded Minneapolis-based Dayton's department store. For rolling acreage in Medina, Minnesota, Howe designed a five-thousand-square-foot house with a dominant, sloping asymmetrical gable that shelters main living areas. On the south side of the house, an uninterrupted wall of glass rises to meet the gable. As a result, flowing interior spaces are open to light and expansive views. As he had done in the Goodale House, Howe included a second-floor balcony that slices through the glass wall, thereby linking the interior of the house to the surrounding natural landscape. A one-story bedroom wing anchors the dwelling, which is constructed of Kasota stone, redwood, and glass, to the site.

In 1971 Howe designed the First Church of Christ, Scientist in New Brighton, Minnesota. The program for the small church called for seating for 150 people and a Sunday school to accommodate 150 children. Howe's stated goal for the auditorium was that it "be kept intimate" with an "atmosphere of warmth and uplifting harmony."[38] Howe believed that congregants in most churches tended to gravitate to back rows, thereby leaving seats in the front of the worship space unoccupied. To address this issue, he chose to replace these potentially vacant seats with a planter in the center front of the church. "This and the lectern provide the focal point for the congregation," he explained. As he had done in the circular studio of the Tucson Creative Dance Center, Howe clear-spanned the angular auditorium of the church but, uniquely, exposed its laminated wood beams and trusses. This allowed placement of clerestory windows within the trusses to provide natural light for the auditorium. He roofed the space with overlapping fibrous panels, which remained exposed on the underside for better acoustics and to create "a decorative ceiling."[39] Brick and saw-textured cedar were used on both the exterior and interior of the church. Glass sidewalls invited contemplative views of the wooded site and nearby Pike Lake.

Howe and the congregation worked together closely and cooperatively to produce a building that "should prove to be an ever-increasing delight to those who worship there and

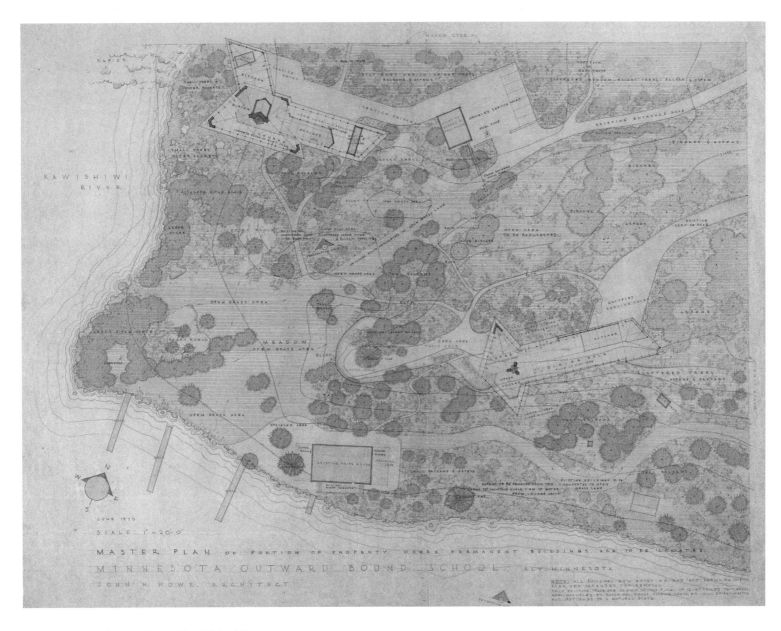

Master plan for the Minnesota Outward Bound School, Ely,
Minnesota (1970). Howe considered the natural attributes
of the rugged site when locating the buildings. The project
was not realized.

VIEW FROM SOUTH
MAIN DINING HALL AND LOUNGE BUILDING
MINNESOTA OUTWARD BOUND SCHOOL ELY, MINNESOTA
JOHN H HOWE, ARCHITECT

Howe's perspective for the main dining hall and lounge for the Minnesota Outward Bound School evokes the beauty of northern Minnesota and the Boundary Waters Canoe Area Wilderness.

Top A prominent asymmetrical gable is a defining feature of Howe's design for the Edward and Kit Dayton House, Medina, Minnesota (1970).

Bottom The two-story living room of the Dayton House derives its architectural drama from the intersection of stone, wood, and glass.

a continuing expression of Divine Fellowship."[40] The First Church of Christ, Scientist was one of two church commissions Howe received during his career and the only one that was built.[41]

Although Howe's practice was thriving during the late 1960s and early 1970s, the era was not kind to some of Frank Lloyd Wright's buildings; two of his major works were demolished within a four-year period. Howe was still mourning the loss of the Imperial Hotel (1913–23) in Tokyo, Japan, which he and Lu visited shortly before its destruction in 1968, when he learned of the impending demise of the Francis W. and Mary Little House (1912), known as "Northome," in Deephaven, Minnesota. In 1972 former Taliesin fellow Edgar Tafel contacted Howe to enlist his help during the dismantling of the grand house, considered by many to be one of the last great houses of Wright's Prairie era. The high-profile preservation case was both a blow and a wake-up call to Minnesota's architectural community.

No longer able to manage the large property that stood on the shore of Lake Minnetonka, and unable to find a buyer for it, the Littles' daughter, Eleanor Stevenson, and her husband, Raymond, sold the house to the Metropolitan Museum of Art. Thomas Hoving, then director of the museum, planned to move the Little house living room to New York, where it would become the centerpiece of the institution's new American Wing.[42] The New York–based Tafel, who was instrumental in the salvage effort and worked with Hoving and others during the process, urged the museum to hire the Minnesota-based Howe to create measured drawings of the house, to "guard the place" during demolition to prevent theft, and to supervise the packing and crating of those parts of the house to be shipped to various destinations.[43] Don Lovness, a Wright client from Minnesota, also lobbied the museum to involve Howe, who was more than interested in being part of the undertaking. Although Howe was in an ideal position to carry out the task, Hoving did not invite him to participate in the effort. "It's a shame that the Museum did not take the suggestions of both Don and myself to employ you," wrote Tafel. "They just don't understand when we tell them something, that our thoughts come from our deep experience with the situation, and with Mr. Wright."[44]

Above First Church of Christ, Scientist, New Brighton, Minnesota (1971), is Howe's only church design that was built.

Opposite Howe's intricate geometric plan for the auditorium of the First Church of Christ, Scientist shows seating arrayed around a centrally placed planter and lectern.

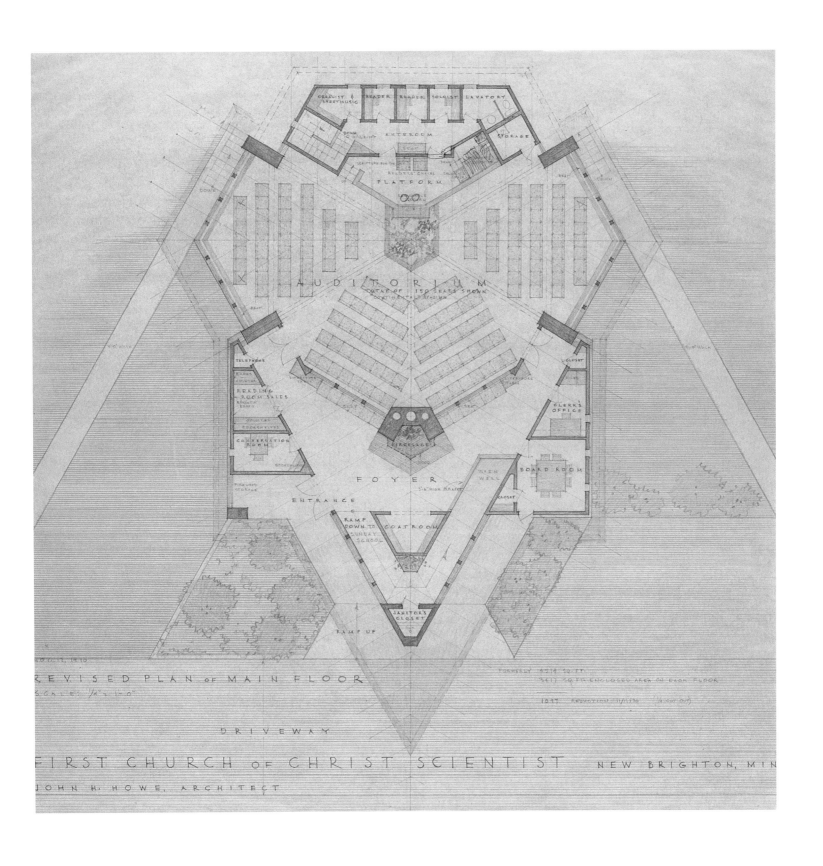

FIRST CHURCH OF CHRIST SCIENTIST   NEW BRIGHTON, MINN

JOHN H. HOWE, ARCHITECT

A NEW CAREER IN MINNESOTA

Above Howe placed clerestory windows within exposed trusses, as seen in this photograph of the church from the 1970s.

Opposite Longitudinal and cross sections of the church show the intimate scale of the auditorium. The lower level comprises a Sunday school, nursery, and office.

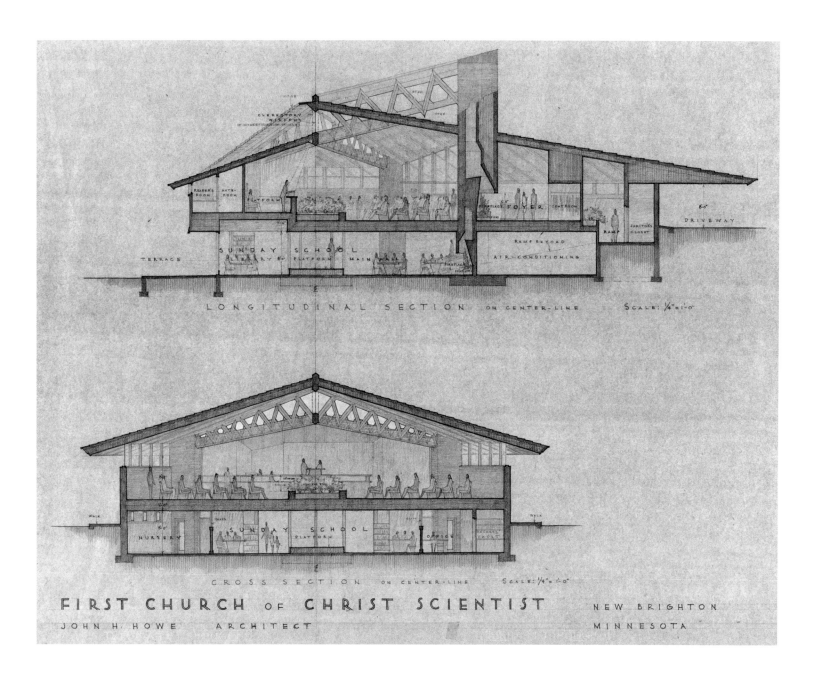

LONGITUDINAL SECTION ON CENTER-LINE   SCALE: ¼"=1'-0"

CROSS SECTION ON CENTER-LINE   SCALE: ¼"=1'-0"

FIRST CHURCH OF CHRIST SCIENTIST   NEW BRIGHTON

JOHN H. HOWE   ARCHITECT   MINNESOTA

Sankaku, the John and Lu Howe House in Burnsville, Minnesota, completed in 1972, is a built expression of the principles of organic architecture.

SANKAKU

In 1971 Howe designed a residence for Lu and himself on a secluded two-and-one-half-acre site on Horseshoe Lake in Burnsville, Minnesota. Howe named the house "Sankaku" after the Japanese word for triangle. The modest dwelling is one of the masterworks of Howe's career.

Before he began to design the house, he acquainted himself with the land. "As with all of my houses," he wrote, "the site was the primary governing factor in the design. The steep slope of the land determined the placement of the house on site and the various floor levels of the residence, which step down the approximately twenty-degree slope."[45]

The approach to Sankaku unfolds slowly. The site is located off a cul-de-sac from which a driveway slopes steeply to a carport. A stepped walkway further descends toward the house. After crossing a small footbridge, one is poised to enter Sankaku. Much of the spatial dynamism of the 1,700-square-foot dwelling, which is constructed of brick, gypsum board, cedar, and glass, derives from the use of an equilateral triangle to generate the modular plan. Howe demonstrated masterful control of all elements of the complex design.

The main living areas of the multilevel house are sheltered by one sweeping roof plane, angled to parallel the slope of the hillside. The south-facing glass walls of the living and dining areas invite panoramic views of the lake and the lakeshore beyond. From the vantage point of the study on the mezzanine level, the views are equally scenic.

Sankaku has few rooms in the traditional sense; instead, spaces flow together. Howe credited the triangular module with amplifying the expansive feel of some rooms: "The angles created within the house, and the flow of space they allow, give a liberating quality and make the house seem much larger than it is," he wrote.[46] "The openness of the plan stimulates the imagination, giving glimpses of the space beyond and increasing the sense of spaciousness." Howe also believed the triangular module "enhanced the orientation of the house in the various seasons . . .

Before entering Sankaku, one passes through a garden
and over a bridge.

169

A NEW CAREER IN MINNESOTA

Above From the viewpoint of the second-floor loft, the horizontal and vertical flow of space at Sankaku can be well understood. Ample glass expanses connect the interior of the house to the surrounding woods and lake.

Right The design of Sankaku is based on an equilateral triangle. There are only a few right angles in the house.

A NEW CAREER IN MINNESOTA

Consistent with his principle of unified design, Howe
created the furniture and fireplace grate at Sankaku.

A NEW CAREER IN MINNESOTA

interestingly illuminating the interior of the house." Almost no right angles can be found in Sankaku, and few doors interrupt the horizontal and diagonal flow of spaces. Howe designed the cabinetry, built-ins, furniture, wood fretwork over the dining room table, and art glass in the study.

Howe sited the house to maximize passive solar opportunities. South-facing glass expanses allow the sun to warm interior spaces in the winter, whereas overhanging eaves block the summer sun and associated heat. Conversely, he sheltered the house on the north and west by minimizing the size of windows. Howe wrote that he protected interiors "from the cold winter winds by roofs which extend to within a few feet of the ground."

Whereas several areas of the house provide extensive views of the lake and woods, a few impart a sense of refuge, notably the west facade of the house, which is built into a hill. Howe underscored the secure feeling of being recessed in the earth in the kitchen, where windows positioned just above the counter offer an eye-level view of the forest floor. From almost any vantage point (and there are many), the house and the land meld into a unified composition—so much so that it is difficult to imagine one without the other.

Japanese architect and former Taliesin apprentice Raku Endo assessed Sankaku in this way: "It is not luxurious, but once a person enters this house built on a slope along a lake, he feels a warm, peaceful atmosphere beyond expression in words. . . . Why? It is impossible to explain, but it must be the mystery of architecture."[47]

Sankaku is perhaps Howe's most eloquent essay on organic architecture.[48]

WORKING FOR THE JOHNSONS AGAIN

In 1973 John Howe designed a second house for George and Norma Johnson when the family was in need of more space to accommodate a lifestyle that included two teenage sons. Although they considered adding on to their current Howe-designed house, they decided against it, "as they felt any changes would detract from the original design," Howe later recalled.[49] Instead, they chose to build a new house on one parcel of a large tract of land they owned on a peninsula on Lake Minnetonka's Maxwell Bay, in Orono, Minnesota.

In 1971 George Johnson acquired the land, which was located just across the public road from the Johnsons' current home. In addition to hiring Howe to design their future dwelling, the couple commissioned him to develop a master plan for a residential neighborhood on the tract to be named "Partenwood." Howe subdivided the property into one-acre lots and reserved land for wildlife areas. Ultimately the Johnsons selected the most spectacular site in the tract for their home. Howe also designed an entry gate and several other houses in Partenwood, including the Raymond Poage residence (1972) and the Dr. John Allenburg residence (1975).[50]

Like all of Howe's designs, the second Johnson house is wedded to its site. Situated on the north slope of a hill, the structure invites nature inside through large expanses of lakeside windows. Interior walls and floors of stone echo the natural surroundings. Howe zoned the house according to use, creating a master bedroom wing for the parents and a lower-level suite of rooms for the Johnsons' sons.

As he had done at Wintertree, Howe planned the Johnson House II on a triangular module and oriented major living areas to maximize lake views. The Johnsons requested "local stone . . . with matching colored stucco" be used to construct the house. For the interior, Howe chose

The intimate dining space at Sankaku is illuminated by a perforated-board light fixture designed by Howe.

Philippine mahogany for wood finishes and stone for floors in noncarpeted areas. By his own account, he provided "considerable richness of detail . . . in the continuous ornamental lighting deck," which encircles the living and dining areas, and enhanced illumination through the use of "specially designed stained glass windows and skylights."[51]

Always responsive to site conditions and sensitive to solar orientation, Howe placed the house "to get as much morning sun as possible." To that end, he rotated the entrance wing forty-five degrees from the house itself to create a "sun pocket." In a departure from his earlier work (and in acknowledgment of rising concerns in the 1970s about energy use), he did not include two-story spaces or vast expanses of glass in his design for the house. The Howe–Johnson association was productive and satisfactory for all involved. "Close collaboration with the owners resulted in complete harmony in details and furnishings, suitable to the architecture and to the lifestyle of the family," Howe later wrote.

In 1982 newly widowed Norma Johnson commissioned Howe to design a residence for her on the north shore of Lake Superior near Grand Marais. The two-story, three-bedroom

HOUSE FOR MR. AND MRS. GEORGE R. JOHNSON
PARTENWOOD, LONG LAKE, MINNESOTA
JOHN H. HOWE, ARCHITECT 1/1/74

Above Howe's perspective for the George R. and Norma Johnson House II, in the Partenwood neighborhood of Orono, Minnesota (1973). Howe had designed the master plan for Partenwood two years earlier.

Opposite top The Raymond Poage House (1972) is one of three Howe-designed residences built in Partenwood.

Opposite bottom View to the Johnson House II from Lake Minnetonka's Maxwell Bay.

house, which Howe dubbed "Seagull," is perched on a rocky rise just above the shore of the lake. The lakeside facade of house is wrapped in a continuous band of windows, and, as a result, from the free-flowing living areas dramatic views open to the largest of the Great Lakes. Gull-wing balconies further expand the floor plan of the house and connect living spaces to the natural world beyond.

As was often his practice, Howe specified the same materials for exterior and interior surfaces. The massive floor-to-ceiling fireplace that stands in the center of the house and anchors it to the rocky site is constructed of Carlton Peak granite, a local stone quarried near Tofte. Howe specified red cedar for walls, light shelves, and the vaulted ceiling that runs the length of the main floor. Between rooms, he avoided full-height walls and doors as much as possible. As a result, primary living areas flow one into the other and views between rooms are unimpeded.

In the late 1980s Norma Johnson commissioned Howe to design a hotel and multihouse complex on Terrace Point Bay, just south of Grand Marais, portions of which were built.

PROJECTS FOR NORTH OAKS AND MENOMONIE

In the early 1960s, when Bob Willow was a young associate in the Twin Cities law firm of Johnson and Eastlund, he and his wife, Jan, began to think about building a home for their family. At about the same time, Norma and George Johnson, the latter of whom was a partner in Johnson and Eastlund, were working with Howe on the design of Wintertree. When George Johnson shared his new house plans with office colleagues, Willow was favorably impressed.

When finances allowed, the Willows approached Howe about designing a house for a lot in North Oaks, Minnesota. After walking the wooded site with the couple, Howe agreed to

VIEW FROM NORTHWEST
HOUSE FOR MR. AND MRS. RAYMOND R. POAGE
PARTENWOOD, LAKE MINNETONKA, MINNESOTA
JOHN H. HOWE, ARCHITECT

Above An ornamental lighting deck warms and animates the living room of the Johnson House II.

Right Howe designed the furniture for the intimate seating area of the Johnson House II.

Opposite top The Norma Johnson House, known as Seagull, stands above the rocky shore of Lake Superior north of Grand Marais, Minnesota. The house was completed in 1984.

Opposite bottom At Seagull, Howe used Carlton Peak granite, a locally quarried stone, for the fireplace and red cedar for interior wood surfaces.

A NEW CAREER IN MINNESOTA

Above Seagull and Lake Superior in the evening.

Opposite top Howe responded to the contours of Bob and Jan Willows' site in North Oaks, Minnesota (1971), by designing a house that steps down the hillside. As a result, the entrance to the residence, on the upper level, is accessed via a bridge that spans the terrain.

Opposite bottom In 1977 Howe designed a second house for the Willows, this time in Menomonie, Wisconsin. It sits on a ridge with panoramic views of the town and countryside.

do so. He asked the Willows to describe some of their favorite activities and how they envisioned living in the house, while "he took notes on a yellow legal pad," recalled Jan. "With John, you didn't talk about how a house would look, but how you would use it." When Howe delivered the presentation drawings to the couple, "he had placed a sheet of tissue paper on the top, permitting only a glimpse—a tease—of the drawings beneath," said Bob. When all was revealed, "we just had to have it," he stated.[52]

As the bids revealed, the house cost a little more than the couple could afford at the time. Although Howe suggested alterations to lower cost, including the removal of a bridge that spanned the contours of the landscape and led from the drive to the entrance of the house, the Willows opted to reduce costs in another way. They did so by providing labor, notably all the finish work on the extensive mahogany paneling and woodwork in the residence. Other materials used in the construction of the 1971 house include brick, cedar, and glass.

The multiple levels and angles in the house, a result of site contours and the triangular module used to generate the plan, created a residence that was "wonderful to entertain in," said Jan. The intimate connection between interiors and the natural surroundings made for exceptional wildlife watching. The couple, who lived in the dwelling for three years, said Howe numbered them among his favorite clients because "there wasn't anything about the house they wanted to change." Subsequent owners of the residence included former U.S. vice president Walter Mondale and his wife, Joan, who purchased it in 1983. That same year, Mondale declared his candidacy for the presidency of the United States. Photographs of the house appeared in numerous articles about the candidate and his family in the local and national press. As a result, Howe enjoyed a surge of interest in his architectural services.

The Willows commissioned Howe to design a second house for them on a site overlooking Lake Menomin, in Menomonie, Wisconsin, in 1977. Over the next two years, he also designed two commercial buildings in Menomonie for Willow, including the Bob Willow Motors

VIEW FROM THE SOUTHWEST

HOUSE FOR MR AND MRS ROBERT E. WILLOW
MENOMONIE, WISCONSIN
JOHN H. HOWE, ARCHITECT

HOUSE FOR DR. AND MRS. JACK GRABOW

ROCHESTER, MINNESOTA

VIEW FROM THE EAST

JOHN H. HOWE, ARCHITECT

HOUSE FOR DR. AND MRS. JACK GRABOW ROCHESTER, MINNESOTA

JOHN H. HOWE, ARCHITECT MINNEAPOLIS, MINN.

Used Car Sales building and a second, larger facility for the company that was not built. As first chairman of the Menomonie Public Library board, Willow was instrumental in Howe's receiving the commission to design the new building for the institution. "To get planning started and the discussion going," Willow asked Howe to design a scheme and create presentation drawings for the building committee's consideration. Ultimately, Howe would design two more schemes for the library, which was built in 1986.[53]

Although the Willows were well aware of Howe's long history with Wright, they didn't believe he felt, in any way, in Wright's shadow. "We always appreciated the confidence he had in himself. He was his own person," Jan said. "John had a lot of integrity," Bob added. "He stood for his principles."

PROJECTS FOR ROCHESTER, MINNESOTA

Frank Lloyd Wright designed three houses that stand in Rochester, Minnesota.[54] The Thomas E. and Betty Keys House (1951) attracted the attention of Mayo Clinic neurologist Dr. Jack Grabow and his wife, Gloria, when they were looking for an architect to design a home for their family. After visiting a 1970 exhibition of Howe's drawings at the Sons of Norway building in Minneapolis, and liking what they saw, the Grabows hired Howe to design their home.[55] The house, which is built of brick and cedar and planned on a rectangular module, features tall expanses of south-facing glass. The living, dining, and kitchen areas of the house flow together and are united under a vaulted ceiling. A bedroom wing, which intersects the house at a right angle, is recessed into the earth to the north. It is further sheltered by a roof plane that stops just short of contact with the ground.

The Grabow House was the first of seventeen commissions in Rochester for Howe. Several of them were houses for Mayo Clinic physicians, including a residence for Dr. John Service and his wife, Shirley.[56] Impressed with Howe's work, the Services contacted him in 1985 to design a house for their family of six. They owned a unique site in a former quarry not far from Mayowood, the original estate of Dr. Charles H. Mayo, a cofounder of the renowned Mayo Clinic in Rochester. The lot is particularly distinctive because of a dramatic cliff to the east and sloping woods to the west. Howe's first scheme for the site was an L-shaped plan, which created a courtyard that opened to the cliff. When bids came in significantly over budget, Howe designed a more linear plan that arranged living areas and a master bedroom on the main floor and children's rooms on a lower level. He also reduced the amount of stone used in construction by substituting stucco. The Services complemented Howe's design by incorporating a Japanese-inspired garden.

Howe received commissions to design four commercial projects in Rochester, although none were constructed. Among them were a multistory motor hotel (1970) and several schemes for apartment buildings and towers (1970–80) for Norman O. Hilleren.[57]

A MASTER, THREE APPRENTICES, AND A CONTRACTOR

Just as Howe had gone to Taliesin to learn from Wright, three men apprenticed with Howe for the same purpose. He recruited none of them—they all found him.

When Mark Hagedorn was still in architecture school at the University of Minnesota, he saw the Howe-designed Grabow House in his hometown of Rochester and was curious to know more about its architect. He eventually contacted Howe, who would become "a friend and mentor," according to Hagedorn.[58] Because he felt he had not learned to draw in

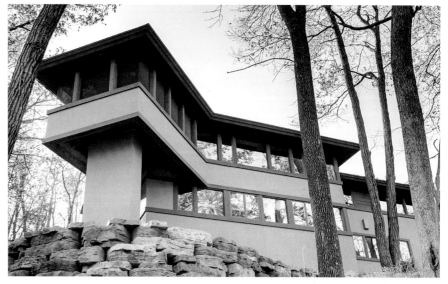

Opposite top left The living room of the Dr. John and Shirley Service House, Rochester, Minnesota (1985), features a vaulted ceiling, expansive bands of windows, and a massive fireplace, the stone of which resembles that of the quarry formerly on the site.

Opposite top right The screen porch of the Service House extends from the top floor at the level of the tree canopy.

Opposite bottom The Services' home site (a former stone quarry) offered a dramatic setting for Howe's design. He placed the house between a cliff that rises to the east and woods that slope to the west. His choice of building materials and Japanese-inspired landscaping enhance the harmonious relationship between the residence and its natural setting.

Right Howe designed the abstract pattern of the multi-colored rug for the Services' living room.

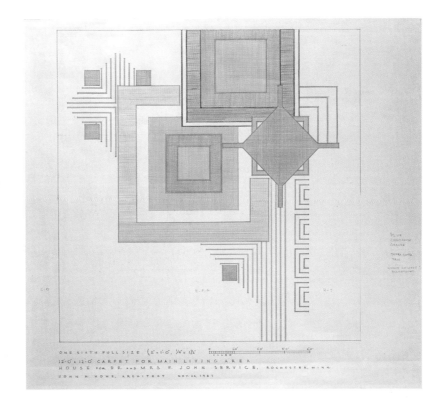

architecture school, he asked Howe if he could study the craft by apprenticing with him. As Hagedorn explained, Howe said he "was welcome to come to the office and learn by doing," but there were certain conditions if he did so. "Under absolutely no circumstances," Howe said, "do I feel obligated to teach anyone anything; I take a nap after lunch and your job is to make sure clients do not catch me napping. Your other job is to answer the phone; never expect to be paid; and any work you bring in is yours." Hagedorn came to the office in 1974 and remained there for six years. Although Howe called him his "sidekick," Hagedorn preferred to think of himself as an apprentice.

As Howe had learned to draw from Wright, Hagedorn said his "introduction to drafting was John Howe." By observing and doing, he "learned how hard to press the pencil, how to add line weight, and how to ink a drawing." When Howe showed Hagedorn how to do color pencil renderings and add foliage to drawings, he said, "This is the way [Louis] Sullivan taught Wright to do it and the way Wright taught me to do it," Hagedorn recalled. Coincidentally, in 1974, the first project Hagedorn worked on for Howe was a radiator screen for the Willey House in Minneapolis—the project on which Howe learned to draw in 1934.

According to Hagedorn, Howe was a disciplined, practical, and efficient architect who generally "worked out the architecture in his head and had an ability to clearly conceive in three dimensions" before committing a design to paper. When he did begin to draw, he did so rapidly, Hagedorn said. "He didn't do any speculative sketching. He believed your first idea was generally your best idea. And he generally hit the nail on the head." In addition to "being the business end of the business," Hagedorn believes "Lu played an important part in her husband's architecture and could be a gentle critic of his work." He added, "She was an integral part of the firm."

In 1975, during Howe's six-week tenure as visiting professor at Nihon University in Tokyo, Hagedorn ran Howe's Minneapolis office. Although he believed the invitation to teach in Japan was motivated by "very sincere interest in Howe's contemporary work," he also thinks it may have been triggered by some "soul searching in Japanese architectural circles over the tearing down of the [Wright-designed] Imperial Hotel a few years earlier . . . and a nostalgia for the work of Frank Lloyd Wright." Howe was determined to focus his Japanese lectures on the "present and the future, and to [convey] his ideas through his own work," Hagedorn recalled.[59]

According to Hagedorn, toward the middle of the 1970s there was a shift in Howe's approach to residential design with regard to the use of materials and massing. Owing to the energy crises of the era, Howe was mindful "about creating more energy efficient houses," Hagedorn stated. As a result, he began to avoid the use of "the tall glass window walls and tall glass mitered corner windows, single glazed by necessity," which Howe had employed to dramatic effect in some of his earlier houses, including the McLellan House (1969), the Goodale House (1969), and Sankaku (1972). Instead, he added, Howe began to favor "a somewhat more conservative but elegant aspect with regard to window sizes and fenestration." Massing and materials were also more reflective of "Wright's Prairie Style houses of the teens," said Hagedorn, as the Johnson House II (1973) and the Service House (1985) exemplify. Howe's renewed interest in Wright's architecture of that period may have been triggered by in-depth office conversations on the subject, Hagedorn said.

Hagedorn eventually chose to leave Howe's office because he was beginning to get work of his own and "did not want in any way to compete with John Howe's practice after all he had done for me."[60] He deeply respected his mentor and remained friends with the Howes long after his departure from the firm.[61]

Yoshiteru "Teru" Kusaka, a young architect from Tokyo, whom Howe met at Nihon University, came to Minnesota to apprentice in the late 1970s. For a period of time he and Hagedorn overlapped in the office, but Howe said it was "not his style" to have more than one apprentice.[62]

Following Kusaka's two-year tenure, Geoffrey Childs joined Howe in 1980. When he was an architecture student at the University of Nebraska, Childs became attracted to the work of Frank Lloyd Wright and began visiting Wright-designed houses in the Midwest. He sometimes asked the homeowners, "Where do you go to get [architecture like] this today?"[63] The answer Childs often received was "John Howe." When Childs visited the Robert Sunday House (1955) in Marshalltown, Iowa, for which Howe prepared drawings and designed an addition, Mrs. Sunday gave Childs Howe's contact information, and he subsequently asked Howe for the opportunity to learn from him. "The only way to really learn an art," Childs said, "is to find somebody who does well whatever it is you would like to do. Then you ask them, 'Will you show me how to do this?'" According to Childs, his apprenticeship was an "extremely humbling experience because you have to give up what you are to become what you want to be. He was the master, I was the apprentice."

Howe put Childs to work right away reassembling the dismantled interior of his former office in Minneapolis in its new location in Burnsville. In the wake of the energy constraints of the time, Howe moved his office from its former location to Burnsville to reduce his fifty-mile round-trip commute.[64] When Childs showed up at the new office space at 151 Burnsville

John Howe's Minneapolis office, circa 1968. Howe designed a mahogany partition (with cove lighting) to subdivide his small office into a public reception area and a private studio. A Japanese screen and textile and a Tiffany Studio bronze and glass box (a receptacle for business cards) adorned the space.

Parkway (a little over four miles from Howe's home), he saw "a pile of lumber in the corner and a drawing on the table, and Mr. Howe said, 'Here's your first project.' " Once he completed it, Childs moved on to other endeavors.

Early in his apprenticeship, Childs said he "had Mr. Howe to myself because little of his work was being constructed." Howe, who believed in learning by doing, encouraged his apprentice to pick out a site plan and design a house for it. Then Howe would critique (or erase) the scheme. Childs learned to master pencil work by coloring blue line reproductions of Howe's designs, using a completed drawing—colored by Howe—as the exemplar. What he could not emulate was Howe's speed of drawing: "He could draw so fast, I couldn't even trace as fast as he drew. He was absolutely unbelievable." One skill he did not learn from Howe was the craft of making an architectural model. According to Childs, Howe did not make them because his designs already lived three-dimensionally "in his brain and heart."[65] Surprisingly, Howe claimed to be incapable of drawing cars or people. "He said Mr. Wright told him his people always looked as if they were in gunny sacks," Childs recalled.[66]

In May 1986 Howe was diagnosed with Guillain-Barré syndrome, a disorder that affects the nervous system and can cause paralysis. He spent several weeks as an inpatient at the Sister Kenny Institute, a rehabilitation facility in Minneapolis, before being transferred to its outpatient facility, the Wasie Institute, to continue therapy. During Howe's hospitalization and ensuing convalescence, Childs supervised the construction of the Menomonie Public Library and assisted in the office in other ways.[67]

Another longtime associate of Howe's was contractor Kenneth Drangstveit of Orchard Builders in Burnsville. The two men were introduced by Marlene and Walter Schmidt, who hired Drangstveit to build their Howe-designed home in Credit River Township. It was a good match. Of Drangstveit, Howe later recalled, "The first thing that really appealed to me was his integrity. . . . He was just straightforward and when he said something, I knew that was it. He wasn't playing games."[68] The feeling was mutual. After constructing his first Howe house, Drangstveit said, he was "pretty impressed with John. From then on whenever John got a design for a house, I was the builder," he recalled.[69] Drangstveit, who later worked with his son Roy, built twenty-nine of Howe's designs.

Drangstveit and his wife, Helen, owned several acres of property around Horseshoe Lake in Burnsville. In 1971, when they decided to build a house on the lake, they asked Howe to design it for them. "I drew up a sketch of what we wanted," said Drangstveit, "but [Howe] threw it away."[70] As Howe walked the Drangstveits' property to get acquainted with the land and consider how best to situate the house on it, he expressed interest in building a home for himself and Lu on the adjacent property. Howe purchased the land and designed both houses simultaneously. Although the houses were both completed in 1972, the Howes' home, Sankaku, was finished first. That same year, Howe also designed a master plan for the Woodhome subdivision in which both homes were located.[71]

According to Drangstveit, Howe's designs were interesting to build because the plans varied greatly and no two houses were the same. "They may all have been two- or three-bed-room houses, but they were all different because John always took the land into consideration," he noted.[72]

The two men enjoyed a good working relationship and got along well, recalled Drangstveit; "and sometimes he even listened to me."[73]

VIEW FROM THE WEST
HOUSE FOR MR. AND MRS. SIDNEY R. BOWEN
DEEPHAVEN, LAKE MINNETONKA, MINNESOTA
JOHN H. HOWE, ARCHITECT   BUILT IN 1974

In 1974 Howe designed this house in Deephaven, Minnesota, for Sidney and Judy Bowen, the first of three he would create for the couple.

THREE HOUSES FOR SIDNEY AND JUDY BOWEN

Sidney Bowen has lived a life surrounded by significant architecture. He grew up in a house designed by architect Einar Broaten in the planned Prairie School neighborhood of Rock Crest–Rock Glen in Mason City, Iowa, within sight of houses designed by Wright and Walter Burley Griffin.[74] After earning an MBA at Dartmouth College, Bowen worked as a brand manager for General Mills in Minneapolis. An avid sailor, he wanted to purchase a house near Lake Minnetonka. Unable to find anything suitable, he decided to build a home of his own. In 1974 Bowen hired Howe to design a two-thousand-square-foot house for him and his wife, Judy, on a small wooded lot in Deephaven. It was the first of three houses Howe would design for the Bowens over the next ten years.

Shortly thereafter, the Bowens transferred to Chicago, where their architectural good fortune continued. There they lived in a house designed by Prairie School architect William Drummond on the former grounds of the Wright-designed Avery and Queene Ferry Coonley estate (1907) in Riverside.[75] In 1979 another transfer took the Bowens to the New York City area, where the couple commissioned Howe to design a house for a seven-acre parcel of land they purchased in New Canaan, Connecticut. They requested Howe design a house that had a casual, intimate feel. "Drama and playfulness" were also desired qualities.[76]

Sidney Bowen was particularly impressed by Howe's Goodale House, a variant on Wright's solar hemicycle designs, and asked that their new house reflect some of its design features, notably the two-story curvilinear glass wall. Howe acceded.

Within the house's double-height space, second-floor bedrooms overlook living areas below and have expansive views to the property beyond. Howe counterpointed the height and openness of some spaces with intimate areas defined by low ceilings, including a one-story

HOUSE FOR MR. AND MRS. SIDNEY R. BOWEN
NEW CANAAN, CONNECTICUT
JOHN H. HOWE, ARCHITECT   EDGAR A. TAFEL, ASSOCIATE ARCHITECT

Above At the owners' request, the Sidney and Judy Bowen House II, New Canaan, Connecticut (1980), took inspiration from Howe's design for the Goodale House of 1969.

Left Exposed stone, an upholstered banquette, and a dropped stained glass ceiling plane provide a feeling of intimacy in the fireplace nook of the Bowen House II.

The Bowen House in New Canaan, Connecticut, features a two-story glass wall and flowing space, seen from the balcony above.

fireplace seating nook, which is animated by an overhead plane of stained glass and patterned wood. The kitchen is uniquely circular in plan. As was his preference, Howe limited the palette of colors and materials used on both the interior and exterior of the house to sand-colored stucco, cypress, cedar shingles, glass, and handsomely set stone. Edgar Tafel, a former Taliesin apprentice who was working in Manhattan at the time, supervised the construction of the house.

In 1982, not long after the completion of their house in New Canaan, the Bowens acquired a large waterfront lot on Shippan Point in nearby Stamford. The property offered panoramic views across Long Island Sound to Manhattan's skyline. Once again, the Bowens commissioned Howe to design a new house for the site. Believing he preferred clients "who would let him [design] without interference," they gave Howe the freedom to create.[77]

Howe designed a second hemicycle scheme for the site, in which main living areas cluster in a two-story, curved volume that is wrapped in glass on the waterfront side. The second-floor bedroom area, which is accessed by a curved staircase, offers views to the living room below and connection to an outdoor balcony with vistas to the Sound. Two one-story wings, which house the garage and master bedroom, flank the central portion of the house. In contrast to the openness and view provided on the waterside of the house, the entry facade is relatively closed and has smaller and fewer windows. Howe used standardized Andersen window units and stone, stucco, gypsum board, and teak in the construction of the house. In-floor radiant heating warms exposed aggregate floors.

As a result of building three houses with Howe, Sidney Bowen became fascinated with design and construction. At age forty he enrolled at the School of Architecture and Planning at the Massachusetts Institute of Technology in Cambridge, Massachusetts. Upon hearing of Bowen's new career path, Howe humorously lamented, "I need more clients like you—not more competition."[78]

Opposite The hemicycle plan of the Sidney and Judy Bowen House III, Stamford, Connecticut (1983), offers passive solar advantages. Double-height window walls allow panoramic views across Long Island Sound to the Manhattan skyline.

Right Howe used simple materials (artist board, gold paint, and wood) and a love of geometric patterning to craft this sign.

IN REFLECTION

There are several astounding aspects to Howe's "second life," as he termed his long and successful practice in Minnesota: it came relatively late in his life (Howe was fifty-four when he established his firm in Minneapolis), and despite the fact that he never advertised his architectural services, he did not lack for clients. Of Howe's two distinct careers, friend and former Taliesin apprentice Louis Wiehle observed, "I marvel at John's ability to have had this unique, first hand presence in the work of Wright for so long, yet to have launched and matured his own highly individual and successful architectural career afterward."[79]

Howe thrived in Minnesota during the twenty-five years he practiced in the state, designing more than 200 commissions, approximately 120 of which were built. All projects, whether realized or not, were rendered by Howe in superbly crafted, hand-colored drawings—a lost art today. They are not only important records of his architectural designs; many are singular works of art.

All of Howe's buildings were the result of his belief that "the land is the beginning" of architecture, that architecture cannot exist without a fundamental understanding of the land, that humans and nature must work together. While acknowledging that Howe's architecture was shaped by the land, Japanese architect Raku Endo also believed Howe, the architect and the man, was profoundly influenced by the landscapes on which he lived and worked over the years—the midwestern prairie, the Arizona desert, coastal California. In an essay written in 1984, Endo described Howe's midlife return to the Midwest: "I do want readers to know that John H. Howe, a seed cultivated at Taliesin, has now firmly taken root deep in the soil of Minnesota and bloomed beautifully."[80]

EPILOGUE
A LASTING LEGACY

Howe's health began to decline in the mid- to late 1980s. As the deterioration progressed, apprentice Geoffrey Childs stepped up to assist his mentor by doing design work and preparing presentation and working drawings. Childs left the firm in 1989, and the Howes officially closed the office in 1992. That year the Howes began the process of sorting through the work of a lifetime and finding homes for John Howe's renderings and records. "We are very pleased that the Northwest Architectural Archives wishes to take all of my drawings," Howe wrote to former apprentice Mark Hagedorn.[1] According to Lu Howe, "so something of Mr. Wright's might remain in Wisconsin," they donated Howe's collection of material relating to Frank Lloyd Wright and the Taliesin Fellowship to the State Historical Society of Wisconsin.[2] The following year, the Howes sold Sankaku, their home for twenty years, to former clients and friends Gene and Elenore Streich, then moved to Novato, California.

Over the next five years, Howe's health continued to fail. He died in his home in Novato on September 21, 1997. His memorial service was held at the First Church of Christ, Scientist in New Brighton, Minnesota, the church he designed in 1970. He was later laid to rest in the Unity Chapel cemetery near Taliesin in Spring Green, Wisconsin. His grave is not far from where Frank Lloyd Wright was originally interred.[3]

John Henry Howe, circa 1960.

Tributes to Howe inevitably spoke of his association with Wright, his role as chief drafts-man and head of the Taliesin studio, and his authorship of hundreds of Wright's seminal drawings. But the eulogies also recognized Howe's independent architectural career, the twenty-five years he spent in practice in Minnesota, and the more than 120 built works he designed during that period. Alan Lathrop, then curator and director of the Northwest Architectural Archives, observed that although Howe might not have been one of the most well-known architects in Minnesota, he was "one of the best from the quality of his work and the buildings he did." He added, "Some of his houses, as well as his drawings, were just outstanding." Not a surprising accomplishment given that Howe, as Lathrop pointed out, "was the guy who was doing the drawings for Frank Lloyd Wright."[4]

Without question, Howe possessed extraordinary artistic talents. Architect and former Taliesin apprentice Louis Wiehle believes Howe should be ranked "at the top" of any list of the twentieth century's finest renderers. "There is great beauty in his renderings; his is an art that was built on what Wright started . . . and grew rapidly into a mastery of his own," he said. In the context of the history of the Taliesin Fellowship, Wiehle believes "Howe was the perfect assistant at the best possible time. One has the feeling that without John Howe the work of Wright after the 1930s would not exist."[5]

Reflections on Howe's career at the time of his death invited comparisons of his own work with that of Wright. Although the principles of organic architecture he learned from Wright were at the heart of his designs, Lathrop believed Howe's architecture was characterized by an additional, indefinable something: "Howe's particular gift was to create houses that are strongly styled in the Wrightian manner, yet do not sacrifice comfort to art," he said. "I think he is going to be regarded as one of the most important architects in Minnesota."[6]

John Howe was most eloquently remembered by a brief passage written for his memorial service: "John's work has ended but his spirit returns to Minnesota and finally to Wisconsin. He is with us in his architectural work, the drawings that he made, the buildings he built, the beauty he created. If that isn't immortality, it must come close."

ACKNOWLEDGMENTS

When we resolved to write a book on John Howe, we were both much younger. In the fifteen years between the inception of this project and manuscript completion (with a long hiatus in between), many people provided invaluable assistance. We thank them all, especially those mentioned here.

Neither of us had the opportunity to meet John Howe, but we had the privilege of knowing his wife of forty-six years, Lu Sparks Howe. Following his death in 1997, Lu worked tirelessly to preserve her husband's legacy. She was a generous supporter of this project and believed John Howe's life and work merited a book. We are grateful that she approved of us for the task and appreciate her gift of trust. We have done our best to live up to the faith she placed in us and to produce the book that she and John deserved. We regret she did not live to see its publication. In truth, the book would not have happened without Lu.

John and Lu's nephew, Christian Goepel, generously shared a trove of family photographs and ephemera from his and Lu's personal collections. Every FedEx package he sent brought new insight into the life and personality of John Howe.

As researchers we were fortunate to have several fine archival collections of Howe's work at our disposal. The Frank Lloyd Wright Foundation Archives, which was at Taliesin West when we conducted our research, gave us access to a wealth of material from Howe's twenty-seven years as "the pencil in Wright's hand." The collection of the Frank Lloyd Wright Foundation Archives is world renowned. Perhaps less recognized is the small but mighty team—walking encyclopedias all—who made research at the archives the very special experience it was. We thank Bruce Brooks Pfeiffer, director; Margo Stipe, curator and registrar of collections; Oskar Muñoz, assistant director; and Indira Berndtson, historic studies administrator. We often asked the wrong question, but they always had the right answer. We appreciate the efforts of Elizabeth Dawsari, director of the William Wesley Peters Library at Taliesin West, for providing information on Taliesin Associated Architects.

The Northwest Architectural Archives at the University of Minnesota was an important resource for information on Howe's years in Minnesota. Thanks go to former director Alan Lathrop and assistant archivist Barbara Bezat for their interest in and knowledge of Howe's work, and to Barb and Christine Avery for making folders and boxes magically appear in the research room. The State Historical Society of Wisconsin was another valuable repository of information. We thank Andy Kraushaar and Lisa Marine for their assistance.

Two of John Howe's apprentices, Mark Hagedorn and Geoffrey Childs, helped us understand the experience of learning from and working with him by generously sharing their time and recollections. Former Taliesin apprentices Carl Book, John Geiger, Tom Olson, and Louis Wiehle shed light on Howe's years in the Fellowship. Jan Novie and Walter Medeiros of Aaron Green Associates helped fill in the details of Howe's years in San Francisco. Scott Perkins and Mary Ann Langston shared their considerable knowledge about the

Taliesin box projects, for which we thank them. Scott, a Eugene Masselink scholar, answered any and all questions we had about this important Fellowship member.

Over the years, many homeowners opened their doors and shared recollections of John Howe, as did friends of John and Lu. We thank Sue Amidon, Jeanette and Stanley Bakke, Scott Belmont, Susan Belmont, Larry Berger, Sidney Bowen III, Jane and Russell Burris, Merilyn Cummings, Bob and Ann Davis, Carol Dethmers, Helen and Kenneth Drangstveit, Helen Durand, Harvey Glanzer, Katherine and Robert Goodale, Jack and Gloria Grabow, Norma Johnson, Rita Kirby, Jean and Bill Kotteman, Bill Krebes, Lynn Krebes-Lufkin, David LaBerge, Bernie Lindgren, Don and Virginia Lovness, Stuart Macaulay, Vernon MacIntyre, David and Glenda McLellan, Tom Olson, John and Jan Peterson, John and Lois Rogers, Walter and Marlene Schmidt, John and Shirley Service, Elenore and Gene Streich, Steve Sikora and Lynettte Erickson-Sikora, Walter Smith, Detlef Stroeh, Merle Sykora, Sidney Wear, Stuart and Kim Wear, and Bob and Jan Willow.

Many others deserve thanks for their generous or unique support of this project. They include Rob Barros, John Clouse, Phil Freshman, Robert Goepel, Rod Grant, Mark Hertzberg, Christian Korab, Richard Kronick, Keith Kuckler, Patrick Mahoney, Karen Melvin, William Olexy, Karen Rue, and Susan Stafford.

Todd Orjala, former acquisitions editor at the University of Minnesota Press, was the first to say yes to this book proposal. We thank Erik Anderson, regional trade editor, and Kristian Tvedten, editorial assistant, for guiding us through the delivery of the book. We also express our appreciation to Laura J. Westlund, managing editor, and Mary Byers, copy editor, along with Ana Bichanich, Emily Hamilton, and Rachel Moeller.

In 2000 the Frank Lloyd Wright Building Conservancy held its annual conference in Minneapolis. During the meeting John Howe's architecture was toured by hundreds of attendees; an exhibition of his work was displayed at the Minneapolis Institute of Arts; and Gabberts Furniture and Design Studio sponsored a lecture series on his career. The events raised public awareness and appreciation of John Howe, architect. We are grateful to all three organizations, with special mention to Christopher Monkhouse, Jennifer Komar Olivarez, and Marilyn Garber.

Jane King Hession acknowledges the support of a 2002 Getty Institute Library Research Grant that facilitated early book research on John Howe at the Getty Foundation in Los Angeles. Thanks go to coauthor Tim Quigley, who is both knowledgeable and passionate about the architecture of John Howe. On a personal note, Jane extends thanks to an incomparable team of friends and colleagues, whose interest in this project made all the difference: you know who you are. Fifteen years is a long time to expect loved ones to engage with one's aspiration, yet they did. Although my wise and loving mother, Helen, and my golden-haired son Brendan are no longer here, the lessons they taught inspire each and every day. My deep appreciation and special thanks go to my "sister" Bettina, who is both therapist and superlative baker; Lisa Rhoads, who always keeps the tea kettle warm; my son Connor, who is the reason for it all; and to my husband, Bill Olexy, for playing the final card.

Tim Quigley wishes to thank Narciso Menocal, retired professor of art history at the University of Wisconsin–Madison, who ignited my interest in Sullivan, Wright, and progressive American architecture in a 1974 seminar. Thanks to "Team Willey," whose friendship and enthusiasm renewed my interest in Wright. Thanks, too, to my coauthor, Jane King Hession, for her tactful editorial suggestions; she agreed to this project long ago and made sure we renewed our commitment to it. Thanks to John Clarey and Bob LeMoine, formerly of Quigley Architects, and Alyssa Portz and Pamela Sax, currently of Quigley Architects, who put up with my passion for things Wright and Howe and the workplace absences that pursuit caused. Thanks to my parents for their support of my architectural quests through the years. Special thanks go to my daughters, Eva Q. Timmons and Allie O'Quigley, who have tagged along on many architectural odysseys over the years yet remain wonderfully supportive. The same goes for Bernadine Bauer, their grandmother, for all her assistance and sustenance during my research. Finally, thanks to my partner, Susan Throndrud, for her tolerance of this passion, even though she "doesn't like brown houses!"

ACKNOWLEDGMENTS

1913
John Henry Howe born in Evanston, Illinois, to Clarence and Edith Howe

1932
Graduates from Evanston High School

1932
Joins Frank Lloyd Wright's Taliesin Fellowship as a charter member

1936
Becomes head of the drafting room at Taliesin

1940
First field supervision in Kansas City, Missouri

1943
Arrested for refusing conscription into military service during World War II. Sentenced to serve four years in the Federal Correctional Institution at Sandstone, Minnesota

1946
Released from prison after serving thirty-three months

1949–1950
Field supervision of Usonian houses in Michigan and Indiana

1951
Marries Lu Sparks Howe in Kansas City, Missouri

1953–1958
Designs and builds Inwood, the John and Lu Howe Cottage in Wyoming Valley, Wisconsin

1958
Becomes a registered architect in the state of Arizona

1959
Frank Lloyd Wright dies in Phoenix, Arizona. Upon his death Howe becomes a principal designer for Taliesin Associated Architects (TAA).

1964
Travels to Europe with the Taliesin Fellowship. Leaves TAA and Taliesin

1964
Joins Aaron Green Associates in San Francisco

1966
Travels to Japan for the first time

1967
Establishes the firm John H. Howe, Architect, in Minneapolis, Minnesota

1971
Designs and builds Sankaku, the John and Lu Howe House in Burnsville, Minnesota

1976
Visiting professor at Nihon University, Tokyo, Japan

1992
Closes his Minnesota practice. Donates his drawings and papers to the Northwest Architectural Archives at the University of Minnesota, Minneapolis, and the State Historical Society of Wisconsin

1993
Retires, sells Sankaku, and moves with Lu to Santa Rosa, California

1997
Dies in Novato, California, and is buried at Unity Chapel near Taliesin, after a memorial service at the First Church of Christ, Scientist in New Brighton, Minnesota

2013
Lu Howe dies in Novato, California. In 2014 a memorial service is held at Unity Chapel, where her ashes were buried.

*A single asterisk denotes unbuilt projects.
A double asterisk denotes an addition
to or a companion structure for a house
designed by Frank Lloyd Wright.*

AT TALIESIN, 1932–1943

Many of these projects were box projects
submitted to Frank Lloyd Wright.

N.D.

Clarence and Edith Howe, house*
Arizona

1932

Clarence and Edith Howe, alterations*
Evanston, Illinois

1934

House for Cedar Point*
Wyoming Valley, Wisconsin
John H. Howe, Taliesin bridge room
Wyoming Valley, Wisconsin

1936

Taliesin Fellowship, proposed
desert camp*
Scottsdale, Arizona

1937

Clarence and Edith Howe, house*
unknown location
Clarence and Edith Howe, silver
anniversary house*
Arizona

1939

Cabin to be Built of Square Logs*

1940

House for South Hill of Dick Jones Farm*
Wyoming Valley, Wisconsin
Summer Cottage*
Shawano, Wisconsin

AT SANDSTONE FEDERAL CORRECTIONAL INSTITUTION, 1943–1946

Airport*
The Big Project*
Sanctum*
Fabric House*
Community Center or Church*
A Writer's Farm for J. F. Powers*
Motel for Wisconsin Dells*
Cinder Block and Plywood Houses *
Speculative Brick Houses
Church*
Quarry House*
House for Phoebe Point*
Cooperative Community Project*
Recreational Vehicle*
Heath Company Factory
in the Country*
A House for I. M. Timid*
Summer House for a Writer*
Harvey Johnson, cottage
(demolished)
Genoa City, Wisconsin

AT TALIESIN, 1946–1959

1948

John H. Howe, desert cabana
Scottsdale, Arizona

1949

Concrete Block House*

1951

John H. Howe, desert cabana addition
Scottsdale, Arizona

1952

Three Arizona houses*

1953–1958

John and Lu Howe, cottage, Inwood
Wyoming Valley, Wisconsin

1955

Irvin L. and Sue Sparks,
house alterations*
Charleston, Illinois

1958

Bryant and Marjorie Denniston, house
Newton, Iowa

TALIESIN ASSOCIATED ARCHITECTS, 1959–1964

1959

Dr. Paul and Helen Olfelt, house
(associated architect)
St. Louis Park, Minnesota
E. Clarke and Julie Arnold, house addition**
Columbus, Wisconsin
Quintin and Ruth Blair, house addition* **
Cody, Wyoming

1960

Joe Paul Frazier, house*
Enterprise, Alabama
Robert and Millicent Hawkins, house
(two schemes)*
Missoula, Montana
George Hovland, house*
Duluth, Minnesota
Kenneth and Phyllis Laurent,
house addition**
Rockford, Illinois
Robert and Rae Levin, house addition**
Kalamazoo, Michigan
David I. and Christine Weisblat,
house addition**
Galesburg, Michigan

1961

James and Patricia Jeffords, house
(four schemes)
Elm Grove, Wisconsin
William and Genevieve Bancroft,
house and hangar
Waunakee, Wisconsin

Paul R. and Jean Hanna, house addition**
Palo Alto, California
Horace F. and Beverly Hardy,
house alterations*
Lake Forest, Illinois
Byron E. and Joyce Harrell, house
Vermillion, South Dakota
Willard and Karen Keland,
house additions**
Racine, Wisconsin
David and Jane Tilford LaBerge,
house
Stillwater, Minnesota
Frank and Louise Lagomarsino,
house (two schemes)*
San Jose, California
Unity Temple, renovation
(renovation architect)
Oak Park, Illinois
Frederic and Toby Royston, cottage
Exton, Pennsylvania
Philip and Sidney Wear, house (demolished)
Wayzata, Minnesota

1962
S. C. Johnson Foundation, Wingspread
Renovation (restoration architect)
Racine, Wisconsin
Dr. George Ablin and Associates,
doctors' park*
Bakersfield, California
Gordon and Ruth Bogart, house
(two schemes)*
Cedarburg, Wisconsin
Mr. and Mrs. Robert Chapman, house*
Old Lyme, Connecticut
Adobe House*
Embudo, New Mexico
Kermit L. and Evelyn Greenley, house*
Dassell, Minnesota
Roscoe Hall, Oasis Bar and Restaurant*
El Paso, Texas
John H. and Lu Howe,
cottage addition

Wyoming Valley, Wisconsin
Leonard Jankowski, house
(two schemes)*
Dearborn Heights, Michigan
Stewart and Jackie Macaulay, house
Madison, Wisconsin
Leroy and Myrtle Senneff, house*
Freeport, Illinois
Dr. H.F. Stevens, house*
Morrisburg, Ontario, Canada

1963
George R. and Norma Johnson, house I
Orono, Minnesota
Barbara Mettler, Tucson Creative
Dance Center
Tucson, Arizona
Robert Sunday, Marshall Lumber Company
Marshalltown, Iowa

1964
John H. and Lu Howe, desert cottage*
Scottsdale, Arizona
Harland and Ursula Kanouse,
entrance terrace
Spring Green, Wisconsin
Patrick and Margaret Kinney,
house additions**
Lancaster, Wisconsin
William B. and Mary Palmer, teahouse**
Ann Arbor, Michigan
Donald and Mary Lou Schaberg,
house additions**
Okemos, Michigan
John and Pat Peterson, addition to
Armstrong House**
Ogden Dunes, Indiana

WITH AARON GREEN ASSOCIATES, SAN FRANCISCO, 1964–1967
1965
Paul C. and Betty Mobley, house
(two schemes, done independently)
Novato, California

Sausalito Library*
Sausalito, California
Mrs. Arthur F. Bridge Town Houses*
Tiburon, California

1966
Herbert C. and Erica Johnson,
house* (done independently)
Edina, Minnesota
Richard and Carol Helstad, house*
(associate architect)
Oconto Falls, Wisconsin
Lum Yip Kee Office Building*
Honolulu, Hawaii
Santa Clara County Peace Officers
Association, Woelffel Youth Center*
Cupertino, California
Santa Clara Peace Officers
Association, Association Building*
Cupertino, California
Santa Clara County Peace Officers
Association, Training Academy*
Cupertino, California
Newark Community Center
Newark, California
Newark Park Pavilion
Newark, California
Victor and Virginia Ohta, house
Soquel, California

1967
Judd Ringer, corporation offices
Eden Prairie, Minnesota
Donald and Mary Lou Schaberg,
house addition* **
East Lansing, Michigan
Dr. Daniel and Lucienne Seftel,
house*
Santa Cruz, California
Philip and Sidney Wear,
house alterations (carriage house)
Wayzata, Minnesota
John H. Howe Architect, office
Wayzata, Minnesota

George R. and Norma Johnson,
guest cottage
Orono, Minnesota
Donald and Virginia Lovness,
storage house* **
Stillwater, Minnesota

1968

Curtis and Arleen Carlson,
residential master plan*
Orono, Minnesota
James and Merilyn Cummings,
house (LaBerge) additions
Stillwater, Minnesota
H. L. and Marge Jerpbak, house
Edina, Minnesota
Johnson and Eastlund,
law offices*
Minneapolis, Minnesota
Patrick and Margaret Kinney,
house alterations**
Lancaster, Wisconsin
Wesley and Lucille Libbey, house
Grand Rapids, Minnesota
Macalester College, master plan*
St. Paul, Minnesota
Stewart and Jackie Macaulay,
house addition
Madison, Wisconsin
Barbara Mettler and Minnie
Warner, house*
Tucson, Arizona
Richard D. and Mary Nelson,
house I, Windscape (four schemes)*
Afton, Minnesota
Toby L. Royston, house addition
(art gallery)
Exton, Pennsylvania
Walter M. and Marlene Schmidt,
house
Credit River Township, Minnesota
Leroy and Myrtle Senneff,
garage and utility building addition*
Freeport, Illinois

1969

E. Clarke and Julie Arnold House,
alterations* **
Columbus, Wisconsin
Russell and Jane Burris, Willey
house additions* **
Minneapolis, Minnesota
Dr. Robert L. and Katherine Goodale,
house, Towerhouse
Excelsior, Minnesota
Norman O. and Ruth Hilleren,
house addition
Edina, Minnesota
Dr. Bruce and Diana Lewis, house
Golden Valley, Minnesota
Fred C. and Alenor Lewis, house*
Excelsior, Minnesota
David and Glenda McLellan, house
Holly, Michigan
Cecil and Lenore March,
Mini Museum*
North Oaks, Minnesota
Robert and Betty Sunday,
house addition**
Marshalltown, Iowa

1970

Arnold and Sylvia Aronson, cottage*
Sturgeon Bay, Wisconsin
Merlin H. Berg, cottage*
Grand Marais, Minnesota
Jean Bollenbach, house alteration*
North Oaks, Minnesota
Edward and Kit Dayton, house
Medina, Minnesota
Dr. Jack and Gloria Grabow, house
Rochester, Minnesota
Robert Graves, weekend cottages*
Spring Green, Wisconsin
Norman O. Hilleren,
apartment building*
Rochester, Minnesota
Hilleren Associates, motor hotel*
Rochester, Minnesota

David and Glenda McLellan,
house addition, utility building,
parking court
Holly, Michigan
Herman T. and Gertrude Mossberg,
burial garden (two schemes)*
South Bend, Indiana
Minnesota Outward Bound School*
Ely, Minnesota

1971

William P. Boswell, office alterations*
Cincinnati, Ohio
Kenneth Drangstveit, Woodhome
master plan
Burnsville, Minnesota
Kenneth and Helen Drangstveit, house
Burnsville, Minnesota
First Church of Christ, Scientist
New Brighton, Minnesota
John H. and Lu Howe, house, Sankaku
Burnsville, Minnesota
George R. and Norma Johnson,
Partenwood master plan
Orono, Minnesota
George R. and Norma Johnson,
Pacesetter house I*
Orono, Minnesota
George R. and Norma Johnson,
Pacesetter house II*
Orono, Minnesota
Dr. Paul C. and Helen Olfelt,
cottage alterations
Grand Marais, Minnesota
Eugene and Elenore Streich, house
(two schemes)*
Eagle River, Wisconsin
Dr. Heinz and Dietlind Wahner,
additions to Keys house and garage**
Rochester, Minnesota
Mary Waterhouse, house*
Evergreen, Colorado
Dr. Leslie Webster, cottage
Spring Green, Wisconsin

Robert E. and Jan Willow, house I
North Oaks, Minnesota

1972
Russell and Jane Burris,
town house interior
Roseville, Minnesota
Bryant and Marjorie Denniston,
carport addition
Newton, Iowa
Norman O. and Ruth Hilleren, house
Bay City, Wisconsin
Dr. Thomas E. and Betty Keys,
apartment
Daytona Beach, Florida
Dr. Thomas F. and Cheryl Keys,
mountain retreat*
Red Feather Lakes, Colorado
Mr. and Mrs. Kurt Lysne, house*
Rainy Lake, Ontario, Canada
Mr. and Mrs. Raymond Poage, house
Orono, Minnesota
Paul E. and Mary Waibel, house
North Oaks, Minnesota

1973
William and Mary Krebes, house I*
Minneapolis, Minnesota
Vernon E. and Virginia Barker, house*
Red Wing, Minnesota
George R. and Norma Johnson, house II
Orono, Minnesota
Marshalltown Savings and Loan,
branch office*
Marshalltown, Iowa
Richard D. and Mary Nelson,
house alterations
Richfield, Minnesota

1974
Stanley and Jeanette Bakke, house
Bald Eagle Lake, Minnesota
Sidney and Judy Bowen, house I
Deephaven, Minnesota

James C. and Mary Jo Gerondale, house*
Orono, Minnesota
Harvey Glanzer, Willey House
kitchen alterations**
Minneapolis, Minnesota
Carlos Hudson, farmhouse*
Chesterton, Indiana
Inver Grove Heights, park shelters (two)
Inver Grover Heights, Minnesota
John and Dottie Ireton, house*
Exton, Pennsylvania
Clyde Reedy, garden center
and restaurant*
North Oaks, Minnesota
Lois Seeden and Group, Taiga Toft
commune house and farm building
Rogers, Minnesota
Dr. John and Maaja Washington,
house (two schemes)
Rochester, Minnesota

1975
Dr. Thomas J. Allenburg, house
Long Lake, Minnesota
Dr. Robert and Katherine Goodale,
carport addition
Excelsior, Minnesota
Byron E. and Joyce Harrell,
 solar annex
Vermillion, South Dakota
W. Thomas and Karen Mahood,
 solar house
Vermillion, South Dakota
Walter and Marlene Schmidt,
garage addition
Credit River Township, Minnesota
Martin Swensen, house
Brookline, Maine

1976
David and Barbara Knudson, house
Burnsville, Minnesota
Mrs. Ward Parten, house
 Orono, Minnesota

Prototype Solar House*
R. V. Hannem Corporation,
Zumbro Square project*
Rochester, Minnesota
Stephen and Diane Gulbrandson,
house
Inver Grove Heights, Minnesota
Menomonie Public Library
(three schemes)
Menomonie, Wisconsin
Ralph Thompson, workshop and
tool house building*
Bismarck, North Dakota
Gabriel Jabbour, house additions
and alterations
Orono, Minnesota

1977
William and Mary Krebes,
house alterations*
Minneapolis, Minnesota
Dr. Robert and Katherine Goodale,
house addition*
Excelsior, Minnesota
Dr. Thomas F. and Cheryl Keys, house
Rochester, Minnesota
Robert and Jan Willow, house II
Menomonie, Wisconsin
Nicholaus and Jutta Uhl, house
Farmington, Minnesota
R. V. Hannem Corporation,
alterations and additions*
Rochester, Minnesota
William and Grace Atkins, house
Minnetonka, Minnesota
Dr. William and Jeannine Karnes, house
Rochester, Minnesota
Thomas Savoie and Jean Swanson, house*
Excelsior, Minnesota

1978
James C. and Mary Jo Gerondale,
house addition and alteration*
Orono, Minnesota

Dr. John Allenburg, clinic addition
and alteration*
St. Paul, Minnesota
Ed Wyner, apartments*
St. Louis Park, Minnesota
Sidney and Judy Bowen,
house alterations*
Deephaven, Minnesota
Bob Willow Motors Used Car Sales,
building
Menomonie, Wisconsin
William Krebes, house, Redleaf
Lakeville, Minnesota
Richard Nelson, garage display room*
Richfield, Minnesota
Norton and Patsy Whitchurch, house*
New Brighton, Minnesota
George R. and Norma Johnson,
Partenwood gate
Orono, Minnesota
Phil and Delores Bowe, house
Lakeville, Minnesota
Dr. Bruce and Jane Trimble, house
Menomonie, Wisconsin
Dr. Manfried and Doris Muenther,
house*
Rochester, Minnesota
Advent Christian Church*
Maplewood, Minnesota
George R. and Norma Johnson, marina*
Hastings, Minnesota
Donald and Mary Lou Schaberg, cottage*
Mecosta City, Michigan

1979

John J. and Pamela Weston, house
Edina, Minnesota
James A. and Audrey Miller, house
Lakeville, Minnesota
Hilleren Towers (four schemes)*
Rochester, Minnesota
David and Glenda McLellan,
house revisions
Holly, Michigan

Ray and Sue McKenna, house
Charleston, Illinois
Robert and Janet Brackey, house*
Inver Grove Heights, Minnesota
Bob Willow Motors, large building*
Menomonie, Wisconsin
David and Barbara Knudson, house II*
Burnsville, Minnesota
Dr. Robert and Katherine Goodale,
water tower alterations
Excelsior, Minnesota
Robert Graves, cluster houses for
Wisconsin River Development
Corporation*
Spring Green, Wisconsin
Roger and Susan Bestland House*
Inver Grove Heights, Minnesota
Paul and Mary Waibel, carport
alterations*
North Oaks, Minnesota

1980

Sidney and Judy Bowen, house II
New Canaan, Connecticut
William Boswell, house*
Fishers Island, New York
Harvey Glanzer, A.D. German
Warehouse, alterations**
Richland Center, Wisconsin
Robert Graves, Spring Green Hotel
Spring Green, Wisconsin
Weekes Lumber, office and sales building*
Eden Prairie, Minnesota
Hilleren Apartments, scheme III*
Rochester, Minnesota
Hans and Bobbie Bernet, house
Monroe, Wisconsin
University of Wisconsin, Stevens Point
Irvin L. Young Center
Tomahawk, Wisconsin

1981

Ed and Barbara Tilford, house I
Eagan, Minnesota

Judd Ringer, master plan for
commercial property*
Long Lake, Minnesota
Norma Johnson, Little House
cottage addition**
Deephaven, Minnesota
Dr. John and Laurel Allenburg, house II*
Orono, Minnesota
Walter and Marlene Schmidt, porch
and bridge addition*
Prior Lake, Minnesota
Dr. William J. and Jean Kottemann,
Johnson I house storage addition
Orono, Minnesota

1982

Tony and Dianna Hofstede, house
Minneapolis, Minnesota
John H. and Judith Jax, house
(four schemes)*
Menomonie, Wisconsin
Norma Johnson, house, Seagull
Grand Marais, Minnesota
William Krebes, condominium apartment
Minneapolis, Minnesota

1983

Sidney and Judy Bowen, house III
Stamford, Connecticut
Tom Monaghan, Domino's Pizza,
world headquarters*
Ann Arbor, Michigan
Casey and Anne Randall, house
Burnsville, Minnesota
John Kerwin, condominium
town houses*
Minneapolis, Minnesota
Dr. John and Maaja Washington,
house addition
Rochester, Minnesota
John Iacano, house*
Grand Marais, Minnesota
Chiropractic Clinic*
Eden Prairie, Minnesota

Reverend Jack and Lorene Busby, house*
near Dallas, Texas
Jurgen Stielow, Parten house alteration*
Orono, Minnesota

1984
John and Pam Weston,
screened porch
Edina, Minnesota
William Krebes,
condominium apartment
Phoenix, Arizona
Michael and Sharon Ahern, house
Sunfish Lake, Minnesota

1985
John and Cheryl Rachac, house
Inver Grove Heights, Minnesota
Dr. F. John and Shirley Service, house
Rochester, Minnesota
Jerry Fischer, Orchids Unlimited,
greenhouse*
Plymouth, Minnesota
G. Weber and H. Huffer,
Greenstreets Restaurant*
Burnsville, Minnesota

1986
Edward and Rosemarie Edwards,
house
Healdsburg, California
Norma Johnson/Wintertree, Inc.,
Inn at Terrace Point houses and hotel
(two hotel schemes, houses built)*
Grand Marais, Minnesota
Robert O'Grady and Elizabeth Eide,
 house*
Burnsville, Minnesota
Leland and Marie Adams, house*
Shorewood, Minnesota
Wendy Willow, house
Hood River, Oregon
Larry and Carol Klapmeier, house
Baraboo, Wisconsin

1987
Paul and Gwenyth Brutlag, house
Wendell, Minnesota
Richard and Catherine Wornson,
house
New Prague, Minnesota

1988
William Krebes, house*
Scottsdale, Arizona
Leland and Marie Adams, house II
Fontana, Wisconsin
Carl and Nancy Manson, house
(in association with Geoffrey Childs)
Eden Prairie, Minnesota

1989
John and Lois Rogers,
Johnson house I alterations
Orono, Minnesota
Robert and Ross Graves,
model homes for Spring Green
Golf and Country Club*
Spring Green, Wisconsin
Ed and Barbara Tilford, house II*
Asheville, North Carolina
David and Barbara Knudson, house*
Burnsville, Minnesota
Glennis TerWisscha and
James Lano, house
St. Paul, Minnesota
Robert Hebbell, Waibel
House alterations*
North Oaks, Minnesota

1990
Mark and Diane Gorder, house*
North Oaks, Minnesota
William Krebes and Helen Durand,
condominium II at Lake Point
Minneapolis, Minnesota
Scott Robinson and Tom Segar,
house*
Hastings, Minnesota

1991
Ada McAllister and Lloyd Nielsen, house
Winthrop, Washington
Kenneth Drangstveit, spec house*
Burnsville, Minnesota

1992
William and Mary Palmer, waiting room
and tool house* **
Ann Arbor, Michigan
Dr. William and Jeannine Karnes,
house addition*
Rochester, Minnesota

NOTES

Sources and individuals frequently cited are identified by the following abbreviations.

AGA
Aaron Green Associates

EM
Eugene Masselink

FLW
Frank Lloyd Wright

FLWFA
The Frank Lloyd Wright Foundation Archives (Museum of Modern Art | Avery Architectural & Fine Arts Library, Columbia University)

JHCP
The John Howe Collected Papers, 1887–2001, Wisconsin Historical Society

JHH
John Henry Howe

JHHP
The John H. Howe Papers, Northwest Architectural Archives, University of Minnesota Libraries, Minneapolis

JHHVI
John H. Howe video interviews with Indira Berndtson and Greg Williams, Phoenix, Arizona. The Frank Lloyd Wright Foundation Archives (Museum of Modern Art | Avery Architectural & Fine Arts Library, Columbia University)

NAA
Northwest Architectural Archives, University of Minnesota Libraries, Minneapolis

SFPC
The Sandstone Federal Prison Correspondence, 1943–46: Eugene Masselink to John (Jack) Howe, unpublished collection. The Frank Lloyd Wright Foundation Archives (Museum of Modern Art | Avery Architectural & Fine Arts Library, Columbia University)

WHS
Wisconsin Historical Society

INTRODUCTION
THE LAND IS THE BEGINNING

1 All drawings that left the Taliesin studio were signed or initialed by Wright. Over the years, Howe and others, including former apprentices, documented the authorship of many of the drawings produced at Taliesin.
2 JHH, undated and untitled essay, JHHP.
3 JHH, "The Contributions of Frank Lloyd Wright Re-examined," lecture delivered in Tokyo, Japan, November 1966, JHHP.
4 Richard Kronick, "The Pencil in Frank Lloyd Wright's Hand," *Journal of the Taliesin Fellows* 55 (1998): 9.
5 Ibid.
6 All quotes in this paragraph, except as otherwise noted, are from ibid.
7 Geoffrey Childs, interview with Jane King Hession, September 13, 1999, Minneapolis.
8 Raku Endo, untitled essay, March 27, 1984, JHHP. Endo was the son of Arata Endo, the Japanese architect who worked with Wright on the Imperial Hotel (1913–23) in Tokyo.
9 JHH, interview with Alan Lathrop, August 30, 1989, JHHP. In the interview Howe said he learned the technique from Wright.
10 Kronick, "The Pencil in Frank Lloyd Wright's Hand."
11 Generally from Geoffrey Childs, telephone interview with Jane King Hession, November 24, 2013.
12 Childs, interview with Jane King Hession, September 13, 1999.
13 JHH, "The Contributions of Frank Lloyd Wright Re-examined." In the lecture Howe cited the Lao Tzu saying as, "The reality of a cup is the space within." There are many versions of the quote.
14 Endo, untitled essay.
15 Quotes in this paragraph and the next two paragraphs are from Marlene Schmidt, ed., "To Our Architect John Henry Howe, a Small Belated Note of Gratitude in Appreciation of His Elegantly Eloquent Life," *Journal of the Taliesin Fellows* 55 (1998): 21, 24.

1 THE TALIESIN FELLOWSHIP

1 Wright designated Howe "Jack" upon his arrival at Taliesin, as there were many "Johns."
2 "FLW Colony Will Study Modern Life, Develop Machine Age Art," *Chicago Daily News*, September 19, 1932.
3 JHHVI, March 12, 1991.
4 Morgan's motives in recommending the Taliesin Fellowship to Howe were not entirely altruistic. Wright conned Morgan into signing the loan documents for Wright's 1929 Cord automobile. Consequently, Wright's precarious financial situation became of paramount importance to Morgan; steering students to Taliesin benefited both.
5 Notably, Morgan rendered the street-level presentation perspective of Wright's unbuilt National Insurance Building, Chicago (1924).
6 JHH, letter to FLW, July 27, 1931, FLWFA.
7 JHH, interview with Alan Lathrop, September 1989, JHHP. Late in Howe's life, he and Lathrop, then NAA director at the University of Minnesota, became friends. Howe bequeathed his Minnesota practice drawings, photographs, project files, and correspondence to the NAA.
8 JHH, "Notebook of Organic Architecture, the Taliesin Fellowship." Unpublished scrapbook, n.d. (late 1930s), JHHP. Subject Prairie buildings include Griffin's Reid House, Evanston, Illinois (circa 1912), Wright's Lake Geneva Hotel (1911), Wright's Emil and Anna Bach House (1915) and the Oscar and Katherine Steffens House (1909), both in Rogers Park, Chicago, and Wright's Frank and Rose Baker House (1909), in suburban Wilmette.
9 Howe's father, Clarence Williams Howe, born and raised in Lancaster, Wisconsin, eschewed a career as an opera singer and became a sportswear sales representative with his own company, Terry and Howe, located in the Merchandise Mart in Chicago; Terry and Howe specialized in women's wear. The family resided at 1315 Church Street, Evanston.
10 Roger Friedland and Harold Zellman, *The Fellowship* (New York: Regan, 2006), 187.
11 JHHVI, February 27, 1991.
12 *Taliesin Fellowship Prospectus* (1933), JHCP. These self-published pamphlets were, like Wright, unfailingly optimistic: always inflating the number

of student positions and key participants.

13 JHHVI, February 27, 1991.

14 JHH, "Reflections of Taliesin," *Northwest Architect,* July–August 1969, 26. This is a tribute to Wright on his presumed centennial (in fact, he was born in 1867). A long article by Howe is augmented by features on many of the Wright buildings in Minnesota and elsewhere, along with client recollections.

15 Kamal Amin, *Reflections from the Shining Brow* (McKinleyville, Calif.: Fithian Press, 2004), 67.

16 William Wesley "Wes" Peters, from Evansville, Indiana, by way of MIT, became, along with Howe, one of Wright's most valuable apprentices, helping primarily with engineering the buildings and leading the constant construction and reconstruction campaigns at the two Taliesins. The son of a well-to-do newspaper publisher, he married Wright's stepdaughter, Svetlana, and, under Olgivanna Lloyd Wright, led Taliesin after Wright's death. Edgar Tafel, from New York City, was instrumental in the early years of the Fellowship, particularly in supervising construction of the S. C. Johnson & Son Administration Building and other notable structures. Robert Mosher, from Bay City, Michigan, was also instrumental early on, most notably with site supervision at Fallingwater. Abe Dombar of Cincinnati was another key apprentice in the drafting room during the first decade of the Fellowship. The same can be said of Yen Liang of China and, to a lesser extent, William Bernoudy of St. Louis. Dombar and Bernoudy led successful architectural practices in their home cities after World War II.

17 Wright's stepdaughter was just fifteen and, according to the initial *Taliesin Fellowship Prospectus,* hailed from "Hillcrest H.S.," undoubtedly a fictional place.

18 JHH, "Reflections of Taliesin," 26.

19 JHH, interview with Alan Lathrop, September 1989, JHHP.

20 *Taliesin Fellowship Prospectus* and Curtis Besinger, *Working with Mr. Wright: What It Was Like* (Cambridge: Cambridge University Press, 1995), 14.

21 Friedland and Zellman, *The Fellowship,* 159–63. Wijdeveld hoped to start his own progressive school and held Wright in the highest esteem. The Dutch architect and educator wrote the introduction

for the 1926 issue of *Wendingen* that featured Wright's work.

22 *Taliesin Fellowship Prospectus.* The professional men included a woman—Yvonne Renalier—as well as Karl Jensen, Henry Klumb, Rudolph Mock, George Steckmesser, Yuan Hsi Kuo, and Sam Ratensky. The initial Fellowship brochure omits several of these names yet includes Robert Goodall, Michael Kostanecki, and Takehiko Okami.

23 JHH, "Reflections of Taliesin," 27.

24 Ibid.

25 Edgar Tafel, *Apprentice to Genius: Years with Frank Lloyd Wright* (New York: McGraw-Hill, 1979), 140.

26 Ibid.

27 JHHVI, February 19, 1991.

28 Bruce Brooks Pfeiffer, *Frank Lloyd Wright: The Heroic Years* (New York: Rizzoli, 2009), 226.

29 The two constructed residences are Graycliff, the Isabelle Martin Residence, Derby, New York (1927), and Westhope, the Richard Lloyd Jones House, Tulsa, Oklahoma (1929).

30 Tafel, *Apprentice to Genius,* 23 and 144.

31 Ibid., 164.

32 Ibid., 46 and 98.

33 Ibid., 165.

34 JHHVI, February 27, 1991.

35 Earl Nisbet, *Taliesin Reflections* (Petaluma, Calif.: Meridian Press, 2006), 53.

36 JHHVI, February 19, 1991.

37 Tafel, *Apprentice to Genius,* 164.

38 Ibid., 169.

39 JHH, "Reflections of Taliesin," 27.

40 Tafel, *Apprentice to Genius,* 69, and JHH, "Reflections of Taliesin," 28.

41 JHH, "Reflections of Taliesin," 30.

42 Nancy Willey, letter to FLW, June 27, 1932, FLWFA.

43 "Usonian" was the name Wright gave these modest dwellings that formed much of his residential work beginning in 1936. The term reputedly refers to "the United States of North America."

44 Richard Kronick, "The Pencil in Frank Lloyd Wright's Hand," *Journal of the Taliesin Fellows,* Summer 1998, 17.

45 JHHVI, February 19, 1991.

46 JHH, "Notebook of Organic Architecture," JHCP. This unpublished notebook contains mostly photographs and is not to be confused with another

scrapbook of the same name in the JHHP. The latter has material dating from Howe's school years and an abundance of newspaper clippings from 1932.

47 JHHVI, February 19, 1991. The luxury resort project brought Wright to Arizona for the 1928–29 winter at Ocatillo, his improvised redwood-and-canvas desert camp.

48 JHH, "Notebook of Organic Architecture," JHCP.

49 Ibid.

50 JHHVI, February 19, 1991.

51 JHH, interview with Alan Lathrop, September 1989, JHHP.

52 JHH, "Notebook of Organic Architecture," and JHHVI, February 19, 1991.

53 JHH, "Notebook of Organic Architecture," and JHHVI, February 19, 1991.

54 Besinger, *Working with Mr. Wright,* 41.

55 JHH, "Notebook of Organic Architecture."

56 The textile block houses are the Alice Millard House, La Miniatura, Pasadena, California (1923); John Storer House, Hollywood, California (1923); Samuel and Harriet Freeman House, Los Angeles, California (1923); and Charles and Mabel Ennis House, Los Angeles (1923). Frank Lloyd Wright Jr. (better known as Lloyd Wright) became both an architect and landscape architect, settling in Los Angeles, where he helped pioneer concrete, textile block houses. Late in his career he designed three houses built in the Minneapolis suburbs.

57 Kronick, "The Pencil in Frank Lloyd Wright's Hand," 12.

58 JHHVI, February 14, 1991.

59 Ibid.

60 Maureen Dowd, "As Time Goes By," *New York Times,* March 10, 2013.

61 Tafel, *Apprentice to Genius,* 185.

62 William Allin Storrer, *The Architecture of Frank Lloyd Wright: A Complete Catalog* (Chicago: University of Chicago Press, 1974), 240.

63 Tafel, *Apprentice to Genius,* 175.

64 JHHVI, February 14, 1991.

65 Bruce Brooks Pfeiffer, *Frank Lloyd Wright, 1943–1959: The Complete Works* (Los Angeles: Taschen, 2009), 575.

66 This technique was also utilized for the presentation drawings for Wright's Herbert and Katherine Jacobs House I, Madison, Wisconsin (1936), and

the *Life* house for Albert Blackbourn, Minneapolis, Minnesota, 1938, among others.

67 JHHVI, February 19, 1991.

68 JHH, "Reflections of Taliesin," 27. Howe commented that if Wright were "grounded" from other diversions by a cold, it helped his architecture. It forced him to be more focused and disciplined. In those instances, Wright would spend considerably more time working out the schematic design.

69 JHHVI, February 14, 1991, and Besinger, *Working with Mr. Wright*, 175.

70 JHHVI, February 14, 1991.

71 JHHVI, February 27, 1991.

72 Ibid.

73 Ibid.

74 JHH, "Reflections of Taliesin," 63.

75 Besinger, *Working with Mr. Wright*, 104. The author points out the constant battle with leaks in the drafting studio canvas roof and the many, mostly failed, attempts to remedy the situation, much to Wright's embarrassment and frustration.

76 Ibid., 68.

77 Ibid., 27.

78 Bruce Brooks Pfeiffer, *List of Projects by Assigned Number*, unpublished document, n.d., FLWFA.

79 Besinger, *Working with Mr. Wright*, 144.

80 Besinger, *Working with Mr. Wright*, 35.

81 Bernard Eisenschitz, *Nicholas Ray: An American Journey* (Minneapolis: University of Minnesota Press, 2011), 20.

82 Tafel, *Apprentice to Genius*, 206.

83 Besinger, *Working with Mr. Wright*, 140.

84 Ibid., 149. Those departing included Tafel, Mosher, Peter Berndtson and Cornelia Brierly, and Blaine and Hulda Drake. Brierly would return after World War II.

2 A SANDSTONE EXILE

1 Lewis Mumford, letter to FLW, May 30, 1941, Bruce Brooks Pfeiffer and Robert Wojtowicz, *Frank Lloyd Wright + Lewis Mumford: Thirty Years of Correspondence* (New York: Princeton Architectural Press, 2001), 181.

2 FLW, letter to Lewis Mumford, June 3, 1941, ibid., 183. The men reconciled in 1952 over lunch at the Plaza Hotel in New York.

3 Robert McCarter, *Frank Lloyd Wright* (London: Reaktion Books, 2006), 158. According to a declassified 1954 FBI report, *Frank Lloyd Wright—Sedition*, by October 16, 1940, the month the draft began, all members of the Fellowship had registered for the draft. "Federal Bureau of Investigation, Frank Lloyd Wright," National Archives and Records Administration, College Park, Maryland.

4 Besinger, *Working with Mr. Wright*, 95.

5 Robert Carroll May, letter to "To whom it may concern," January 14, 1943. Calvin B. Howard, *Frank Lloyd Wright*, March 3, 1943, and FBI, *Federal Bureau of Investigation, Frank Lloyd Wright*. Howard's report is part of a 124-page FBI investigative file summarizing "pertinent available information concerning Frank Lloyd Wright" over a forty-two-year period. "Highlights" include Wright's "background of promiscuity" and desertion of his wife and family in 1909, a 1915 charge—and arrest in 1926—for violation of the White Slave Traffic Act, an accusation in 1918 that he was a "German Sympathizer," and a "long history of affiliation with communist-type groups and activities." According to the report, Wright was not prosecuted for any crime. All quotes and information in this paragraph and the next paragraph are from the petition contained in this report.

6 The signees were Anton Bek, Frederic Benedict, Peter Berndtson, Curtis Besinger, Alfred Bush, Carey Caraway, Gordon Chadwick, James Charlton, Allen L. Davison, Benjamin Dombar, Blaine Drake, Herbert Fritz, Burton J. Goodrich, Aaron Green, Norman Hill, John H. Howe, John E. Lautner Jr., Kenneth Lockhart, Rowan Maiden, Eugene Masselink, Robert C. May, Robert Mosher, William Wesley Peters, Charles F. Sampson, Edgar A. Tafel, and Marcus Weston.

7 Furthermore, they argued that the work of the Fellowship was on behalf of the "completely legal, non-profit" Frank Lloyd Wright Foundation.

8 Jack El-Hai, "The FBI's File on Frank Lloyd Wright," http://www.el-hai.com.

9 FBI, *Federal Bureau of Investigation, Frank Lloyd Wright*.

10 Besinger, *Working with Mr. Wright*, 111.

11 FBI, *Frank Lloyd Wright—Sedition*; FBI, *Federal Bureau of Investigation, Frank Lloyd Wright*. In the *Herald Tribune* article, as he was wont to do, Wright shaved two years off his birthdate by claiming

to have been born in 1869 instead of, correctly, 1867.

12 The apprentices Masselink refers to are Wes Peters, Cornelia Brierly, Peter Berndtson, Svetlana Peters (Olgivanna Lloyd Wright's daughter and Peters's wife), Burton Goodrich, Lee Kawahara, and John deKoven Hill. "Del" was possibly Delton Larson. EM, letter to JHH, May 22, 1944, SFPC. Wright also used the phrase "The Upkeep of the Carcass" as a section heading in his autobiography to refer to the Fellowship and Taliesin. Masselink likely would have been aware of this reference.

13 JHH, letter to Mrs. C. W. Howe, April 16, 1942, JHHP. No documentation could be found of a meeting between Wright and President Franklin Delano Roosevelt on the subject of Taliesin COs. Once source reported that Wright's son Robert Llewellyn Wright, a lawyer with the Department of Justice in Washington, D.C., secured the services of Scher. Priscilla J. Henken, *Taliesin Diary: A Year with Frank Lloyd Wright* (New York: W. W. Norton, 2012), 101.

14 Besinger and Ten Brink CPS service source: http://www.civilianpublicservice.org. Conscientious Objector classification was relatively rare: "Of the estimated 43,000 World War II objectors, 25,000 served in the military as non-combatants, 6,000 went to prison, and 12,000 were inducted into the Civilian Public Service camps." *The War Within*, University of California Irvine Libraries, http://www.lib.uci.edu.

15 Weston was convicted on January 11, 1943. Howe and Davison were arrested on February 25, 1943, released on thousand-dollar bonds, and convicted in Wausau on June 16, 1943. "Taliesin Pair Get Four Years on Draft Charges," *Wisconsin State Journal*, June 17, 1943. Marcus Weston's imprisonment caused a deep rift between Weston's father, Will, a carpenter who had helped build Taliesin, and Wright. Weston blamed Wright for his son's refusal to report for induction. The events ended Weston's long professional relationship with Wright. Besinger, *Working with Mr. Wright*, 142. His son's imprisonment might have been more than Will Weston could endure. Marcus's older brother, Ernest, was killed in August 1914 in the massacre at Taliesin in which Wright's lover, Mamah Borthwick Cheney, and five others also were murdered.

16 FBI, *Federal Bureau of Investigation, Frank Lloyd Wright.*

17 JHH, letter to William Howe (Howe's brother), February 6, 1943, JHHP.

18 Wendell Berge, letter to Arthur L. Weatherly, March 30, 1943, JHHP. Weatherly, Howe's uncle, had been a CO during World War I. He unsuccessfully tried to plead his nephew's case with the U.S. Department of Justice.

19 Ibid.

20 "Strip Judge of Authority, Wright Asks," *Wisconsin State Journal,* December 20, 1942.

21 FBI, *Federal Bureau of Investigation, Frank Lloyd Wright.* In addition to summaries of numerous interviews with several members of local selective service boards, the file also contains personal letters written by Davison to his parents in which he chronicles his journey from petition signee to jail. The investigator underlined several sentences of interest in the letters, including Davison's statement in a letter dated September 11, 1940, that "Mr. Wright claims the government will have to take all of his boys over his dead body."

22 The Iowa County Veterans Service Office currently does not have World War II draft records on file. Jeffrey Lindeman, e-mail to Jane King Hession, March 12, 2014. The whereabouts of Howe's draft file is not known.

23 JHH, letter to Mr. and Mrs. C. W. Howe, January 19, 1942, JHHP. In a letter to John Howe dated June 3, 1942, his father wrote, "There is no place for any 'C.O.s' in the country now. . . . It is the most cowardly thing I can think of and I can't believe that you are seriously considering it." John Howe's nephew Christian Goepel confirmed the family rift: "Jack's father was not the least bit understanding or supportive of Jack's conscientious objector status and brave stance during World War II." Goepel, e-mail to Jane King Hession, January 4, 2013.

24 Weston served six months of his sentence at Sandstone. Subsequently he was reassigned to work with other conscientious objectors in the kitchen of the University of Michigan hospital. El-Hai, "The FBI's File on Frank Lloyd Wright."

25 JHH, letter to Mrs. C. W. Howe, June 27, 1943, JHHP.

26 Ibid.

27 Lu Sparks Howe, letter to Jane King Hession, July 18, 2000. In the letter, Howe provided excerpts from her husband's written recollections about his years at Sandstone.

28 Ibid. One "so minded" person was William "Bill" Krebes, a CO who had "never heard of Frank Lloyd Wright" before meeting Howe at Sandstone. Krebes was in Howe's furniture design class there. William Krebes, interview with Jane King Hession, June 15, 2000. Beginning in 1967 Howe designed eleven projects for Krebes, including "Redleaf" (1978), his residence in Lakeville, Minnesota.

29 Quotes in this paragraph are from Lu Sparks Howe, letter to Jane King Hession.

30 FLW, letter to JHH, January 5, 1943, FLWFA.

31 FLW, letter to JHH, August 16, 1944, FLWFA.

32 EM, letter to JHH, July 18, 1943, SFPC.

33 The apprentices Masselink references are "Ted" Bower, "Johnnie" deKoven Hill, and "Kenn" Lockhart.

34 EM, letter to JHH, April 30, 1944, SFPC.

35 Information in this paragraph is sourced from an unpublished "narrative" by Scott W. Perkins, curator, *Fellowship: 75 Years of Taliesin Box Projects,* Price Tower Arts Center, Bartlesville, Oklahoma, 2010.

36 Mary Ann Langston, e-mail to Jane King Hession, September 24, 2012. Langston, a Taliesin box project historian, wrote, "Apparently Mr. Howe was usually too busy to do drawings for the gift boxes."

37 FLW, letter to JHH, January 5, 1944.

38 EM, letter to JHH, June 12, 1944, SFPC. In his drawing, Howe sited the Quarry House above the Wyoming Valley near Spring Green, Wisconsin, with a view to Taliesin in the distance. Less than ten years later, Howe designed Inwood, a cottage for him and his wife, Lu, on approximately the same site.

39 FLW, letter to JHH, January 5, 1944.

40 Lu Sparks Howe, letter to Jane King Hession.

41 Powers, who spent thirteen months at Sandstone for his pacifist views, later settled in Minnesota as writer in residence and professor of English at Saint John's University in Collegeville.

42 In the early 1940s Hudson was the editor of the *Industrial Organizer,* a publication of Minneapolis Teamsters Local 544. In December 1943 he was one of eighteen defendants convicted in Minneapolis of advocating the overthrow of the government, among other charges. The charges stemmed from a dispute between Minneapolis Teamsters Local 544 and Teamsters International. See Elizabeth Raasch-Gilman, "Sisterhood in the Revolution: The Holmes Sisters and the Socialist Workers' Party," *Minnesota History,* Fall 1999, 358–75. Hudson and Howe remained friends after being released from Sandstone. In 1974, Howe designed a farmhouse for Hudson near Chesterton, Indiana. It was not built.

43 In concept the Big Project may be compared to America's first indoor shopping mall, Southdale Center in Edina, Minnesota, designed in 1956 by Victor Gruen, and the multiuse Mall of America in Bloomington, Minnesota, which opened in 1992.

44 At least two of Wright's unbuilt projects fully embraced the automobile: the Gordon Strong Automobile Objective (1925) and Broadacre City (1934). Wright's largest and most ambitious design for a multiuse complex was the Pittsburgh Point Park Civic Center (1947, unbuilt). It postdates the Big Project by several years.

45 Howe recalled there was a store at Sandstone where inmates could buy yarn. Roughly one hundred men were housed in each dormitory. JHHVI, March 25, 1991.

46 Krebes interview with Jane King Hession.

47 JHH, letter to Mr. and Mrs. C. W. Howe, May 10, 1943, JHHP.

48 The exact date of Howe's release from Sandstone could not be determined by the authors. According to E. Frie, SST/executive assistant, Bureau of Prisons, Sandstone prison records "do not go back that far." E. Frie, e-mail to Jane King Hession, September 25, 2012. However, Masselink wrote his last letter to Howe at Sandstone on March 4, 1946.

49 Lu Sparks Howe, letter to Jane King Hession.

3 RETURN TO TALIESIN

1 Besinger, *Working with Mr. Wright,* 157.

2 Amin, *Reflections from the Shining Brow,* 68.

3 Ibid.

4 Besinger, *Working with Mr. Wright,* 154.

5 Ibid., 156.

6 Ibid.

7 Ibid.

8 JHHVI, February 14, 1990.

9 Ibid.

10 Ibid.

11 Ibid.

12 Ibid.

13 JHH, "Reflections of Taliesin," 27.

14 Ibid., 27.

15 JHHVI, February 14, 1990.

16 *Arizona Highways,* October 1949.

17 Ibid., 9. "Coil of concrete" was a term used in *House and Home, III,* June 1953, 99–107, which featured it on the cover.

18 Besinger, *Working with Mr. Wright,* 176.

19 A&P refers to the Great Atlantic & Pacific Tea Company, a grocery store chain, once the nation's largest.

20 JHHVI, February 14, 1990.

21 Ibid.

22 Ibid.

23 Besinger, *Working with Mr. Wright,* 176.

24 JHHVI, February 14, 1990.

25 Besinger, *Working with Mr. Wright,* 183.

26 Carl Book, interview with Tim Quigley, April 12, 2013, Santa Rosa, California.

27 Besinger, *Working with Mr. Wright,* 182 and 23.

28 Ibid., 162.

29 JHHVI, February 19, 1991.

30 Mary Jane Hamilton, "Frank Lloyd Wright and His Automobiles," *Frank Lloyd Wright Quarterly* 21, no. 1 (Winter 2010), 5.

31 Besinger, *Working with Mr. Wright,* 225. This section relies heavily on his account.

32 JHH, "Reflections of Taliesin," and JHHVI, February 19, 1991.

33 Besinger, *Working with Mr. Wright,* 202.

34 JHHVI, February 14,1990.

35 JHCP.

36 Ibid.

37 The others are the Eric Brown House (1949) and the Helen and Ward McCartney House (1949).

38 *Architectural Notes* from "Wright on the Inside" published by the Frank Lloyd Wright Building Conservancy, 2013.

39 JHHVI, February 14, 1990.

40 Lu Sparks Howe, interview with Tim Quigley, October 3, 2001, Minneapolis, Minnesota.

41 Lu Sparks Howe, interview with Tim Quigley, April 12, 2013, Novato, California.

42 JHH, interview with Alan Lathrop, September 1989, JHHP.

43 JHHVI, March 12, 1991.

44 Lu Sparks Howe, interview with Tim Quigley, April 12, 2013.

45 Carl Book, interview with Tim Quigley, April 12, 2013, Santa Rosa, California.

46 Amin, *Reflections from the Shining Brow,* 73.

47 Ibid., 74.

48 Lu Sparks Howe, interview with Tim Quigley, April 12, 2013.

49 Besinger, *Working with Mr. Wright,* 273.

50 JHHVI, February 19, 1991.

51 Ibid.

52 Bruce Brooks Pfeiffer, *List of Projects by Assigned Number,* unpublished document, n.d., FLWFA.

53 Lu Sparks Howe, interview with Tim Quigley, April 12, 2013.

4 AFTER WRIGHT

1 JHH, letter to H. Allen Brooks, September 5, 1966, JHHP. Howe chastised Brooks for suggesting Wright may have been senile in his later years: "Anyone who knew or worked with Mr. Wright in the last years of his life could only laugh at the use of the word 'senility' in connection with his work."

2 Due to the frequency of apprentice arrivals at and departures from Taliesin, Fellowship member counts changed on an almost monthly basis. For that reason it is difficult to ascertain the exact number of fellows who were in residence at any one point in time.

3 Louis Wiehle, e-mail to Jane King Hession, March 2, 2014. Louis Wiehle was known as Alvin Wiehle when he was at Taliesin.

4 As part of the restructuring of the Frank Lloyd Wright Foundation, Olgivanna Lloyd Wright created two "operating divisions" within it: Taliesin Associated Architects (TAA) and the Frank Lloyd Wright School of Architecture. Elizabeth Bauer Kassler, *The Taliesin Fellowship: A Directory of Members, 1932–1982* (Princeton, N.J.: E. B. Kassler, 1982), 2.

5 Louis Wiehle, e-mail to Jane King Hession.

6 Ibid.

7 "Weekly Work Assignments," notebook, JHCP.

8 "TAA Projects Attributed to John H. Howe," complied November 5, 2013, by Elizabeth Dawsari, director, William Wesley Peters Library, Frank Lloyd Wright Foundation. TAA also took on the task of completing projects that were unfinished at the time of Wright's death.

9 Other fellows took credit for their designs in a similar manner.

10 Kronick, "The Pencil in Frank Lloyd Wright's Hand," 15–16.

11 Don Lovness (Wright client), interview with Tim Quigley, January 28, 2000, Grant, Minnesota. Lovness contended Howe designed two of Wright's Minnesota houses: the A. H. and Wilhelmine Bulbulian House in Rochester (1947) and the Dr. Paul and Helen Olfelt House in St. Louis Park (1958). According to one client, Howe told him that during the last five years of Wright's career, many [Wright] houses were not designed by Wright. Stewart Macaulay (Howe client), interview with Tim Quigley, April 14, 2001, Madison, Wisconsin.

12 Curiously, "Harvey Johnson" was an alias for client John Harvey; he requested Howe use the pseudonym in their dealings. Harvey claimed he had been "so thoroughly blacklisted in the metal trades" owing to his involvement in the labor movement that he had to plan and construct his house under an assumed name. John Harvey, letter to JHH, JHHP, undated.

13 Howe acquired the land for the cottage, which was originally part of Aldebaran Farm, from Peters. Prior to Peters's ownership, the land belonged to a member of the Lloyd Jones family, relatives of Wright's on his mother's side.

14 Ultimately Howe was registered in three other states: Wisconsin (1959), Minnesota (1965), and California (1966). Original certificates in the Lu Sparks Howe Collection, in the possession of Christian J. Goepel.

15 Gordon made the statement in the June 1946 issue of *House Beautiful.*

16 The other apprentices who worked for *House Beautiful* included Curtis Besinger, Kenneth Lockhart, and Robert Mosher. Diane Maddex, *Frank Lloyd Wright's House Beautiful* (New York: Hearst Books, 2000), 36.

17 The list identified six men as TAA architects: Peters, Howe, Davison, Lockhart, Masselink, and Mendel Glickman. Eight men and one woman were listed as "associate architects on staff": Edmond T. Casey, John Rattenbury, Kamal Amin, Jim Pfefferkorn, John Amarantides, Alvin (Louis) Wiehle, Cornelia Brierly,

Kelly Oliver, and Robert Beharka. "Architects Who Understand and Use Wrightian Principles," *House Beautiful*, October 1959, 266.

18 The article also featured photographs by Parker (a frequent *House Beautiful* contributor) of the Mrs. J. G. Ashman House in Midland, Michigan, designed by Alden Dow, and of Lloyd Wright's Wayfarers Chapel in Palos Verdes, California. "Beyond the Functional—into the Poetic," *House Beautiful,* October 1959, 228–31, 308–9.

19 Royston Distributors, Inc. v. Moore-McCormack Lines, Inc., United District Court E.D. Pennsylvania, June 4, 1965. The suit involved damages to cars in transit from England to the United States. An inventory of 488 automobiles was provided.

20 Vernon MacIntyre, interview with Tim Quigley, March 13, 2013, Exton, Pennsylvania. MacIntyre is the current owner of the Royston cottage.

21 The Wright Barney plan was also the basis for several Wright-designed properties, including the Helen and Ward McCartney House in Kalamazoo, Michigan (1949), and the Howard and Helen Anthony House in Benton Harbor, Michigan (1949). William Allin Storrer, *The Frank Lloyd Wright Companion* (Chicago: University of Chicago Press, 1993), 327–28.

22 Royston ordered several pieces from Nakashima's Conoid line of furniture, including a table with bar stools, a bench, and four cushion chairs. JHHP. Nakashima, who earned a master's of architecture degree from the Massachusetts Institute of Technology, once worked for Antonin Raymond, an architect who formerly worked with Frank Lloyd Wright at Taliesin and in Japan.

23 Over time, Toby Royston sold off parcels of land surrounding the cottage. The current owner of the house, who "grew up in the shadow of the Beth Sholom Synagogue," is renovating the buildings, which were damaged over the years by flooding and roof leakage.

24 This quote and all quotes in this section are from David LaBerge, e-mail to Jane King Hession, November 7, 2013.

25 LaBerge led the Bach Society of Minnesota from 1959 to 1980. He also revived the Bach Society Chorus in which John Howe sang tenor for a number of years.

26 LaBerge said Howe "jokingly" offered a solution: "We put the roof point on a hinge and drop the point when the building inspectors visited the site."

27 LaBerge approached the search with scientific precision: "I wrote to the national survey office in Washington and obtained topographical maps of the land areas around the University, stretching out twenty-five miles in all directions. We learned to spot a 'rise of land over a south-west exposure,' far from the madding crowd."

28 Wright was guided by the Welsh word "Taliesin," meaning "shining brow," when it came to siting a building on hilly terrain. As such, he favored placing a building below the crest of a hill, rather than on top of it.

29 In 1952, Sidney Wear earned an MBA from Harvard Business School.

30 Sidney Wear, interview with Tim Quigley, April 12, 2009, Edina, Minnesota. "Poet in stone," quote also from Sidney Young Wear obituary, *Minneapolis Star Tribune,* November 21, 2010.

31 Sidney Wear was related on her mother's father's side of the family to Algernon Sidney Washburn, one of six brothers of Cadwallader C. Washburn, who opened the first flour mill in Minnesota in 1866. Minnesota Milling Company was renamed the Washburn Crosby Company when Washburn partnered with John Crosby. The company became General Mills in 1928. Linda Courtney, "History of General Mills," July 30, 2012, http://www.insidebusiness360.com.

32 All quotes in this and the next paragraph are from Howe, "House No. 1 for Mr. and Mrs. George R. Johnson, 'Wintertree,' " unpublished and undated description, JHHP. George Johnson would also become Howe's attorney.

33 The projects were the George and Norma Johnson House I (1963); George and Norma Johnson House I, guest cottage (1967); Johnson and Eastlund law offices (1968, not built); Partenwood master plan (1971); Pacesetter houses I and II (1971, not built); marina (1978, not built); Partenwood gate (1978, not built); George and Norma Johnson House II (1973); Northome cottage alterations of the Francis W. and Mary Little House outbuilding (1981); Norma Johnson House (1982); houses and hotel (1986); six houses for Wintertree, Inc. (1987); Inn and townhouses at Terrace Point, for Wintertree, Inc. (1989). Howe also designed an undated treehouse at Wintertree for the Johnsons' sons, Merritt and Marshall, and a birdfeeder in 1970 for a school project of Merritt's.

34 The house is not far from the former site of the Frank Lloyd Wright–designed Francis W. and Mary Little House (1912), which was demolished in 1972.

35 Howe, "House No. 1 for Mr. and Mrs. George R. Johnson."

36 Ibid.

37 Prior to the Tucson Creative Dance Center, Howe designed two nonresidential projects that were not built: a Doctors' Park for Dr. George Ablin for Bakersfield, California (1961); and a bar for Roscoe A. Hall for El Paso, Texas (1962). In 1961 a combined house and hangar for William Bancroft was built in Waunakee, Wisconsin.

38 Barbara Mettler, *Dance as an Element of Life* (Tucson: Mettler Studios, 1985), 30.

39 Rob Dobson, "A Leap to the West: Barbara Mettler and the Making of the Tucson Creative Dance Center," http://www.dancecreative.org.

40 The Barbara Mettler Archive, Hampshire College, http://www.hampshire.edu.

41 Mettler, *Dance as an Element of Life,* 29.

42 Wes Peters served as project engineer for the dance center. JHHVI, March 25, 1991.

43 One such client was Loren Pope, who was unable to acquire conventional financing for his 1940 Wright-designed Usonian house in Alexandria, Virginia. Instead, he secured a loan from his employer, the *Washington Evening Star* newspaper, which allowed him to build the house.

44 Mettler, *Dance as an Element of Life,* 31.

45 Of the Tucson Creative Dance Center Howe once declared, "I think that's my favorite building." Kronick, "The Pencil in Frank Lloyd Wright's Hand," 17. On her death in 2002, Mettler willed the property to the Nature Conservancy.

46 Barbara Mettler, letter to JHH, December 16, 1963, JHHP. Mettler also thanked Howe for designing her letterhead, one of the many "unbilled helps" he provided. Howe's papers include documentation and designs for business cards, letterheads, stationery, holiday cards, and other graphics he created for clients.

47 The houses, and the years the additions were designed, are the Clarke Arnold House, Columbus, Wisconsin (1959); the Kenneth Laurent House, Rockford, Illinois (1960); the Robert Levin House, Kalamazoo, Michigan (1960); the David Weisblat House, Galesburg, Michigan (1961); the Paul Hanna

211

House, Palo Alto, California (1961); the Willard Keland House, Racine, Wisconsin (1961); the Patrick Kinney House, Lancaster, Wisconsin (1964); the Andrew Armstrong House, Ogden Dunes, Indiana (1964–74); and the Donald Schaberg House, Okemos, Michigan (1964). A design for the Quintin Blair House, Cody, Wyoming (1959), was not built.

48 Historical American Buildings Survey, Unity Temple (the Unitarian-Universalist Church), HABS no. ILL-1903, National Park Service, 1967. According to the HABS report, "Because of financial problems, the refurbishing was done on a do-it-yourself basis with the cooperation of William Wesley Peters and John Howe."

49 Information and quotes in this and the next paragraph are from Grant Hildebrand, *Frank Lloyd Wright's Palmer House* (Seattle: University of Washington Press, 2007), 26–27.

50 Don Lovness (Wright client) interview with Tim Quigley, October 14, 2001, Grant, Minnesota. Lovness additionally noted, "John and Lu never smiled at Taliesin [during those years]."

51 Wiehle, e-mail to Jane King Hession.

52 According to Lovness, Olgivanna dismissed Howe as being "no architect." Lovness, interview with Tim Quigley, January 28, 2000, Grant, Minnesota.

53 JHHVI, March 25, 1991.

54 Lu Howe also acknowledged experiencing personal and professional challenges during that period. Of the typing assignments Olgivanna gave her, she commented, "I typed those awful books of hers a thousand times." Lu Howe, interview with Tim Quigley, April 12, 2013, Novato, California.

55 John Howe, interview with Alan Lathrop, September 6, 1989, JHHP.

56 Ibid.

57 Quotes in this paragraph are from "Transcription of Mr. John Howe's lecture at the Milwaukee Art Center," JHHP.

58 Wiehle, e-mail to Jane King Hession.

59 In addition to providing the inscription, Wright identified the artwork as "Actor print (Hosoye) by Shunsho 1770." Katsukawa Shunshō was a Japanese painter and printmaker. A print of the same name is listed in the catalog for the 1917 Wright-curated exhibition, *Antique Colour Prints from the Collection of Frank Lloyd Wright,* held at the Arts Club of

Chicago Exhibition and Fine Arts Building. After her husband's death, Lu Howe gave the print to Howe's former apprentice Mark Hagedorn. Mark Hagedorn, e-mail to Jane King Hession, November 26, 2013.

5 THE FREEDOM OF CALIFORNIA

1 Carl Book, interview with Tim Quigley, April 12, 2013, Santa Rosa, California.

2 Lu Sparks Howe, interview with Tim Quigley, April 12, 2013, Novato, California.

3 Jan Novie, telephone interview with Tim Quigley, November 11, 2012.

4 Unpublished letter, JHH to William Palmer, August 22, 1982, JHHP.

5 JHH, interview with Kronick, *Journal of Taliesin Fellows,* Summer 1998, 17.

6 Lu Sparks Howe, interview with Tim Quigley, April 12, 2013, Novato, California.

7 The office interior is credited to Wright as his West Coast Field Office. The Wright-designed interior was sold to collector Tom Monaghan, then acquired by the Carnegie Museum, Pittsburgh, where it was installed for display by curator Christopher Monkhouse in 1993, prior to being dismantled and relegated to storage by his successor.

8 Walter Medeiros and Jan Novie, interview with Tim Quigley, April 11, 2013, Berkeley, California.

9 Rose Pauson House, Shiprock, Phoenix, Arizona (1939). This house burned to the ground in 1942 and remained a notorious ruin for years.

10 Walter Medeiros and Jan Novie, interview with Tim Quigley, April 11, 2013, Berkeley, California.

11 Ibid.

12 Ibid.

13 Ibid.

14 Ibid.

15 Information on these projects is from both JHHP and AGA.

16 Information on these projects is from both JHHP and AGA.

17 "Aaron Green Designs a Mountain Retreat for a Crest Above Santa Cruz," *House Beautiful,* October 1965, 218–19.

18 The Ohta House is associated with a particularly violent mass murder that occurred on the afternoon of October 19, 1970. According to newspaper accounts,

a "hippie-deranged environmental terrorist" confronted and then murdered Ohta, his wife, their two sons, and his secretary at the house and burned it to the ground. This Charles Manson–like slaying terrified the community and left Green grieving. A subsequent owner rebuilt the house to the original plans, but Green could never bring himself to visit.

19 Wright's Harold and Carolyn Price Jr. House, Bartlesville, Oklahoma (1953), and Howe's George and Norma Johnson House I, Orono, Minnesota (1963), are examples in which this feature is striking. The silhouette of Wright's Russell and Ruth Kraus House, St. Louis, Missouri (1951), also comes to mind.

20 JHHP project lists reveal Howe designed four versions of the Richard Nelson House, Afton, Minnesota, 1968–74, before both owner and architect resigned themselves to remodeling an existing house in 1978, rather than building a new structure.

21 JHHP.

22 JHHVI, February 14, 1991.

23 Lu Sparks Howe, interview with Tim Quigley, April 12, 2013, Novato, California.

24 JHH, interview with Kronick, 5.

25 Ibid.

26 Walter Medeiros and Jan Novie, interview with Tim Quigley, April 11, 2013, Berkeley, California.

27 "The Pacifica Radio/UC Berkeley Social Activism Sound Recording Project: Anti-Vietnam War Protests in the San Francisco Bay Area & Beyond," Media Resources Center, UC Berkeley.

6 A NEW CAREER IN MINNESOTA

1 Charles Fredeen, "Howe Designs in the (W)right Style," *Burnsville This Week,* June 27, 1983.

2 Ibid.

3 When the Howes first moved to Minnesota they stayed in an apartment owned by Krebes on West 32nd Street and Bryant Avenue South in Minneapolis. William Krebes, interview with Jane King Hession, June 15, 2000, Lakeville, Minnesota.

4 Kronick, "The Pencil in Frank Lloyd Wright's Hand," 9.

5 Ibid. The Howes did not buy the house because they found the noise from nearby Interstate 94, completed in 1968, to be intolerable, despite a noise barrier installed to mitigate the problem. In 1969

the Burrises hired Howe to design an addition to the Willey House. It was not built.

6 "Recollections," http://www.thewilleyhouse.com. Harvey Glanzer purchased the house in 1972 and owned it until 2002.

7 The exhibitions also increased his client base. The venues included Augsburg College (1968); Northwestern National Bank Skyway (1969); Sons of Norway (1970), all in Minneapolis; and Carleton College (1974), in Northfield, Minnesota, south of the Twin Cities; JHHP.

8 Lu Sparks Howe, note to Jane King Hession, undated.

9 Dentley Haugesag, "John Howe and the Usonian Touch," *Twin Citian*, August 1967, 52–53.

10 Ibid.

11 John H. Howe, "Architectural Criteria," for AIA student chapter publication, Catholic University of America, JHHP.

12 Ibid.

13 All quotes in this and the following paragraph are from JHH, interview with Alan Lathrop, September 6, 1989, JHHP.

14 John Howe, "Preliminary Remarks to the Society of Architectural Historians," October 11, 1984, JHHP.

15 Geoffrey Childs, interview with Jane King Hession, September 13, 1999, Minneapolis.

16 Unless otherwise noted, all quotes in this section are from Walter and Marlene Schmidt, interview with Jane King Hession, October 2, 2013, Prior Lake, Minnesota.

17 "Informal warmth," from Howe's notes from a meeting with Walter and Marlene Schmidt, October 17, 1967, JHHP.

18 JHH, interview with Lathrop, September 6, 1989.

19 The Schmidts claim responsibility for introducing two sets of clients to Howe. When two of Walter's Univac colleagues saw the Schmidts' house, they hired Howe to design their houses: the Ed and Barbara Tilford House, Eagan, Minnesota (1981), and the John Rachac House, Inver Grove Heights, Minnesota (1985).

20 David and Glenda McLellan, interview with Tim Quigley, October 20, 2013, Holly, Michigan.

21 David McLellan, sometimes referred to as "Mr. Corvette," is the author of *Corvettes from the Inside,* published in 2002. His contributions are featured prominently in the Corvette Hall of Fame in Louisville, Kentucky.

22 All quotes in this and the next paragraph are from "McLellan House," podcast with David and Glenda McLellan, September 2008, http://corvettechief.com.

23 The house was originally designed for a different site. When a two-story Colonial was built in the subdivision, in direct view of where their house would stand, the McLellans purchased a second site twenty miles from the first one on which their Howe-designed house would be built.

24 Ibid.

25 Due to illness, Howe closed his practice in 1992.

26 Quotes in this paragraph are from David McLellan, e-mail to Tim Quigley, November 2, 2013. Today the house remains in near-original condition. Low-E thermopane windows and new countertops were installed in 2002.

27 Goodale House project files, JHHP.

28 As Wright's chief draftsman, Howe was involved in the creation of several of Wright's solar hemicycle designs and their variants, including the Herbert and Katherine Jacobs House II, Middleton, Wisconsin (1944); Lillian and Curtis Meyer House, Galesburg, Michigan (1948); Kenneth and Phyllis Laurent House, Rockford, Illinois (1949); Wilbur C. Pearce House, Bradbury, California (1950); Robert D. Winn House, Kalamazoo, Michigan (1950); Clifton and George Lewis House, Tallahassee, Florida (1952); Ethel and Luis Marden House, McLean, Virginia (1952); Elizabeth and Robert Llewellyn Wright House, Bethesda, Maryland (1953); Andrew and Maude Cooke House, Virginia Beach, Virginia (1953); John L. Rayward House, New Canaan, Connecticut (1955); and Dudley and Dorothy Spencer House, Wilmington, Delaware (1956).

29 It was a technique Wright had used before him, notably for the screen porch of the Loren Pope House in Alexandria, Virginia (1940).

30 All quotes in this paragraph are from Robert and Katherine Goodale, interview with Tim Quigley, April 2000.

31 The other nonresidential projects—all unbuilt—from the era are Law Offices for Johnson and Eastlund, Minneapolis (1968); an apartment project for Norman O. Hilleren and a motor hotel for Hilleren Associates, both in Rochester, Minnesota (1970); two schemes for a burial garden for Herman T. and Gertrude Mossberg, South Bend, Indiana (1970);

office alterations for the Boswell Oil Company, Cincinnati, Ohio (1971); and the Marshalltown Savings and Loan branch office, Marshalltown, Iowa (1973). The last three projects listed all had associations with clients for whom Wright designed houses.

32 Learning Resources Consultants, *Preliminary Plans for Macalester College, Learning Resources Center,* undated report, JHHP. The three-man committee was chaired by Russell Burris, owner of the Willey House; Ervin Gaines was the third committee member.

33 JHH, interview with Lathrop, September 6, 1989.

34 Ibid. Humphrey returned to Minnesota in 1969 after an unsuccessful presidential run.

35 JHH, letter to Marshall Erdman, November 6, 1969, JHHP.

36 List of "Building Requirements," prepared by Alan Hale for JHH, May 15, 1970, JHHP.

37 Thomas M. Crosby Jr., letter to JHH, April 2, 1970, JHHP.

38 All quotes in this paragraph are from an undated program description by John Howe, JHHP.

39 Howe used the same material and approach for the roof of the Byron E. and Joyce Harrell House in Vermillion, South Dakota (1961).

40 Untitled document, April 16, 1972, JHHP. Although the document is unsigned, it is likely that Howe authored the piece.

41 The other was a project for the Advent Christian Church in Maplewood, Minnesota (1978).

42 The Metropolitan Museum of Art sold two parts of the Little House to other institutions: the library was purchased by the Allentown Art Museum, Allentown, Pennsylvania; and a hallway was purchased by the Minneapolis Institute of Arts.

43 "Secret Project" memo, Edgar Tafel to John Howe, December 2, 1971. The project initially was somewhat clandestine. In his memo, Tafel cautioned: "Should Mrs. W. get wind, we all would be in the soup." Howe agreed that once demolition began, it would be essential to have "a watchman on duty around the clock." He cited the 1970 demolition of Wright's Lake Geneva Hotel (1911) in Lake Geneva, Wisconsin, as a cautionary tale. "People backed station wagons up to the building at night and took whatever they wanted for free." JHH, letter to Edgar Tafel, January 6, 1972, JHHP.

44 Edgar Tafel, letter to JHH, April 20, 1972, JHHP.

45 John Howe, "House for Mr. and Mrs. John H. Howe—'Sankaku,'" undated, JHHP.

46 Quotations in this and the following paragraph are from ibid.

47 Raku Endo, untitled essay, March 27, 1984.

48 The Howes lived in Sankaku until 1993.

49 John Howe, "House No. 2 for Mr. and Mrs. George R. Johnson—'Partenwood,'" unpublished and undated description, JHHP.

50 In 1971 Howe also designed the Pacesetter I and II houses for Partenwood. They were not built.

51 All quotes in this and the next paragraph are from Howe, "House No. 2 for Mr. and Mrs. George R. Johnson—'Partenwood.'"

52 All quotes in this section are from Jan and Bob Willow, telephone interview with Jane King Hession, November 18, 2013. When he presented schemes to clients, Howe generally topped his drawing sets with a blank sheet of semitransparent paper to pique their interest and allow for a more dramatic unveiling of his designs.

53 Willow said Howe, like Wright, "did not like committees, and declined to come to Menomonie to present his work." That responsibility fell to Willow. In 1986 Howe designed one final project for the Willow family: a house for daughter Wendy on the Hood River, in Oregon.

54 Wright depicted perspectives of three of the houses—the Dr. and Mrs. B. Marden Black House, the Dr. and Mrs. Thomas E. Keys House, and the Dr. and Mrs. A. H. Bulbulian House (all designed in 1947)—in a single drawing. The Black House was not built. Wright's fourth house was for James B. and Kathleen McBean (1957).

55 Jack and Gloria Grabow, interview with Jane King Hession, June 6, 2000, Rochester, Minnesota.

56 In addition to the Grabow and Service Houses they include the Dr. William and Jeannine Karnes House (1977); the Dr. Thomas F. Keys House (son of Dr. Thomas E. Keys; 1977); and the Dr. John and Maaja Washington House (1975). A fifth house, for Dr. Manfried Muenther (1978), was not built.

57 Howe was also hired by a subsequent owner of the Wright-designed Keys house to design five alterations and additions to that house, three of which were completed. Two commercial projects for the R.V. Hannem Corporation, designed in 1976 and 1977 in association with Howe apprentice Mark Hagedorn, were not constructed.

58 All quotes in this and the next two paragraphs are from Mark Hagedorn, interview with the authors, May 18, 2013, Edina, Minnesota. In 1974 Hagedorn received a bachelor of environmental design degree from the School of Architecture and Landscape Architecture at the University of Minnesota.

59 All quotes in this and the next paragraph are from Mark Hagedorn, e-mail to Jane King Hession, November 26, 2013.

60 Mark Hagedorn, undated note. After leaving Howe's office, Hagedorn established his own design practice in Key West, Florida.

61 Some years after John Howe's death, Lu presented Hagedorn with a gift that had originally been given to Howe by Wright: a print by Japanese painter and printmaker Katsukawa Shunshō dating from 1770, inscribed by Wright, "To Jack—the Senior True." Mark Hagedorn, e-mail to Jane King Hession, November 26, 2013.

62 Kronick, "The Pencil in Wright's Hand," 14.

63 All quotes in this and the next two paragraphs are from Geoffrey Childs, interview with Jane King Hession, September 13, 1999, Minneapolis.

64 The constraints were a result of the disruption of oil production in Iran following the Iranian Revolution of 1979.

65 Geoffrey Childs, telephone interview with Jane King Hession, November 24, 2013.

66 Ibid.

67 JHHVI, March 5, 1991.

68 JHH, interview with Lathrop, September 6, 1989.

69 Kenneth and Helen Drangstveit, interview with Jane King Hession, November 22, 2013, Burnsville, Minnesota.

70 Ibid.

71 In 1976 Howe also designed a house for David Knudson in Woodhome.

72 Drangstveit, interview with Jane King Hession, November 22, 2013. Among the other Minnesota houses Drangstveit built were the Goodale House, the Johnson House II, the H. L. and Marge Jerpbak House (1968, Edina), the Dayton House, and the Paul E. and Mary Waibel House (1972, North Oaks).

He also constructed the First Church of Christ, Scientist (1971, New Brighton).

73 Drangstveit, interview with Jane King Hession, November 22, 2013.

74 Wright's designs for Mason City include the George Stockman House (1908), the City National Bank and Hotel (1909), and the Joshua and Minnie Melson House (1908, not built).

75 Drummond was an associate in Wright's studio in Oak Park in the early 1900s.

76 Sidney Bowen, interview with Tim Quigley, September 24, 2012, Boston.

77 Ibid.

78 Bowen now heads a nationally recognized architecture firm in Boston. Parenthetically, Bowen's string of architecturally significant residences continues. He and his second wife now live in a Walter Gropius–designed house near Boston, and they own a second home, designed by a Gropius student, on Cape Cod. General information in this section, ibid., and from project files, JHHP.

79 Louis Wiehle, e-mail to Jane King Hession, March 2, 2014.

80 Endo, untitled essay, March 27, 1984.

EPILOGUE
A LASTING LEGACY

1 JHH, letter to Mark Hagedorn, May 11, 1992, Mark Hagedorn personal collection.

2 Lu Sparks Howe, interview with Tim Quigley, April 12, 2013, Novato, California.

3 Frank Lloyd Wright's body was originally interred in the Unity Chapel cemetery. In accordance with Olgivanna Lloyd Wright's dying wish, his remains were exhumed, and his ashes were comingled with hers and reburied at Taliesin West in Scottsdale. Iver Peterson, "Reburial of Frank Lloyd Wright Touches Off Stormy Debate," *New York Times*, April 10, 1985.

4 Linda Mack, "Prominent Architect John Howe, 84, Dies." *Star Tribune*, September 23, 1997.

5 All quotes in this paragraph are from Louis Wiehle, e-mail to Jane King Hession, March 2, 2014.

6 Ibid.

ILLUSTRATION CREDITS

220

JANE KING HESSION, an architectural historian and curator specializing in modernism, is a founding partner of Modern House Productions. She is coauthor of *Frank Lloyd Wright in New York: The Plaza Years, 1954–1959* and *Ralph Rapson: Sixty Years of Modern Design*. She is a former president of the Frank Lloyd Wright Building Conservancy and recently wrote and produced (with William Olexy) the documentary *Wright on the Park: Saving the City National Bank and Hotel*.

TIM QUIGLEY, AIA, is principal of Quigley Architects, a residential design firm in Minneapolis. He is a former president of the Frank Lloyd Wright Building Conservancy, vice president of the Minnesota chapter of Docomomo, and president of the advisory board of the Goldstein Museum of Design at the University of Minnesota. He taught architectural studio and history courses for twenty years at the University of Minnesota and Ball State University.

BRUCE BROOKS PFEIFFER is vice president and director of the Frank Lloyd Wright Archives at Taliesin West. He is the author of more than forty books on Wright, including *Frank Lloyd Wright: Complete Works* and *Frank Lloyd Wright Designs: The Sketches, Plans, and Drawings*.